Digital Classroom:
InDesign
CS3

Digital Classroom:
InDesign
CS3

AGI Creative Team

AGITRAINING.COM · AQUENT GRAPHICS INSTITUTE

Digital Classroom: InDesign CS3   By The AGI Creative Team

Writing: **Christopher Smith, Larry Happy, Chad Chelius, Haziel Olivera, Jeff Ausura, Robert Underwood**

Series Editor: **Christopher Smith**

Technical Editors: **Caitlin Smith, Jeremy Osborn, Linda Forsvall, Jerron Smith**

Video Project Manager: **Jeremy Osborn**

Video Editor: **Trevor Chamberlain**

Cover Design: **Jennifer Smith**

Interior Design: **Jennifer Smith, Ron Bilodeau**

Graphic Production: **Lauren Mickol**

Additional Production: **Aquent Studios**

Indexing: **Lauren Mickol**

Proofreading: **Jay Donahue**

Print History: May 2008, First Edition.

Contents

Lesson 3: Building Documents and Master Pages

Lesson 4: Working with Text and Type

Lesson 5: Working with Styles

Lesson 6: Working with Graphics

Lesson 7: Creating and Using Tables

Lesson 8: Using Color in Your Documents

Lesson 9: Using Effects

Lesson 10: Advanced Document Features

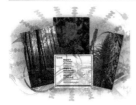

Lesson 11: Document Delivery: Printing, PDFs, and XHTML

Lesson 12: Using XML

Starting up

About Digital Classroom

Adobe® InDesign® CS3 lets you create print layouts for brochures, magazines, flyers, marketing and sales sheets, and more. InDesign CS3 provides tight integration with other Adobe products such as Photoshop® CS3, Illustrator® CS3, and Dreamweaver® CS3.

Digital Classroom: InDesign CS3 is like having your own personal instructor guiding you through each lesson while you work at your own speed. This book includes 12 self-paced lessons that let you discover essential skills and explore the new features and capabilities of InDesign CS3. Each lesson includes step-by-step instructions and lesson files available on the Digital Classroom web site at *agitraining.com/digitalclassroom*. The *Digital Classroom: InDesign CS3* lessons are developed by the same team of Adobe Certified Instructors and InDesign experts that have created many of the official training titles for Adobe Systems.

Prerequisites

Before you start the lessons in *Digital Classroom: InDesign CS3,* you should have a working knowledge of your computer and its operating system. You should know how to use the directory system of your computer so that you can navigate through folders. You need to understand how to locate, save, and open files. You should also know how to use your mouse to access menus and commands.

Before starting the lessons files in *Digital Classroom: InDesign CS3*, make sure that you have installed Adobe InDesign CS3. The software is sold separately, and not included with this book. You may use the 30-day trial version of Adobe InDesign CS3 available at the *Adobe.com* web site, subject to the terms of its license agreement.

System requirements

Before starting the lessons in *Digital Classroom: InDesign CS3*, make sure that your computer is equipped for running Adobe InDesign CS3, which you must purchase separately. The minimum system requirements for your computer to effectively use the software are listed on the following page.

System requirements for Adobe InDesign CS3:

Windows OS

- Intel® Pentium® 4, Intel Centrino®, Intel Xeon®, or Intel Core™ Duo (or compatible) processor
- Microsoft® Windows® XP with Service Pack 2 or Windows Vista™ Home Premium, Business, Ultimate, or Enterprise (certified for 32-bit editions)
- 512MB of RAM (1GB recommended)
- 1.8 GB of available hard-disk space (additional free space required during installation)
- 1,024x768 monitor resolution with 16-bit video card
- DVD-ROM drive
- QuickTime 7 software required for multimedia features
- Internet or phone connection required for product activation

Macintosh OS

- 1GHz PowerPC® G4 or G5 or multicore Intel® processor
- Mac OS X v10.4.8–10.5 (Leopard)
- 512MB of RAM (1GB recommended)
- 1.6 GB of available hard-disk space (additional free space required during installation)
- 1,024x768 monitor resolution with 16-bit video card
- DVD-ROM drive
- QuickTime 7 software required for multimedia features
- Internet or phone connection required for product activation

Starting Adobe InDesign CS3

As with most software, Adobe InDesign CS3 is launched by locating the application in your Programs folder (Windows) or Applications folder (Mac OS). If you are not familiar with starting the program, follow these steps to start the Adobe InDesign CS3 application:

Windows

1 Choose Start > All Programs > Adobe InDesign CS3.

2 Close the Welcome Screen when it appears. You are now ready to use Adobe InDesign CS3.

Mac OS

1 Open the Applications folder, and then open the Adobe InDesign CS3 folder.

2 Double-click on the Adobe InDesign CS3 application icon.

3 Close the Welcome Screen when it appears. You are now ready to use Adobe InDesign CS3.

Menus and commands are identified throughout the book by using the greater-than symbol (>). For example, the command to print a document would be identified as File > Print.

Fonts used in this book

Digital Classroom: InDesign CS3 includes lessons that refer to fonts that were installed with your copy of Adobe InDesign CS3. If you did not install the fonts, or have removed them from your computer, you may substitute different fonts for the exercises or re-install the software to access the fonts.

If you receive a Missing Font Warning, press OK and proceed with the lesson.

Resetting the InDesign workspace and preferences

To make certain that your panels and working environment are consistent, you should reset your workspace at the start of each lesson. To reset your workspace, choose Window > Workspace > Default Workspace (Windows) or Window > Workspace > Default (Mac OS).

You can reset the settings for InDesign at the start of each lesson to make certain you match the instructions used in this book. To reset the InDesign preferences, Start Adobe InDesign, and immediately press Shift+Alt+Ctrl (Windows) or Shift+Option+Command (Mac OS). Press OK to reset the preferences.

Loading lesson files

Digital Classroom: InDesign CS3 uses files that accompany the exercises for each of the lessons. You may download the entire lessons folder from the *Digital Classroom: InDesign CS3* web site, *agitraining.com/digitalclassroom*, to your hard drive, or download only the lesson folders for the individual lessons you wish to complete.

For each lesson in the book, the files are referenced by the file name of each file. The exact location of each file on your computer is not used, as you may have placed the files in a unique location on your hard drive. We suggest placing the lesson files in the My Documents folder (Windows) or at the top level of your hard drive (Mac OS).

Macintosh users may need to unlock the files after they are installed. This only applies to Mac OS computers. After copying the files to your computer, select the idlessons folder, then choose File > Get Info. In the idlessons info window, click the You can drop-down menu labeled Read Only, which is located in the Ownership section of this window. From the You can drop-down menu, choose Read & Write. Click the arrow to the left of Details, then click the Apply to enclosed items... button at the bottom of the window. You may need to click the padlock icon before the Mac OS allows you to change these permissions. After making these changes, close the window.

Additional resources

The Digital Classroom series goes beyond the training books. You can continue your learning online, with training videos, at seminars and conferences, and in-person training events.

Video training series

Expand your knowledge of the Adobe Creative Suite 3 applications with the Digital Classroom video training series that complements the skills you'll learn in this book. Learn more at *agitraining.com*.

Seminars and conferences

The authors of the Digital Classroom seminar series frequently conduct in-person seminars and speak at conferences, including the annual CRE8 Conference. Learn more at *agitraining.com*.

Resources for educators

Visit *agitraining.com* to access resources for educators, including instructors' guides for incorporating Digital Classroom into your curriculum.

Lesson 1

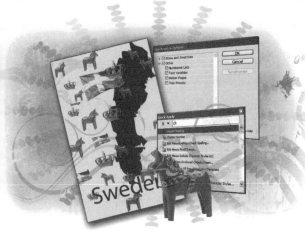

What you'll learn in this lesson:

- Boosting your InDesign productivity

- Enhancing text formatting

- Expanding your creative capabilities

- Using enhanced table formatting tricks

What's New in InDesign CS3?

InDesign CS3 is a significant step forward in page-layout software. Whether you are a creative professional or a production artist, InDesign CS3 includes enhancements that make it easier to produce and distribute compelling content. We've highlighted some of the program's key new features in this lesson, and included references to the lessons in which they're discussed in more detail.

Starting up

This lesson provides an overview of the new features of CS3. If you are new to InDesign, or prefer to get started with the hands-on projects, skip to Lesson 2, "Essential Skills."

Before starting, make sure that your tools and panels are consistent by resetting your preferences. See "Resetting the InDesign workspace and preferences" on page 3.

You will work with several files from the id01lessons folder in this lesson. Make sure that you have loaded the idlessons folder onto your hard drive. See "Loading lesson files" on page 4.

See Lesson 1 in action!

Explore more of the features shown in this lesson using the supplemental video tutorial available online at agitraining.com/digitalclassroom.

Improved styles

When designing your layouts, you may want to create the same border for all the picture frames or assign the same text attributes, such as color, size, and font, to all the headlines. InDesign makes it easier than ever to save a snapshot of these attributes, called Styles, for repeated use. You can save an enormous amount of time and maintain consistency in your layouts by using styles to apply formatting. You can create text styles for individual characters, such as the numbers used in the step-by-step instructions in this book, or for an entire paragraph. Object styles can include attributes such as the border or drop shadow applied to a graphic frame.

InDesign CS3 introduces styles for tables and the cells within a table. This allows you to quickly and easily format tables so they maintain a consistent look.

1   Open Adobe InDesign CS3.

2   Choose File > Open. In the Open a File dialog box, navigate to the id01lessons folder within the idlessons folder you placed on your desktop, then double-click the id01.indd file to open it.

This is a one-page brochure with information about Stockholm, Sweden. If you receive any warnings relating to missing fonts, press OK and don't worry about them, as you'll be formatting the text over the next few steps.

3   From the Tools panel, choose the Type tool (T). Click the cursor anywhere in the table listing city names in the upper-right corner of the document so that the insertion point is blinking within the table.

4   Press the Table Styles button (⊟) in the dock on the right side of the workspace to display the Table Styles panel. You can also choose Window > Type & Tables > Table Styles to display the panel.

5 In the Table Styles panel, select the City Table Style to apply this style to the table where the cursor is located. The table formatting, including rules (lines), background color, and text formatting, changes. You will work more with table styles in Lesson 7, "Creating and Using Tables."

City	Population
Stockholm	1,500,000
Gothenburg	490,000
Malmo	278,000
Uppsala	185,000

Table styles let you quickly format an entire table, including cell and text attributes.

Styles applied to text characters and paragraphs can be grouped together into a nested style. Nested styles let you quickly and easily apply multiple formats to text in a single step. InDesign CS3 now lets you repeat nested styles in a paragraph, such as a list, in a single step.

6 With the Type tool still activated, click anywhere within the text listing statistics about Sweden, located along the bottom of the document.

7 Press the Paragraph Styles button (◻▯) in the dock, or choose Type > Paragraph Styles. The Paragraph Styles panel opens.

8 In the Paragraph Styles panel, click to select the Nested List Style and apply it to the text. Notice that two alternating formats apply to the text. This is called a nested style, or a style that accommodates multiple styles within it. You will learn more about nested styles in Lesson 5, "Working with Styles."

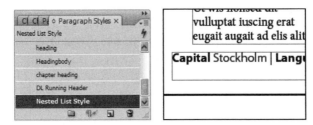

Use nested styles to apply repetitive formatting to text.

9 Choose File > Save As. In the Save As dialog box, type **id01_work.indd** into the Name text field. Navigate to the id01lessons folder, then press Save.

Quickly apply formatting to text and objects

Styles and other commands can be applied using the enhanced Quick Apply option to speed up the formatting of your documents. Simply select the object or text you wish to format, then press Ctrl+Enter (Windows) or Command+Return (Mac OS) to access the Quick Apply feature. When the Quick Apply panel opens, type the first few letters of the style you want to apply, and when that style is highlighted, press Enter (Windows) or Return (Mac OS) to apply it to the object or text.

1   From the Tools panel, choose the Type tool (T) and click the cursor in the blue headline text so the blinking insertion point appears anywhere within the word *Stockholm*.

2   Using your keyboard, press Ctrl+Enter (Windows) or Command+Return (Mac OS). The Quick Apply panel appears.

3   Type **ch** and the Quick Apply panel lists all styles that start with the letters *ch*, including the chapter heading style. Click on the chapter heading style to apply it to the *Stockholm* text.

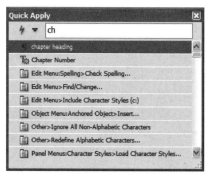

Use Quick Apply to easily format text or objects.

Quick Apply lets you apply character, paragraph, object, and table styles. It also lets you apply key commands and scripts. You can learn more about working with styles in Lesson 5, "Working with Styles."

4   Choose File > Save to save your work. Keep this file open for the next part of the lesson.

You can use the arrow keys on your keyboard to scroll through the various Quick Apply options, then press Enter (Windows) or Return (Mac OS) to apply the desired style or command.

Importing files

When designing a page, you need to pull together assets from different locations. These can include a variety of content, such as images, illustrations, and text. InDesign CS3 took a process that had been relatively unchanged for the past decade, and improved it dramatically. You can now import multiple files in a single instance, obtain a preview of text or graphic files as they are being placed, and cycle through files before they are placed into your document. These capabilities save you time, and help ensure that you are importing the correct file before you place it into your document.

Additionally, you can now place native InDesign files, which means that it is no longer necessary to create a PDF of an InDesign page that you wish to use in your layout. This is useful if you have a cover design, created using InDesign, for a book or magazine that you want to promote in a brochure.

Import InDesign documents into your layout
without converting them to another file format.

You'll find these features demonstrated throughout this book, especially in Lesson 4, "Working with Text and Type," and Lesson 6, "Working with Graphics."

Fitting frames

In the past, you would have to manually fit the frames of text and images placed into your layout to the content. While this level of manual control is still possible within InDesign CS3, you can now set your text and graphics to automatically fit to a specific size.

If you have dozens, or hundreds, of images to import into a catalog layout, InDesign can now automatically reduce or enlarge each item automatically to the appropriate size as it imports the image.

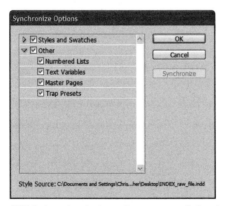

You can define frames' fitting settings even before you import the content.

Synchronizing master pages

Book publishers need to keep their individual sections and chapters consistent. In previous editions of InDesign, this involved building one template file and hoping that all designers working on the file maintained the original design. If a master page needed to be changed, all chapters had to be manually updated.

InDesign CS3 makes this a one-step process; master pages can be defined in a single document and then distributed to all documents that are part of a book. You can learn more about these capabilities in Lesson 10, "Advanced Document Features."

With book synchronization options, you can easily keep book formatting consistent across multiple InDesign documents.

Text wrap on master pages

Wrapping text around an object is not a new feature. Page layout software has been able to do this for years. But previous versions of InDesign didn't let you place an object on a master page and define a text wrap that would push the text away, regardless of the page on which the object appeared. Instead, you needed to manually apply the text wrap, sometimes referred to as run-around.

With InDesign CS3 you can apply a single text wrap to an object on a master page, and the object is pushed away from the text regardless of the page on which it is used. You can learn more about this in Lesson 3, "Building Documents and Master Pages."

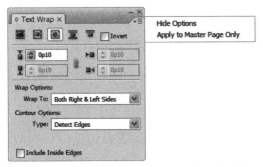

Applying text wraps in InDesign CS3 is easy, and more flexible.

Photoshop transparency effects

InDesign has borrowed some great features from Photoshop CS3, making it easier to design and apply interesting and artistic effects to images and objects from within InDesign. Many effects and designs that previously required you to work in both InDesign and Photoshop can now be achieved in one place.

1   In the id01_work.indd file, choose the Selection tool (**k**) from the Tools panel.

2   Click to select the picture of Stockholm located at the top of the layout.

3   Choose Object > Effects > Gradient Feather. The Effects dialog box opens.

4 In the Effects dialog box, click the Preview checkbox to preview the effect as you make adjustments to the settings in the dialog box. You can see the image adopt the default settings, and fade from full opacity to transparent. Keep all settings unchanged, then press OK.

Apply Photoshop transparency effects without leaving InDesign.

5 Choose Edit > Deselect All so you do not affect this image with future modifications.

6 Choose File > Save, and keep the file open.

Customizable interface

You can customize your version of InDesign yourself, without the need for power tools or safety glasses. Simply make a trip to a couple menus and you can customize most menu choices and some of the panels.

1 Choose Edit > Menus. The Menu Customization dialog box appears.

2 In the Menu Customization dialog box, click the arrow to the left of File to display all the commands available from the File menu.

3 Locate the Save As command and click the eye icon (👁) to the right of this command. When the eye is not visible, the command does not appear in the menu choices. Repeat this process to hide the Check In and the Save a Copy commands from the File menu, then press OK to close the Menu Customization dialog box.

Personalize your menus and navigate through InDesign more quickly and easily.

4 Click the File menu and notice that the three choices you disabled are no longer visible.

5 Choose Edit > Menus. The Menu Customization dialog box appears. Click the area in the visibility column next to Save As, Check In, and Save a Copy so that the eye icon is once again visible. These items now appear in the File menu. Keep the Menu Customization dialog box open.

6 Click to select the Save command, then click the word None in the Color column. The word None becomes a drop-down menu. Click it again and choose Green from the color choices, then press OK to close the Menu Customization dialog box.

7 Click the File menu and notice that the Save option is highlighted in green. This feature makes it easier for you to locate certain commands.

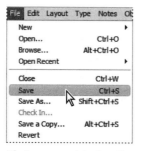

The Save command stands out because of the green highlight you applied.

The Control panel can be similarly customized.

8 From the Tools panel, choose the Selection tool (➤).

9 Click once to select the picture of Stockholm. Notice that the Control panel, located above the InDesign workspace, displays the size, position, and other information about the selected image.

10 At the far-right side of the Control panel, press the panel menu button (•≡) and choose Customize. The Customize Control Panel dialog box opens. Click the checkbox to deselect the Object option; all the Object options become deselected. Click the triangle next to Object to display additional options and click the Transform X-Y-W-H so it is the only item selected. Press OK to close the Customize Control Panel dialog box.

Reselect the image of Stockholm. Notice that the Control panel now only displays the transform information relating to the selected object.

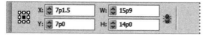

Disabling the Object option leaves only the transform information in the Control panel.

11 Along the far right side of the Control panel, click the panel menu button again and choose Customize. The Customize Control Panel window opens. Click to reselect the Object option. All the Object options are once again selected. Press OK to close the Customize Control Panel dialog box.

Keep the file open; you will continue to work with it in the next exercise.

Exporting HTML

InDesign CS3 makes it much easier to convert your print projects into content for the Web, especially if you use Adobe Dreamweaver CS3.

1   Choose File > Cross-media Export > XHTML/Dreamweaver. The Save As dialog box appears. Navigate to the id01lessons folder, then open the Web folder and press Save. The XHTML Export Options dialog box appears.

2   In the XHTML Export Options dialog box, you can choose options relating to the XHTML file that will be generated from your InDesign document. If it's not already done, set the Export option to Document, not Selection. Keep all other settings unchanged and press Export to generate the XHTML file.

Generate XHTML files from your InDesign documents to put them on the Web.

You can open and edit the XHTML file that was generated using Dreamweaver CS3, or view the file using your web browser.

Improved lists

You may need to create documents that contain different types of lists. Maybe you need to use numbered lists, or perhaps lists with bullets. InDesign CS3 makes it possible to create sophisticated lists, but it does require a little bit of work. You can now create lists with multiple levels, span lists across multiple text frames that are not connected, and use the Paragraph Styles panel to more easily format the numbers or bullets used in a list. In Lesson 4, "Working with Text and Type," these capabilities are covered in more detail.

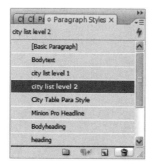

One way to add a more fun, or sophisticated, look to your lists is to use the Paragraph Styles panel.

Text variables

If you create documents with various sections, such as catalogs, magazines, books, or brochures, you can benefit from the variable text capabilities of InDesign CS3.

In order for this exercise to function correctly, you must have formatted the headline using the Styles discussed earlier in the lesson. If you have not already formatted the headline using the chapter heading style, do so now.

1   Using the Type tool (T), click to insert the cursor in the empty text frame in the upper-right corner of the page.

2   Choose Type > Text Variables > Insert Variable > Running Header. The word *Stockholm* appears in the text box.

This is because the style applied to the *Stockholm* text has been defined as a variable. InDesign located the first usage of the text on the page, and then placed it into the running header. You'll discover more about text variables in Lesson 10, "Advanced Document Features."

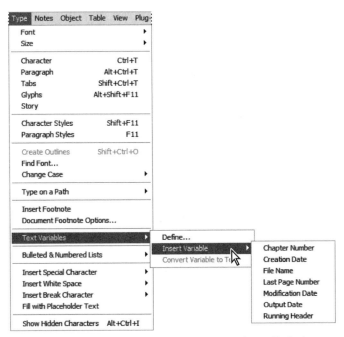

Go to Type > Text Variables > Insert Variable > Running Header to add a header to your Stockholm brochure.

Choose File > Close to close the document. When asked if you want to save your changes, choose No.

Now that you've had a chance to see many of the new and improved features in the latest version of InDesign, let's take a quick tour of all that InDesign has to offer in Lesson 2, "Essential Skills." Throughout the remainder of the book you'll get a more in-depth look at specific features and capabilities of InDesign CS3.

Lesson 2

What you'll learn in this lesson:

- Managing the workspace
- Placing and formatting text
- Repositioning images
- Applying paragraph and character styles
- Using object styles and effects

Essential Skills

In this lesson, you will learn some of the most essential skills for working efficiently inside an InDesign document. To start, you'll learn how to navigate within InDesign and customize its appearance. Later on in the lesson, you will place graphics and add formatting to text to create a finished product. All the topics in this lesson are covered in detail later in this book, so this lesson serves to get you up-and-running quickly, and to preview some of InDesign CS3's amazing features.

Starting up

Before starting, make sure that your tools and panels are consistent by resetting your preferences. See "Resetting the InDesign workspace and preferences" on page 3.

You will work with several files from the id02lessons folder in this lesson. Make sure that you have loaded the idlessons folder onto your hard drive. See "Loading lesson files" on page 4.

InDesign's tools

InDesign is built around the Tools panel. Located in the upper-left corner of your screen by default, the Tools panel provides everything you need to design and edit within InDesign. Every tool in the Tools panel has its own keyboard shortcut that allows you to quickly switch between different tools. If you hover your cursor over one of the tools in the Tools panel, a tooltip appears, displaying the tool's name and keyboard shortcut.

The InDesign workspace

When you open a document in InDesign, the file opens into a window that displays the page(s) contained within the document. In the same window are many panels that perform specific tasks on the document. Managing these panels allows you to easily and more efficiently work with your InDesign documents. The combination of windows and panels is referred to as the InDesign workspace. Let's take a closer look.

The document window

Most of the content in your document window is located within the page area, denoted by a black border. Anything positioned within this area appears on the final printed page. The area outside of the black border is referred to as the pasteboard. Anything that is placed completely outside the black border onto the pasteboard does not print on the final page.

You can place elements on the pasteboard while designing your project, and then move the elements on or off the page to try different variations of layout design. The pasteboard can also be a useful area to put notes to yourself or coworkers working on the same project. To get a better understanding of the InDesign workspace, you'll open up the completed project and reset the workspace.

1 Choose File > Open. In the Open dialog box, navigate to the id02lessons folder and select the id02_done.indd file. Press Open.

2 Choose Window > Workspace > Default Workspace to reset your panels to their InDesign default positions. This ensures that your panels are in position for easy referencing during this lesson.

With your document open in InDesign, your screen should now resemble the figure below.

*A. The document window. **B**. The page (black lines). **C**. The pasteboard. **D**. Bleed guides. **E**. Margin guides. **F**. Column guides.*

Showing and hiding guides

There are elements on the page, called guides, which are non-printing elements used to align and lay objects out on the page. Though useful, they can be distracting when you want to see only the elements on the page that will print.

1 Choose View > Grids & Guides > Hide Guides or use the keyboard shortcut Ctrl+; (Windows) or Command+; (Mac OS) to hide all the guides in the open document.

2 Choose View > Grids & Guides > Show Guides or use the keyboard shortcut Ctrl+; (Windows) or Command+; (Mac OS) to show all the guides in the open document.

By hiding the guides in your document, you can more clearly see the printable parts of your layout. When you need to make adjustments to elements on the page, simply show guides. Now you have the references that the guides provide for laying out elements on the page.

Viewing modes

Content on the pasteboard can be distracting when trying to view only what will print on the final page. Fortunately, in addition to the ability to hide guides, InDesign provides viewing modes that hide all non-printing elements on a page. That includes elements that are on the pasteboard. With one click of a button, you can see your document exactly as it will appear in its final printed form.

1 Click and hold the Mode button (▣) at the bottom of the Tools panel, and choose Preview from the submenu. Notice that the entire pasteboard is now gray and hides any elements located on the pasteboard.

2 Click and hold the Mode button again and choose Bleed from the menu. This shows the allowable bleed area that was specified when the document was created. This is very useful when you need to make sure that all the elements on your page extend to the bleed line.

3 Finally, click and hold the Mode button again and return to Normal.

You can also use the shortcut key W to toggle between Preview and Normal Modes in InDesign. Keep in mind that it will not work if you have the Type tool active and your cursor inside a text frame.

Working with panels

Now that you understand the different pieces of a document, it's time to begin working with the interface and become acquainted with the program's panels.

The Tools panel

The Tools panel is located on the left side of your screen and contains all the tools necessary to draw, set type, modify, and change elements in your document. By default, the Tools panel appears in a single-column strip docked to the left side of your screen. You can modify the appearance and location of the Tools panel to accommodate your needs.

1   Click on the double-arrow icon at the top of the Tools panel to switch from the single-column layout to a double-column layout.

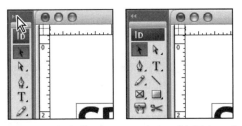

Clicking on the double arrow icon at the top of the Tools panel switches from single-column layout to the double-column layout.

2   Click on the gray bar at the top of the Tools panel and drag to the right. When you release the mouse button, the Tools panel is repositioned at a different area of your screen. You can position and dock this panel anywhere within your document window.

3   Click on the gray bar at the top of the Tools panel and drag the panel to the right so that it is just to the left of the panels. A blue vertical bar appears. Release the mouse button and the Tools panel is docked to the right of your screen.

Managing panels

InDesign contains numerous other panels that perform different tasks. By default, you have several panels that are in a dock at the right side of the document window. InDesign CS3 treats panels differently than in previous versions. For instance, by default, all the panels that are docked at the right of your document window are in collapsed mode, saving you valuable screen space when working on a document. Let's explore how these panels work.

1 Press the double-arrow icon (◀◀) at the top of the docked panels at the right side of the document window. This expands the dock of panels to reveal the contents of every panel. This is similar to what you may have seen in previous versions of InDesign.

2 Press the double-arrow icon again to collapse the dock and return the panels to their previous state.

3 Press the Info button (ℹ) in the dock. This reveals the entire contents of the Info panel.

4 Press the Info button again, and the panel closes to its basic button appearance.

5 Click and drag the Info button to the far left side of the document window until the blue vertical bar appears again. Release the mouse button. The info panel is now docked to the left side of the document window.

You are in no way limited by the appearance of the panels that display when you first launch InDesign. You can customize the panels however you like. Go ahead and experiment a little further. Move them to different areas on your screen to see how you may like them positioned as you work. You can always get back to the defaults, as you'll see later in this lesson.

Customizing the Control panel

The Control panel is the panel that appears across the top of the document window. The Control panel is contextual, meaning its contents change depending on what tool you have chosen in the Tools panel. The options available for each tool can vary from computer to computer, depending on your monitor's size and resolution. The larger your monitor and the higher the resolution, the more options you'll see in the Control panel. With smaller monitors, InDesign simply truncates the number of available options that you see. Fortunately, even if you don't have a large monitor, you can control which options will appear in the Control panel for each type of tool.

1 Choose the Selection tool (▶) in the Tools panel so that its options display in the Control panel. Note that the Text Wrap options are available as shown in the figure below.

The Control panel with the Text Wrap options displayed.

2 Press the panel menu button (◄≡) in the far right side of the Control panel and choose Customize.

3   In the Customize Control panel dialog box, click the triangle next to
Object and uncheck Text Wrap. Press OK.

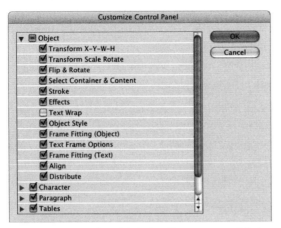

*The Customize Control Panel dialog box allows you to control the items
that appear in the Control panel when different tools are selected.*

The Text Wrap options are no longer displayed in the Control panel because
they have been disabled. Any of the options you see in the Customize
Control panel dialog box can be enabled or disabled to make room for
other options that you would like to appear in the Control panel.

Saving your workspace

Once you have adjusted the panels to display in a way that you prefer, and have
customized the Control panel to your liking, you can save those settings as a
new workspace. This allows you to switch back to it if you ever make changes to
the panels, or if you want to experiment with other panel configurations.

1   Choose Window > Workspace > Save Workspace.

2   In the Save Workspace dialog box, enter Lesson 2 in the name field and
press OK.

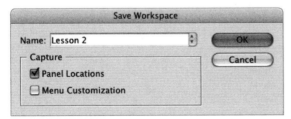

*Saving your workspace allows you to easily restore the panel positions and
Control panel customizations.*

You've now saved the locations of your panels and the Control panel customization as a workspace that you can always revert to if needed. Let's see how.

3   Choose Window > Workspace > Default workspace. All the panels are restored to InDesign's default workspace.

4   Choose Window > Workspace > Lesson 2. All the panels are restored to the Workspace that you saved earlier in step 1.

InDesign allows you to have multiple workspaces that are not document-specific, and can be used in any document that you have open. Before proceeding to the next section, reset your workspace to the default so that the panels match the rest of the lesson.

Navigating an InDesign document

In this exercise, you'll continue working with the id02_done.indd file, which is the completed newsletter that you opened at the beginning of the lesson. You'll explore the tools used to navigate to different pages in an InDesign document, as well as change the document's magnification.

Using the Pages panel

The Pages panel provides a quick glimpse inside an InDesign document by displaying small thumbnails of each page and summarizing how many pages are in a document.

1   Press the Pages button (⊞) in the dock at the right of the workspace to display the Pages panel. The bottom left of the Pages panel indicates that there are four pages in three spreads within this document.

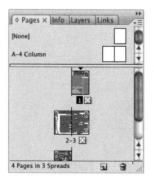

The Pages panel manages and displays the pages within your InDesign document.

2   Double-click on page 2 in the Pages panel to display page 2 of your document within the workspace. The left page of the inside spread (page 2) appears on the document window.

3   Double-click on page 4 in the Pages panel to display page 4 of your document within the workspace.

If you are unable to see all the pages in the Pages panel, you can make the panel larger by clicking and dragging on the bottom-right corner of the panel to enlarge it. In addition, InDesign allows you to scroll through the pages in the Pages panel by using the scroll bar, the scroll wheel on your mouse, or you can click to the side of the page thumbnails and drag up or down to navigate through the pages.

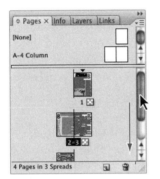

Scroll through the pages in the Pages panel by dragging the scroll bar.

Changing the magnification of your document

So far, you've been viewing this document at the default magnification at which the document was last saved. It is often necessary to get a closer look at components of your document to check things such as alignment, kerning of type, legibility, etc. InDesign provides the tools necessary to do this quickly and easily.

1   Double-click on page 1 in the Pages panel to return to the first page of the document.

2   Select the Zoom tool (🔍), then click in the upper-left area of the Spinnews logo and drag down to the lower-right corner of the logo and release the mouse. InDesign enlarges the area that you just selected.

Click and drag around an area to zoom in on it.

3   You may find that you enlarged the document too much or not enough. To fine-tune the magnification, you can click with the Zoom tool to increase the magnification incrementally or hold down the Alt (Windows) or Option (Mac OS) key while you click with the Zoom tool to decrease the magnification incrementally.

You can quickly zoom in and out of the document incrementally by using the keyboard shortcut Ctrl+plus sign (Windows) or Command+plus sign (Mac OS) to zoom in on a document, or Ctrl+minus sign (Windows) or Command+minus sign (Mac OS) to zoom out.

4   When you are zoomed in on a document, it's often necessary to fine-tune the position of the page within the document window. This can be done easily by selecting the Hand tool (✋) from the Tools panel, then clicking and dragging on your page. This will move the page within the document window, allowing you to focus on specific areas of your page.

You can also access the Hand tool without selecting it from the Tools panel. Simply hold down the spacebar on your keyboard and your cursor changes to the Hand tool. If you have the Type tool selected, you will also need to hold down the Alt (Windows) or Option (Mac OS) key to access the Hand tool.

5   To make your page fit within the document window again, choose View > Fit Page in Window or press Ctrl+0 (Windows) or Command+0 (Mac OS). The currently selected page now fits inside the document window.

6   Choose File > Close to close the document. If asked to save, choose No (Windows) or Don't Save (Mac OS).

Working with type

In this section, you'll explore the excellent typographic tools that InDesign provides when working with type. InDesign provides complete control over the formatting and placement of type on a page and allows you to save formatting in the form of a style to give your project consistency throughout a document or multiple documents. To see the type capabilities, you'll open a new file that is partially completed, then apply text and formatting to complete it.

Entering and formatting type

When working with type in InDesign, it's important to remember that type can only exist inside a frame. A frame is a container that holds text or a graphic that will appear on a page. There are three different types of frames in InDesign: text frames, graphic frames, and unassigned frames. In this exercise, you'll be working with text frames.

1 Choose File > Open. In the Open dialog box, navigate to the id02lessons folder and select the id0201.indd file. Press Open. You will use this partially completed project for the remainder of the lesson.

2 Choose File > Save As. In the Save As dialog box, navigate to the id02lessons folder. In the Name text field, type **id0201_work.indd**, then press Save.

3 Press the Pages button (⬚) in the dock to the right of the workspace to open the Pages panel. In the Pages panel, double-click on page 1 to center the page in the workspace.

4 Select the Type tool (T) from the Tools panel, then click and drag from the left side of the page where the left margin and the first horizontal guide meet, to where the right margin and the second horizontal guide meet. Release the mouse button. You should now see the cursor blinking in the top-left corner of the frame.

5 Type **Fending off the winter blues with cross-training**. The text appears in the font and size that InDesign uses by default.

Type the headline into the newly created text frame.

6 In the dock, press the Paragraph Styles button (⊡) to open the Paragraph Styles panel. Select Heading from the list in the Paragraph Styles panel to apply that paragraph style to the type in the frame.

Apply the paragraph style to the text.

7 Notice that the top line of the sentence is much longer than the bottom line. To balance the lines, press the panel menu button (•≡) in the Control panel and choose Balance Ragged Lines from the submenu. InDesign automatically balances the lines within the frame.

Apply the Balance Ragged Lines command to the headline.

Placing and formatting type

You can add text to an InDesign document by either entering it directly within InDesign, or by placing it into the document from an external file. InDesign accepts several forms of text files including Microsoft Word, ASCII, Rich Text, and InDesign Tagged Text.

1 Press the Pages button (⊡) in the dock to open the Pages panel. Double-click on page 2 in the Pages panel. Using the Type tool (T), click inside the empty frame below the headline *Caring for Those Wheels* to insert your cursor within the frame.

2 Choose File > Place. In the Place dialog box, navigate to the Links folder inside the id02lessons folder and choose the file Wheels.txt. Press Open. The text of the file should appear inside the active frame.

3 Make sure your cursor is at the beginning of the first paragraph, and choose Body from the Paragraph Styles panel to apply the correct formatting to the text.

Note that only the first paragraph of text has been formatted using the style. This is because a Paragraph style only applies formatting to a single paragraph. To apply formatting to multiple paragraphs, several paragraphs must be selected.

4   Use the keyboard shortcut Ctrl+A (Windows) or Command+A (Mac OS) to select all the type within the current frame. From the Paragraph Styles panel, choose Body. All the selected paragraphs are formatted using the Body style.

Flowing type

It is often necessary for text to span multiple text frames and pages in InDesign. In the following steps, you will learn how to flow text into several columns in a layout.

1   Double-click on page 3 in the Pages panel to display page 3 in the document window.

2   Using the Type tool, click inside the first frame on the left side of the page underneath the heading *Race Calendar.*

3   Choose File > Place. In the Place dialog box, navigate to the Links folder inside the id02lessons folder. Select the file Calendar.txt and press Open to place the text from the file into the frame.

4   Activate the Selection tool (✳) from the Tools panel, then select the text frame if it is not already selected.

Every text frame in InDesign contains an in port located in the upper-left corner of the frame and an out port located in the lower right corner of the frame. Currently, the outer edge of the active frame contains a red plus sign. This red plus sign indicates that there is overset text, which is text that doesn't fit into the current frame. Overset text can be fixed by deleting text until there isn't any text that is overset, making the frame bigger, or linking the current frame to another frame.

The newly-placed text on the page is overset.

5 Using the Selection tool, click once on the red plus sign on the outer edge of the frame. A loaded text icon appears.

6 Move your cursor on top of the second frame to the right of the first frame. Notice that the loaded text icon changes to a thread icon.

7 Click inside the second frame to link the first and second frames.

8 Click once on the red plus sign on the outer edge of the second frame, then click inside the third frame to link the second and third frames together.

9 Choose File > Save to save your work.

Using styles

There are several different types of styles in InDesign. Styles provide a method of applying consistent formatting to various aspects of your document, including type, frames, and tables. In this section, you'll use some predefined styles to apply formatting to text and objects in a consistent and efficient manner.

Applying paragraph styles

Paragraph styles apply formatting to an entire paragraph of text. You can't apply a Paragraph Style to a single word unless it is the only word in the paragraph. This is an important distinction to make within InDesign, as it determines how you will create and apply styles to your text.

1 Select the Type tool (T) from the Tools panel and click anywhere inside the word *January* on the first line of the first frame on page 3.

2 In the Paragraph Styles panel, choose Calendar Month to apply the correct formatting to the word *January*. Click within the words *February*, in the second column, then *March*, in the third column and apply the Calendar Month Paragraph Style to these month names as well.

3   Using the Type tool, select all the text between the *January* and *February* headings and select Calendar Event from the Paragraph Styles panel. Repeat this step for the remainder of unformatted text in the calendar text on page 3.

Format the text using the Calendar Event style from the Paragraph Styles panel.

The Calendar Event text includes a nested style, which automatically applies formatting to text within a Paragraph Style. The nested style formats the text based on triggers such as periods and commas that appear within the paragraph. To learn more about nested styles, refer to Lesson 5, "Working with Styles."

Applying character styles

Unlike paragraph styles, character styles can be applied to a word or even a single character. This is useful when applying common formatting, such as bold and italic, to text. You won't find a button anywhere in InDesign to apply bold and italic formatting to text. To properly apply any type of styling to text, you need to either select it from one of the font menus or create a character style to do the work for you.

1   Double-click on page 2 in the Pages panel to display page 2 within the workspace.

2   Using the Zoom tool (🔍), zoom in on the first paragraph of text that starts with *Your wheels*.

3   Select the Type tool (T) from the Tools panel and select the word *wheels* at the top of the first paragraph by double-clicking it.

4 Press the Character Styles button (A) in the dock to open the Character Styles panel. Choose Italic from the Character Styles panel to apply that style to the selected word.

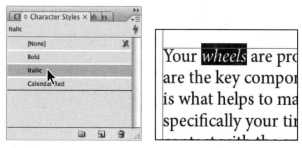

The Character style applies to a word rather than a whole paragraph.

Apply styles using Find/Change

Character Styles make easy work of applying formatting to selected areas of text. In the current story, we want every instance of wheels to be italicized. Finding each of them individually would be very time-consuming, so let's speed up the process a bit.

1 Using the Type tool, right click (Windows) or Ctrl+click (Mac OS) anywhere within the text frame on page 2 and choose Find/Change from the contextual menu.

2 In the resulting Find/Change dialog box, make sure that the Text tab at the top of the dialog box is selected and type **wheels** in the Find what text field.

3 Press the Specify attributes to change button (⚙) in the Change Format section of the dialog box.

Press the Specify attributes to change button.

4 In the resulting Change Format Settings dialog box, choose Italic from the Character Style menu and press OK.

Choose Italic from the Character Style drop-down menu.

5 Press the Change All button. A dialog box should appear indicating that five replacements have been made.

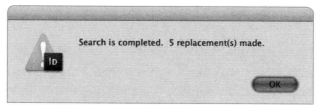

InDesign will notify you how many replacements are made when using the Find/Change option.

6 Press Done.

Applying object styles

Object styles provide a method by which you can consistently apply formatting to frames in your InDesign document. Properties such as effects, fill color, stroke color, and many more can be easily applied to elements on a page. In addition, an object style can automatically apply formatting to type that is contained within a frame. In the following section, you'll place some text into a text frame and then apply an object style to the frame to format it as a sidebar.

1 Double-click on page 1 in the Pages panel. You may need to zoom out a bit to see the full page. Choose the Hand tool (✋) from the Tools panel, then drag from the right to the left until you are able to see the text frame in the pasteboard, located to the right of the page.

2 Select the Type tool (T) from the Tools panel and click to insert your cursor inside the text frame.

3 Choose File > Place. In the Place dialog box, navigate to the Links folder within the id02lessons folder and select the file Sidebar.txt. Press Open.

4 Choose the Selection tool (▸) from the Tools panel and make sure the text frame is selected.

5 Press the Object Styles button (⊞) in the dock to open the Object Styles panel. In the Object Styles panel, choose Sidebar from the list. The entire frame, including the text inside, is automatically formatted.

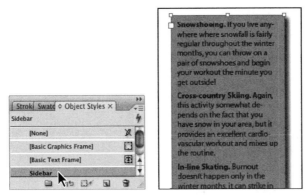

Object styles format entire objects, including text.

6 Using the Selection tool, click and drag the frame to the lower-right portion of page 1 aligning the lower right corner to the margin guides.

Working with graphics

Graphics are an integral part of any design, regardless of what program you use. InDesign provides excellent graphics capabilities and puts the user in complete control of cropping, sizing, and other aspects of the graphic's appearance. InDesign also supports a wide variety of graphic formats to use when placing images on a page, saving you time during the design process. These files include: .pdf, .tif, .jpg, .ai, and .eps. You can even place an .indd file inside an .indd file.

Placing graphics

Just as with text, graphics can only appear within a frame in InDesign. Fortunately, InDesign is flexible when it comes to placing images. If you don't define a frame to begin with, InDesign will create one for you.

1 Double-click on page 4 in the Pages panel to display page 4 within the workspace.

2 Choose File > Place. When the Place dialog box appears, navigate to the Links folder within the id02lessons folder and select the file cyclist.psd. Press Open. Because there was no frame selected, InDesign presents you with a loaded cursor indicating that it has an image that is ready to be placed in the active document.

3 Click once in the upper-left corner of the page where the red bleed guides intersect. This places the image at 100% beginning at the location where you clicked.

4 If the upper-left corner of the image is not in the correct location, simply click and drag the image using the Selection tool (▶).

5 Hold down Shift+Ctrl (Windows) or Shift+Command (Mac OS), then click and drag the lower-right handle of the frame. This scales the frame and the image inside the frame proportionately. Scale the frame until the bottom of the frame touches the bleed guide at the right side of the page.

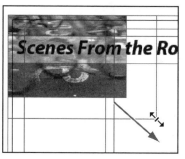

Scaling the image and the frame proportionately.

6 The image is slightly taller than desired, so with the Selection tool, simply click and drag the middle handle at the bottom of the frame upwards until it snaps to the guide in the middle of the page.

Moving the handles of a frame using the Selection tool without any modifier keys simply changes the size of the frame that contains the image, it only adjusts the cropping of the image and doesn't scale the image in any way.

7 If the text is hidden beneath the image, right-click (Windows) or Ctrl+click (Mac OS) the image and choose Arrange > Send to Back. This places the image behind the text.

Positioning graphics within a frame

When placing graphics in InDesign, the image is not always used at its original size. Usually there is a certain amount of cropping and scaling that is required to create the visual appearance that is desired. InDesign provides some visual tools that help when positioning and scaling graphics within a frame.

1   Double-click on page 1 in the Pages panel.

2   Using the Selection tool (✦), select the graphic frame at the bottom-left corner of page 1. InDesign displays graphic frames with an X inside an empty frame.

3   Choose File > Place. In the Place dialog box, navigate to the Links folder within the id02lessons folder and select the snowshoe.psd image. Press Open. The image is placed inside the selected frame.

4   The image is obviously much larger than the frame into which it was placed. But how much larger? Choose the Direct Selection tool (✦) in the Tools panel and select the snowshoe image. The content is displayed with a light brown border. This shows the actual size of the graphic within the frame. Select the Hand tool (✋) from the Tools panel and reposition the page within the document window so that the image's entire border is visible.

5   Using the Direct Selection tool, hold down Shift+Ctrl (Windows) or Shift+Command (Mac OS) and drag the bottom-right corner of the image to scale it proportionately. Scale the image until the width of the image is slightly larger than the width of the frame, and release the mouse button.

6   Move your cursor into the middle of the frame and you'll notice that the cursor changes to a hand (not to be confused with the Hand tool). Click with your mouse and drag to reposition the graphic within the frame. Continue adjusting the position until the graphic is cropped as desired.

The cropped image.

With your Direct Selection tool active, click with your mouse on an image and hold for a second, then begin moving the image. You'll get a dynamic preview of the image as you are moving it, which is extremely useful when positioning a graphic within a frame.

7 Use the keyboard shortcut Ctrl+0 (Windows) or Command+0 (Mac OS) to fit page 1 within the document window.

8 Choose File > Save to save your work.

Applying text wrap

The ability to wrap text around a shape is essential when designing many types of projects in InDesign. InDesign provides intuitive tools to make applying text wrap very easy. In this exercise, you'll continue working on page 1 to apply text wrap to an image.

1 Using the Selection tool (k), select the snowshoe image at the bottom of the page. Notice that the image is partially covering the text in the first column.

2 Choose Window > Text Wrap to open the Text Wrap panel.

3 Press the Wrap around bounding box button (▤) at the top of the panel to apply the text wrap to the selected image. The text wrap of the image forces the text to flow into the second column, making all the text visible.

The Wrap around bounding box button in the Text Wrap panel wraps the text around the bounding box of the shape.

4 To get a better understanding of how the text wrap is being applied to the text surrounding the graphic frame, move the snowshoe image up and down on page 1 using the Selection tool. This gives you an idea of how the image displaces the text around it. When you're finished, move the image back to its original location.

5 Press the X in the upper-right corner of the Text Wrap panel to close it.

Understanding layers

Whenever you create a project in InDesign, you may encounter situations where you have a large number of objects on a page to control. Layers can help organize the visual imagery and the text content that appear on a single page or multiple pages. Think of layers as transparent sheets lying on top of each other. If you put an object on a layer that is below another layer, as long as there aren't any objects covering up the object below it, it shows through the layer above it. Layers can also be used for versioning purposes. You can create two graphics layers with different images on each layer. That way you can hide one of the graphics layers to see one version and then hide the other graphics layers to see the other version.

Another common use for layers is to put your text and graphics on separate layers, so that when you print the document to proofread text, you can hide the graphics layer so that the document prints faster. In the next exercise, you'll see how layers can be used in this way.

1   Double-click on page 2 in the Pages panel, then choose View > Fit Spread in Window to display the entire spread in the workspace.

2   Choose Window > Layers or press the Layers button (◈) in the dock to open the Layers panel.

The Layers panel.

3   There are three layers listed in the Layers panel: Text, Graphics, and Background content. Press the visibility icon (👁) next to the Text layer to hide the content of the layer. All the text is temporarily hidden because that is the content that is on that layer. Press the visibility icon again to show the contents.

4   Turn the visibility of the Graphics and Background Content layers on and off to see the items that are on each layer.

> *It's important to understand that in InDesign, a layer encompasses the entire document. In other words, when you create a layer, that layer is available on every page in the document, including the master pages. So when you hide or show a layer, you are doing so for every page in the document.*

5   In the Pages panel, double-click on page 1.

6   Using the Selection tool (*), select the snowshoe image at the bottom of the page, then open the Layers panel by pressing the Layers button (◈) in the dock. Notice the blue square (■) that appears to the right of the Text layer. This indicates that the currently selected object is located on the text layer.

7   To move the image to the Graphics layer, click and drag the blue square on top of the Graphics layer. The dot moves to the Graphics layer and takes on the color that was assigned to the Graphics layer. In addition, the edge of the frame that contains the snowshoe graphic is now red, indicating that the frame is located on the Graphics layer.

Move the image from the Text layer to the Graphics layer.

8   Toggle the visibility icon of the Graphics layer off and on to hide and show the contents of that layer, verifying that the snowshoe image is on that layer.

9 Another useful feature is the ability to lock a layer to prevent yourself or other users from altering any of the contents on a layer. Click the square immediately to the left of the Graphics layer to lock it.

The padlock icon allows you to lock and unlock a layer, preventing any direct changes to objects on that layer.

10 Activate the Selection tool and try to select the snowshoe image. You cannot currently select it because the layer is locked.

11 Unlock the layer by clicking on the padlock (🔒) immediately to the left of the Graphics layer, then select the snowshoe image using the Selection tool. You can now select the image.

Locking a layer prevents all items on that layer, including ruler guides, from being selected. One way to use this to your advantage is to create a layer that contains all the guides for your document. This provides another method of hiding and showing your guides quickly. In addition, the guides take on the color of the layer on which they reside. This is a great way to consistently color-code the guides in your document.

Applying effects

InDesign has had the ability to apply effects to images and objects on a page for some time now. CS3, however, provides many additional effects that you previously could only accomplish in Photoshop. Effects in InDesign allow you to alter the transparency, as well as the appearance, of objects in a non-destructive manner. This means you can always remove or alter the effect at a later time without permanently affecting the image or object. InDesign CS3 provides a total of nine transparency effects: Drop Shadow, Inner Shadow, Outer Glow, Inner Glow, Bevel and Emboss, Satin, Basic Feather, Directional Feather, and Gradient Feather. Let's apply an effect to an object in this newsletter.

1 In the Pages panel, double-click on page 2.

2 Using the Selection tool (▸), select the blue border in the upper-left corner of the page. The border encompasses the entire spread.

3 Press the Effects button (*fx*) in the dock or choose Windows > Effects to open the Effects panel.

4 New to CS3 is the ability to affect different levels of an object independently of the others. In this case, we can apply an effect to the object, stroke, or fill of the selected object. Make sure that Object level is highlighted, and press the Add an object effect to the selected target button (*fx*) at the bottom of the panel. Choose Bevel and Emboss from the menu that appears.

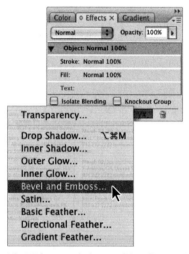

The FX button at the bottom of the Effects panel allows you to choose which effects to apply to the selected object(s).

5   In the Effects dialog box, leave the settings at the defaults and press OK.

The Effects dialog box.

6   Use the keyboard shortcut W to view the document in preview mode. This gives you a view of the final project without any of its non-printing elements.

7   Choose File > Save, then choose File > Close to close the file.

Congratulations! You have completed Lesson 2, "Essential Skills."

Resources for additional help

In-product help

InDesign includes help documentation directly within the application itself. Choose Help > InDesign Help, and InDesign will launch the Adobe Help Viewer, which allows you to search by the topic in question.

On-line help

Adobe makes the documentation for InDesign available on the Web in the form of Livedocs at *http://livedocs.adobe.com/en_US/InDesign/5.0/index.html*. The Livedocs help tends to be more current, as it can be updated very easily. In addition, Livedocs provides you with the ability to add comments to topics that you view and even receive an e-mail when someone else adds a comment to the topic. For many of the help files, you can also download them in PDF format for printing on your desktop printer.

Forums

Adobe on-line forums are an excellent resource for finding solutions to questions you have about InDesign or how InDesign integrates with other applications. Adobe forums are contributed to by a community of beginner, intermediate, and advanced users who may be looking for the same answer as you, or who have already discovered solutions and answers to questions and are willing to share their solutions with other users.

Self study

Place some of your own graphics into the newsletter that you just created, and practice cropping and repositioning the graphics within their frames. Move objects to other layers and create your own layer to further refine the organization of the file.

This lesson has given you a glimpse of the essential capabilities available in the latest version of InDesign. For more in-depth instructions on how to perform many of these tasks in detail, read and work through the other lessons in this book.

Review

Questions

1   What does the red plus sign on a text frame indicate?

2   What tool must be used to reposition an image inside of a frame?

3   How can you ensure that if you reposition the panels in InDesign to your liking, you could always bring them back to that state in the event that the panels got rearranged?

Answers

1   There is more text in the frame than can be displayed within the current frame. This is called overset text.

2   The Direct Selection tool.

3   Save a custom workspace by choosing Window > Workspace > Save Workspace.

Building Documents and Master Pages

Document page dimensions are the most basic and important information needed to create a new layout. InDesign CS3 gives you the ability to save commonly used page dimensions as presets, and create master pages to enhance your productivity and maintain consistency throughout your document pages.

Starting up

Before starting, make sure that your tools and panels are consistent by resetting your preferences. See "Resetting the InDesign workspace and preferences" on page 3.

You will work with several files from the id03lessons folder in this lesson. Make sure that you have loaded the idlessons folder onto your hard drive. See "Loading lesson files" on page 4.

The project

In this lesson, you will create a monthly magazine/newsletter for a company. This lesson takes advantage of InDesign CS3's powerful master page features to create several different layout templates for each of the sections in the magazine, create running headers and footers, and keep a consistent look and feel to the publication.

Planning your document

Before you can begin designing the magazine, you need to get some important information. What is the final trim size? How will the magazine bind? Will the document bleed? The answers to these questions are vital to properly setting up your magazine pages.

The first rule of print design is to always design to final size. The final trim size is the magazine's dimensions, once it has been collated, folded, bound, and trimmed. When you create your new document, you will use these dimensions as the page size. Next you need to determine how the magazine pages will be bound together.

There are several binding options:

- saddle-stiched (pages are stapled together on the fold of the spine)
- perfect bound (pages are glued onto the cover at the spine)
- three-hole punched (to be placed into three-ring binders)
- coil/ring bound (pages are bound together by coils or rings that run through holes punched on the spine of the pages)

The binding information is important for correctly setting up the margins for your documents. For example, if you are designing pages that will be three-hole punched and put into a binder, you need to ensure that the margin at the spine of each page allots enough space for the holes to be punched without cutting any copy. The binding information also helps to determine how the document and bleeds should be set up. Saddle-stiched books can only bleed on three sides (head, foot, outside edge). The other binding options can bleed on all four sides.

Bleeds are images, shapes, or copy that print all the way to the edge of the trimmed page. In order to accomplish this, the items that bleed must extend beyond the edges of your page by a specific amount of space. The US bleed standard is 1/8", but this can vary. It's always a good idea to check with your printer for best results.

Creating custom page sizes

Your document will be an 8.125"W x 10.625"H, saddle-stich magazine with 1/8" bleeds. You'll start by creating a new document with these dimensions and saving it as a preset, which you can then use when creating subsequent issues of the magazine.

Creating a new custom size document

1 Before creating a new document, choose Edit > Preferences > Units & Increments. When the Preferences dialog box appears, choose Inches from the Vertical and Horizontal drop-down menus in the Ruler Units section.

Choose File > New > Document or press Ctrl+N (Windows) or Command+N (Mac OS) to create a new document.

2 In the New Document dialog box, make sure that the Facing Pages checkbox is selected. In the Page Size section, type **8.125** in the Width text field and **10.625** in the Height text field.

3 In the Margins section, make sure that the Make all setting the same button (⧉) is deselected. Type **.5** in the Top, Inside, and Outside margin text fields, then type **.75** in the Bottom text field.

4 If the Bleed and Slug section is not visible, press the More Options button on the left of the dialog box. In the Bleed and Slug section, make sure that the Make all setting the same button is unselected, then type **.125** in the Bleed Top, Bottom, and Outside margin text fields. Because this magazine is saddle-stitched, it won't bleed into the spine of the page.

5   Press the Save Presets button in the upper-right corner of the New
Document dialog box. Type **Newsletter** in the Save Preset As text field.
Press OK. Newsletter appears in the Preset drop-down menu at the top of
the New Document dialog box.

The next time you need to create a new newsletter, select the preset from
the drop-down menu and all the settings are saved for you to use in the
new newsletter. Press OK.

6   A new, untitled document is created with the dimensions you entered.
Choose File > Save As. In the Save As dialog box, navigate to the
id03lessons folder and type **id03_work.indd** in the File name text field.
Press Save and keep the file open. You will now import the style sheets you
need for your magazine.

7   Press the Paragraph Styles button (¶) in the dock on the right side of the
workspace to open the Paragraph Styles panel. Press the panel menu button
(≡) in the upper-right corner of the Paragraph Styles panel and choose
Load All Text Styles.

8   In the resulting Open a File dialog box, navigate to the id03lessons folder
and select the file named id03_styles.indd. Press Open. The Load Styles
dialog box appears.

9   In the Load Styles dialog box, press the Check All button in the bottom-
left part of the dialog box and press OK. This imports all the paragraph and
character styles you need for your magazine.

10   Choose File > Save to save your work. Keep this file open for the
next exercise.

Creating and formatting master pages

The document contains only one page and one master page at the moment. You need to add more pages and master pages to the magazine. You will add a master page for the Table of Contents & Credit/Editorial, Feature Stories, News From the Field, and Classified sections of your magazine. Each of these sections has a different layout (number of columns, margins, headers, etc). Building master pages ahead of time allows you to easily apply the appropriate layout when you create these sections later on.

1 Press the Pages button (⊞) in the dock on the right side of the workspace or press the keyboard shortcut F12 (Windows) or Command+F12 (Mac OS) to open the Pages panel. Double-click on the name A-Master page in the upper division (master pages section) of the Pages panel.

This takes you to the A-Master page and fits the spread in your window.

2 With the A-Master pages still selected, in the Pages panel, press the panel menu button (•≡) and select Master Options for A-Master. This opens the Master Options dialog box and allows you to rename your master page.

3   In the Name text field of the Master Options dialog box, type **Footer**. Leave all other settings at their defaults, and press OK. This changes the name from A-Master to A-Footer. You will now add a footer that runs across the bottom of all the pages of the magazine by using the A-Footer master page.

Master Options

Prefix:	A	OK
Name:	Footer	Cancel
Based on Master:	[None]	
Number of Pages:	2	

Formatting master pages

You now need to format your A-Footer master page. You will base the rest of your master pages off this master page; this will be your parent master page. This means that items on this master page will appear on every page of the magazine. In this case, only the magazine's footer will appear on every page. Items such as the Header and column guides will be added to master pages corresponding to the appropriate sections.

Adding automatic page numbering

InDesign gives you the ability to set up auto page numbering. This handy feature numbers pages according to their positions within the document. This is useful if you reposition pages in a document; the pages renumber themselves.

1   Double-click on the left page icon or your A-Footer master page. This fits the left side of your A-Footer master page in the window. Now you can begin to create footers. You need to make sure that the footer information is at least 3/8" away from the bottom edge of your page, so you will create a guide to help align the footer.

2   If the page rulers aren't visible, choose View > Show Rulers or press Ctrl+R (Windows) or Command+R (Mac OS). Move your Selection tool (⬉) onto the horizontal ruler at the top of the page. Ctrl+click (Windows) or Command+Click (Mac OS) and drag down from the ruler to create a horizontal guide at 10.25". Holding down the Ctrl/Command key while dragging the guide causes it to span the entire spread instead of only one page.

3 Select the Type Tool (T) from the Tools panel and draw a type frame that starts at the bottom-left margin guide and extends down to the guide you just drew. Extend the text frame to the .5 mark in the horizontal ruler at the top of the workspace.

4 You will now use InDesign's Auto Page Number option to create the page number in your footer. Select Type > Insert Special Character > Markers > Current Page Number or press Shift+Alt+Ctrl+N (Windows) or Shift+Option+Command+N (Mac OS).

The Special Characters menu can also be located by right-clicking (Windows) or Ctrl+clicking (Mac OS) anywhere in the workspace, and choosing Special Characters from the contextual menu.

A letter *A* is inserted into the text frame. This letter tells us that your current page is master page *A*.

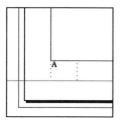

5 Now you'll format the look of your page numbers. Using the Type tool, select the letter *A* that was just inserted into the text frame. From the Character Formatting Controls in the Control panel, choose Myriad Pro Bold from the font drop-down menus, then choose 12pt from the font size drop-down menu. Press the Paragraph Formatting Controls button (¶) in the control panel and press the Align away from Spine button (☰).

6 Choose the Selection tool from the Tools panel and make sure the text frame is selected. Choose Object > Text Frame Options or press Ctrl+B (Windows) or Command+B (Mac OS). In the Text Frame Options dialog box, in the General tab, select Bottom from the Align drop-down menu in the Vertical Justification section and press OK. This aligns the baseline of the text to the bottom of the text frame.

7 Copy the frame by pressing Ctrl+C (Windows) or Command+C (Mac OS). Double-click on the right-hand page of the A-Footer master in the Pages panel and paste the page number by pressing Ctrl+V (Windows) or Command+V (Mac OS). Align the text frame so that the upper-right side of the frame is aligned to the bottom-right guide of the right-hand page. Notice that since you set the text to Align away from spine, the page number automatically changes to align to the right side of the text frame.

Using text variables

InDesign CS3's new text variables feature allows you to insert dynamic text that can be set to change contextually. InDesign comes with seven pre-defined text variables: Chapter Number, Creation Date, File Name, Last Page Number, Modification Date, Output Date, and Running Header. You can also edit any of these variables and create new ones.

Defining new text variables

Next you will use the new text variables feature to create variable text for your magazine title and page footers.

1 Choose Type > Text Variable > Define. The Text Variables dialog box opens.

2 Select Running Header from the Text Variables section of the dialog box and press the New button on the right side of the dialog box.

```
Text Variables

Text Variables:                          Done

Chapter Number                           Cancel
Creation Date
File Name                                Insert
Last Page Number
Modification Date                        New...
Output Date
Running Header                           Edit...

                                         Delete

                                         Convert To Text

                                         Load...

Preview:

<Running Header>
```

The new text variables feature gives you the power to create variable text for your title and page footers.

This opens the New Text Variable dialog box.

3 In the New Text Variable dialog box, type **Magazine Title** in the Name text field. Leave the Type field as Running Header (Paragraph Style), and from the Style drop-down menu choose the MagTitle paragraph style. In the Options section, select the Change Case checkbox, then select the Title Case radio button below it.

Determine the settings for creating your text variables.

Press OK. This formats your magazine's title in title case regardless of how it is typed. A new Magazine Title variable appears in the Text Variables dialog box.

4 Repeat steps 1-2. Name this text variable *Magazine Issue* and select the MagIssue paragraph style from the Style drop-down menu. All the other settings should match the settings used in step 3. You should now see the variables for Magazine Title and Magazine Issue in the Text Variables dialog box. Press Done to save these new variables.

Creating page footers

You will now use the new Magazine Title and Magazine Issue variables you just created to create your footers. Later in this lesson, you'll add some text to the table of contents page that will automatically populate these variables.

1 Double-click on the left page icon of the A-Footer master page. Select the Type tool (T) from the Tools panel and draw a type box that starts at the bottom-right margin guide and extends down and to the left until the bottom of the frame reaches the bottom guide you drew earlier.

2 Using the Character Formatting Controls in the Control panel at the top of your workspace, choose Minion Pro Italic from the font drop-down menu. Choose 12 pt from the font size drop-down menu and set the leading to Auto. Press the Paragraph Formatting Controls button (¶) in the Control panel, then press the Align toward spine button (≣).

3 Choose Type > Text Variable > Insert Variable > Magazine Title, to put variable text <magazine Title> into the frame, then enter a space. Using the Character Formatting Controls in the Control panel, change font to Minion Pro regular.

Choose Type > Text Variable > Insert Variable > Magazine Issue, to put variable text <magazine Issue> into the frame.

4 Choose the Selection Tool (**k**) from the Tools panel and make sure the text frame is selected. Choose Object > Text Frame Options or press Control+B (Windows) or Command+B (Mac OS). In the Text Frame Options dialog box, click on the General tab, and in the Vertical Justification section, select Bottom from the Align drop-down menu. Press OK.

5 Double-click on the right page icon of the A-Footer master page. Select the Type tool from the Tools panel and draw a type box that starts at the bottom-left margin guide and extends down to the bottom guide you drew earlier.

6 Using the Character Formatting Controls in the Control panel, set the font to Minion Pro regular, and choose 12pt from the font size drop-down menu. Select Auto from the Leading text field (A/IA). Leading is the vertical space between the baselines and is covered in more detail in Lesson 4, "Working with Text and Type."

Press the Paragraph Formatting Controls button, and set the paragraph alignment to Align toward spine. Within the text frame, type **Visit us online at www.agitraining.com**, then repeat step 4.

7 Choose File > Save to save your work.

Basing master pages on other master pages

InDesign gives you the ability to create new master pages that are based on other master pages. This feature creates a parent-child relationship between the master pages. The items on the parent (original) master page automatically appear on all the child master pages. This link allows you to update or add items on the parent master page and have them automatically update on all their child pages. In the next exercise, you'll load a number of master pages from another InDesign file and apply the A-Footer master to these pages.

1   Open the Pages panel by pressing F12 (Windows) or Command+F12 (Mac OS) or by pressing the Pages button (⊞) in the dock. In the Pages panel, press the panel menu button (-≡) and select Load Master Pages resulting menu.

2   In the Open a File dialog box, navigate to the id03lessons folder and select the file called id0301_styles.indd. Press Open. Four new master pages are added to your document. These pages correspond to the various sections of the magazine. Next, you'll apply the A-Footer master page you created earlier to these new master pages.

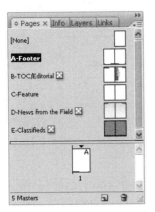

The Pages panel reflects the newly added master pages.

3   Double-click on the B-TOC/Editorial master page in the Pages panel. Make sure to click on the name of the master page instead of the page icon. This allows you to select the entire spread. From Pages panel menu, choose Master Options for B-TOC/Editorial. This opens the Master Options dialog box.

4   In the Master Options dialog box, choose A-Footer from the Based on
Master drop-down menu. Press OK. Notice that the B-TOC/Editorial
master page now features the footer you created earlier. Also, in the Pages
panel, the B-TOC/Editorial pages display capital A's indicating that they are
linked to this master page.

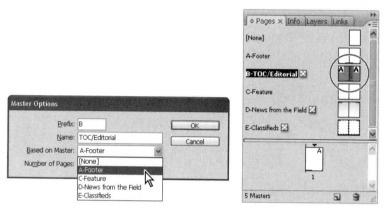

Base the page on the A-Footer master page.

A's indicate that the pages are linked to this master.

5   Master pages can always be applied using the Pages panel menu, but a
faster way to accomplish the same result is to simply drag and drop the
master page icons on the target pages. In the Pages panel, click and drag the
A-Footer master page onto the C-Feature master page. Notice that as with
selecting master pages, dragging the master page by its name instead of its
icon drags the entire spread.

6   Use the panel menu or the drag and drop method to link the remaining
master pages to the A-Footer master page.

Overriding master page items

When a page is linked to a master page, all the content that page inherits
from the master page is locked by default. This prevents you from accidentally
modifying these items and also preserves the special relationship that pages have
to their master pages. It's important to remember that this relationship is a one-
way street. Changes can only be made to master page items on their respective
master pages.

In the next exercise, you'll break the link between the A-Footer master page and
the table of contents section of the TOC/Editorial master page. This allows you
to selectively delete the footer information on this page.

1 In the Pages panel, double-click on the B-TOC/Editorial master page.
Notice that frame edges on this page are dotted lines instead of solid lines.
This indicates that an item is linked to a master page. In this case, some of
the items are linked to the currently active master page (B-TOC/Editorial).
These items are editable as usual. At the bottom of the page, the footer
items are linked to the A-Footer master page. These items are locked and
cannot be edited.

2 Choose the Selection tool (⬉) from the Tools panel. Move your cursor over
the footer on the B-TOC/Editorial page. Notice that clicking on the footer
items produces no result. In order to modify these items, you must first
break the link to the A-Footer master page.

3 Shift+Ctrl+Click (Windows) or Shift+Command+Click (Mac OS) on
the frames containing your page number and footer on the left page of
the B-TOC/Editorial spread. This selects these items and also breaks the
link between the items and the A-Footer master page. Press delete to
remove them.

4 Choose File > Save to save your work.

*Shift+Control+Click (Windows) or Shift+Command+Click (Mac OS) is
known as a local override. It applies only to the items you click on. If you wish to
override every master page item on a page, choose Override All Master Page Items
from the Pages panel menu (-≡).*

Adding empty image and text frames to master pages

You can also set up empty text and image frames on your master pages so that
you can have them in position to place text or images onto your layouts. You
can also use InDesigns CS3's new frame fitting options to determine how the
images will be sized when they are placed into the empty frames. Since the
B-TOC/Editorial master is the one section where the layout itself won't change
from issue to issue, this is a great place to create empty image and text frames.

1 Double-click on the left-hand page of the B-TOC/Editorial master page, if
it is not the main page on the workspace. You will now add a text frame for
the table of contents.

2 Select the Text tool (T) from the Tools panel and drag out a small text box.
The position and dimensions of the box are not important; you'll be setting
these using the Tool options bar in the next step.

3 Choose the Selection tool (↖) from the Tools panel and make sure the text frame you drew in the last step is selected. In the Options bar in the Control panel, set the reference point to top left and type **2.9583"** in the X text field and **1.4028"** in the Y text field. Type **4.6667"** in the W text field and **3.6607"** in the H text field.

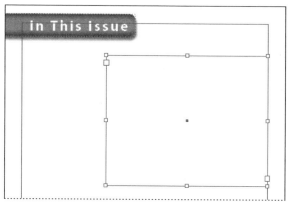

Draw a text frame that you can use for the table of contents.

4 Now you'll add a number of image frames on the left side of the page. Select the Rectangle Frame Tool (⊠) from the Tools panel and draw a small rectangle to the left of the text frame you created in the last step. Once again, you'll use the Options bar to set the exact position and dimensions of this box.

5 Choose the Selection tool from the Tools panel and make sure the frame you created in the last step is selected. In the Tool options bar, make sure the reference point is set to top-left and type the following values into the appropriate text field for the dimension and position: X: -.125" Y: 2.0615" W: 2.3929" H: 1.625". You have created an image frame that is aligned to the top of the text frame and bleeds off the page on the left-hand side. Now you will set the image frame's frame fitting options to Fill Frame Proportionally. This automatically sets the image to fill the entire frame while keeping its original image proportions.

6 Using the Selection tool, select the image frame you just created, and from the menu bar choose Object > Fitting > Frame Fitting Options.

In the Frame Fitting Options dialog box, choose Fill Content Proportionally from the Fitting drop-down menu in the Fitting on Empty Frame section. Press OK.

Choose Fill Content Proportionally in the Frame Fitting Options dialog box.

Now that you have set up the image frame you'll use that formatted frame to create more.

7 With the image frame still selected, choose Edit > Step and Repeat. This feature allows you to duplicate the items selected a specific number of times at a specific distance from each other.

8 In the Step and Repeat dialog box, type **3** in the Repeat Count text field, **0** in the Horizontal Offset text field, and **2.0625"** in the Vertical Offset text field. Press OK.

Set the three duplicates of the text box 2.0625" from each other.

This makes three copies of the frame, and spaces the copies 2.0625 inches apart from each other.

9 Save your file and keep it open for the next exercise.

Setting text wrap and allowing master page item overrides on master page items

InDesign CS3 has the added ability to set text wrap onto master page items and the ability to lock items so they cannot be overridden on subsequent pages. You will use these great new features to set a text wrap around the oval shape on the Editorial page and lock it so that users cannot delete it on the text pages.

1 Double-click on the left hand page of the B-TOC/Editorial master page. Using the Selection tool (▸), select the oval shape on the left hand side of the page and right-click (Windows) or Ctrl+click (Mac OS) on the shape. In the contextual menu that appears, deselect Allow Master Item Overrides.

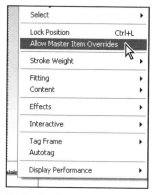

Deselect the Allow Master Item Overrides option.

This removes the ability to break that item's link to the master page from any of its child pages. You will now set up a text wrap around the same image.

2 Choose Window > Text Wrap. This opens the Text Wrap panel. From the panel, select the *Wrap around object shape* option and set the Top Offset to .25 in.

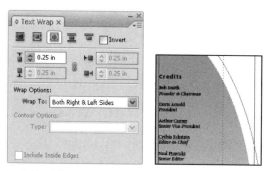

Set the Top Offset to .25 in. and the text wraps above the image, offset by 1/4".

This causes text to wrap .25 inches away from the edge of the oval.

3 Press the X at the top-right corner of the Text Wrap panel to close it.

Adding layout pages

Now that you have created and formatted all the master pages, you can now begin to lay out the magazine. You'll begin by adding pages to the file.

1 Add a page to your document by choosing Layout > Pages > Add Pages, or by using the keyboard shortcut Shift+Control+P (Windows) or Shift+Command+P (Mac OS). A page was added at the end of your file. You will now see two pages in the Pages panel.

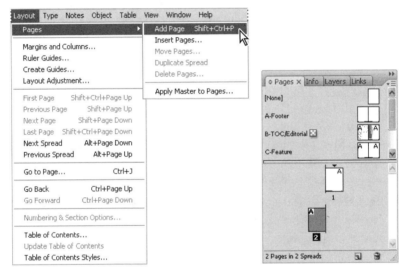

Add a page to the document.

2 You can also add multiple pages to your file at one time and even choose where the new pages will be inserted and what master page to apply to those pages in your file. Next you'll insert the Table of Content and Editorial pages to the file. In the Pages panel, Alt+click (Windows) or Option+click (Mac OS) on the Create new page button (⬓) at the bottom of the Pages panel. This opens the Insert Pages dialog box.

3 In the Insert Pages dialog box, type **2** in the Pages text field. Select After Page from the Insert drop-down menu and type **1** in the text field. Select B-TOC/Editorial from the Master drop-down menu.

Insert Pages

Pages: 2

Insert: After Page 1

Master: B-TOC/Editorial

OK

Cancel

Determine the settings for your Table of Contents and Editorial pages.

This inserts two pages between pages 1 and 2, and applies the B-TOC/ Editorial master page to those new pages. This issue of the magazine will be 12 pages. We will now add the additional pages, but since they won't all be in the same section, you'll insert them without a master page assignment.

4 In the Pages panel, Alt+Click (Windows) or Option+Click (Mac OS) on the Create new page button (📄) at the bottom of the Pages panel. In the Insert Pages dialog box that appears, type **9** in the Pages text field. Select After Page in the drop-down menu next to Insert, and type **4** in the text field. Choose None from the Master drop-down menu. This inserts nine blank pages into your file. You now have 13 pages in the document. Since you don't know which layout section will go on page 4, you can delete that page so that the document is 12 pages.

5 To delete the page, select page 4 by double-clicking on the page icon in the Pages panel. This highlights the page icon in the Pages panel and brings you to that page.

6 Press the Delete selected pages button (🗑) at the bottom of the Pages panel. This deletes page 4 and leave you with the 12 pages you need for this issue.

7 Choose File > Save to save your work. Keep it open for the next exercise.

Setting numbering and section options

Now you have all the pages you need to set up the numbering and sections options. Because you are using InDesign's auto page numbering, the cover is page 1 in the document. You actually want page 1 of the magazine to be the third page of the file. With the numbering and sections options, you can change the document's sections in the document to do just that.

1   In the Pages panel, double-click on the section start icon (-), located over the first page in the Pages panel.

Double-click the section start icon in the Pages panel.

This opens the Numbering & Section Options dialog box.

2   In the Numbering & Section Options dialog box, select I, II, III, IV from the Style drop-down menu in the Page Numbering section and press OK.

Select I, II, III, IV from the Styles drop-down menu.

This changes the document's numbering to Roman numerals. You will now create a new section on the third page and make it start with page 1.

3 In the Pages panel, double-click on page III to select it. Press the panel menu button (-≡) in the Pages panel and select Numbering & Section Options from the contextual menu. In the New Section dialog box, select the Start Page Numbering at radio button and type **1** in the text field. In the Page Numbering section, delete the characters *Sec:1*, in the Section Prefix text field, then select 1, 2, 3, 4 from the Style drop-down list and press OK.

Set the numbering options for your magazine's new section.

This will start a new section on the third page of your document that begins with page number 1.

Placing formatted text

Now that the numbering and section options have been adjusted to compensate for the front and back covers of the magazine, you'll add some content to the editorial page. In this case, you'll place text from a document with placeholder copy and pre-formatted styles. Then you'll finish the editorial page by adding a picture of the esteemed editor himself.

1 In the Pages panel, double-click on the third page of your document, which was set to page 1 in the last exercise.

2 Select the Type tool (T) from the Tools panel and draw a small text frame on the right side of the page. The exact size and location isn't important; you'll use the tool options bar to specify these values next.

3 Choose the Selection tool (↖) from the Tools panel and make sure the text frame is selected. In the Options bar at the top of your workspace, make sure the reference point is set to top left. Type **11.0833"** in the x text field and **3"** in the y text field. Type **4.6667"** in the W text field and **6.875"** in the H text field.

Size your text frame after you draw it.

4 With the text frame still selected, Choose File > Place. Navigate to the id03lessons folder and select the file named Editorial.doc. At the bottom of the Place dialog box, make sure Show Import Options and Replace Selected Item are both checked. Press Open. The Microsoft Word Import Options dialog box opens.

5 In the Formatting section of the Microsoft Word Import Options dialog box, choose the Preserve Styles and Formatting from Text and Tables radio button. Leave all other settings at their defaults and press OK. The Word document is placed into the text frame and all the styles are automatically mapped to the paragraph styles you imported at the beginning of the lesson.

Leave the settings at their defaults.

6 In the Pages panel, double-click on the right page icon of the B-TOC/ Editorial master pages. Since the editor probably won't get a new headshot with each issue of the magazine, it makes sense to place his photo on the master page.

7 Choose File > Place. In the Place dialogbox, navigate to the id03lessons folder and select the file named editor.jpg, then uncheck Show Import Options and Replace Selected Item. Press OK.

8 Move the loaded cursor to the top-right portion of the page, below the *From the Editor* text. Click once to place the photo, then drag the photo until the right side snaps to the right margin. If necessary, use the arrow keys to nudge the photo into place.

Place the editor's photo on the master page beneath the From the Editor text.

9 In the Pages panel, double-click on the editorial page to view the finished page and make sure the photo doesn't overlap the text you added earlier.

10 Choose File > Save to save your work.

Creating the classified page

Local goods and services are often advertised on a classified page toward the back of a magazine. Since most of the space is sold by number of words or characters, layouts typically involve narrow columns to pack as many ads as possible into the space. In this case, a four-column layout with an appropriate header has already been created for you. Next, you'll apply the master and then add the classified text.

1 In the Pages panel, double-click on page 9. Press the Pages panel menu button (-≡), and choose Apply Master to Pages. The Apply Master dialog box opens.

2 From the Apply Master drop-down menu, choose E-Classifieds. The To Pages text field should already be populated with the current page number. If it isn't, type **9** in the text field. Press OK. The header, footer, and four-column layout of the E-Classifieds master page is applied to page 9.

Apply Master

Apply Master: E-Classifieds   OK

To Pages: 9   Cancel

Apply the master page to page 9, your classified page.

3 To flow the copy onto the page, choose File > Place. Navigate to the id03lessons folder and select the file named Classifieds.rtf. At the bottom of the Place dialog box, check Show Import Options and leave Replace Selected Items unchecked. Press Open.

4 In the RTF Import Options dialog box, make sure the Preserve Styles and Formatting from Text and Tables radio button is selected. By default, InDesign uses the settings you last specified in this dialog box, but it's a good idea to check the settings to avoid unexpected results. Leave all the other settings at their defaults and press OK.

5 Move the cursor to the upper-left corner of the first column on page 9. When the cursor approaches the top of the column text frame, the arrow turns from black to white. Hold down the Shift key and click to place the text.

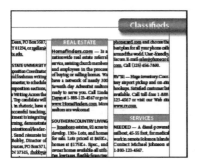

Place the Classified text.

6 Choose File > Save to save your work.

Populating master page image and text frames

Earlier in this lesson, you added some image frames and a text frame to the TOC/Editorial master page. If you recall, it isn't possible to select frames that are linked to a master page without breaking this link. You might be wondering how you can add content to a frame that isn't selectable. Adding content to these frames is actually quite simple. In the next section, you'll add the images and table of contents to the TOC/Editorial spread.

1   Double-click on the table of contents page icon in the Pages panel, which is now labeled with the Roman Numeral II. The image and text frames you added earlier have dotted borders, indicating that they are linked to a master page and, therefore, unselectable.

2   Choose File > Place. In the Place dialog box, navigate to the id03lessons folder and locate the folder named TOC images. Double-click the folder to open and select the file, photo1.jpg. At the bottom of the Place dialog box, uncheck Show Import Options and Replace Selected Item. Press Open.

3   Move your cursor over the topmost image frame on the left side of the page and click to place the image. The image is placed inside the frame and automatically resized. If you recall, when you created this image frame on the master page a little while ago, you chose some fitting options for the frame. These options control how InDesign treats your images when you place them.

After placing images and text in frames originally drawn on the master page, the link to the master page is automatically broken. This is important to note, as changes to the position of the frames on the master page do not affect the position of the populated frames.

4   Repeat steps 2 and 3 to place the remaining images in the TOC images folder.

5   Now you'll finish the TOC/Editorial spread by adding the table of contents to the text frame on the right side of the page. Choose File > Place.

6   In the Place dialog box, navigate to the id03lessons folder. Select the file named TOC.rtf. Make sure that Show Import Options and Replace Selected Item are still unchecked. Press Open.

7 Move your cursor over the text box on the right side of the table of contents page and click to place the TOC.rtf file. Just like the Editorial and Classified sections, the TOC.rtf file is pre-formatted. In this case, the magazine title and section correspond to the text variables that you defined earlier in the chapter. In the next section of this exercise, you'll apply the remaining master pages and see the fruits of your labor reflected in the footer on each page.

Your completed table of contents.

Applying master pages to multiple pages

Many times the content for a publication remains unfinished when the layout is created. In these cases it's often useful to bring the document as close as possible to the finished state to make flowing the content as easy as possible. Next you'll complete your work on this magazine by assigning master pages to the remaining pages in the magazine.

1 In the Pages panel, press the panel menu button (-≡) and choose Apply Master to Pages. In the Apply Master dialog box, choose C-Feature from the Apply Master drop-down menu.

2 In the To Pages text field, type **2-4**. Make sure to add the hyphen between 2 and 4. Press OK. The C-Feature master page is applied to pages two through four.

3 Press the Pages panel menu button again and choose Apply Master to Pages. In the resulting Apply Master dialog box, choose D-News from the Field from the Apply Master drop-down menu.

4 Type **5-8** in the To Pages text field to apply the D-News from the Field master to the remaining pages in the magazine. Press OK.

5 Scroll through the pages and note the text variables inserted in the footer have been automatically populated with the magazine title and issue. Much like master pages, text variables are a convenient way to save time and maintain consistency throughout a document.

6 Choose File > Save to save your work, then choose File > Close to close the file.

Self study

Create a newsletter for your circle of friends or extended family. Include a number of sections like profiles of people, recent stories, favorite quotes, top ten lists, and photo galleries. Think about which of these sections share common elements and which don't. Design a number of master pages to easily manage these common elements. Things to think about: headers, footers, guides, text frames, and picture frames. If you find yourself repeating steps on multiple pages, consider how you can use features like master pages and text variables to streamline your process.

Review

Questions

1 What are the most common methods of binding discussed at the beginning of this lesson?

2 True or False: Automatic page numbers always start on the first page of a document.

3 If you wish to modify content on a page that is linked to a master page, how do you select this locked content?

Answers

1 Saddle-stiched (pages are stapled together on the fold of the spine), perfect bound (pages are glued onto the cover at the spine), three-hole punched (to be placed into three-ring binders), and coil/ring bound (pages are bound together by coils or rings that run through holes punched on the spine of the pages).

2 False. Use the Numbering and Sections dialog box to specify sections of a document where automatic page numbers should begin and end.

3 Using the Selection tool (▶), Shift+Control+Click (Windows) or Shift+Command+Click (Mac OS) on content that is linked to a master page to break the link.

What you'll learn in this lesson:

- Creating and entering text
- Editing text in the story editor
- Customizing the dictionary
- Applying styles
- Using the Quick Apply feature

Working with Text and Type

This lesson covers the essential capabilities necessary to import, format, and flow text using InDesign CS3.

Starting up

Before starting, make sure that your tools and panels are consistent by resetting your preferences. See "Resetting the InDesign workspace and preferences" on page 3.

You will work with several files from the id04lessons folder in this lesson. Make sure that you have loaded the idlessons folder onto your hard drive. See "Loading lesson files" on page 4.

The project

To explore InDesign's text controls, you will be entering and flowing type into a fictitious magazine: *Tech.* You will explore a variety of text formatting tools. You will also create styles for the text.

To view the finished project before starting, choose File > Open, navigate to the id04lessons folder, select id04complete.indd, then press Open. You can keep the lesson open for reference, or close it by choosing File > Close.

Creating and entering text

InDesign provides many ways for you to add text to your design. Text is generally contained within a frame. You can use the Type tool, frame tools, or shape tools to draw a frame, then simply click in the frame using the Type tool to add text. You can also place text by importing a text file without defining a frame. You will do this later in this lesson.

To insert text using the Type tool, you must first define a frame. The fastest way to define a new text frame is to click and drag with the Type tool in the document to create a text frame.

Defining a text frame

You will start by creating a new text frame and entering type.

1   Choose File > Open. In the Open dialog box, navigate to the id04lessons folder, select the file id0401.indd, then press Open. If the document does not open to page 1, press the Pages button (⊞) in the dock on the right side of the workspace to open the Pages panel and double-click on page 1.

    The lower-left section of page 1 has a listing of what stories are featured in this issue of the magazine. You will be making a text frame above this box and entering the text, *Inside this issue.*

2   From the Tools panel on the left side of the workspace, choose the Type tool (T). Directly above the list of stories, click and drag with the Type tool to define a text frame. Try to make it about the same width as the text frame below it.

Click and drag with the Type tool to define a frame.

3 Type **Inside this issue:** into the text frame. If you need to re-position the text frame, choose the Selection tool (➤) from the Tools panel, then click and drag the frame to move it.

When using the Selection tool, you can activate the Type tool (T) by double-clicking on any text frame.

4 Choose File > Save As. In the Save As dialog box, navigate to the id04lessons folder and type **id0401_work.indd** into the Name text field. Press Save.

Changing character attributes

With the type selected, you will see that the Control panel at the top of the workspace now lists all the attributes for the character part of your selection. This is because at the far left of the Control panel there are two buttons; the Character Formatting Controls button (**A**), and, below that, the Paragraph Formatting Controls button (¶). Press the Paragraph Formatting Controls button and the Control panel changes to show all the paragraph attributes, including text alignment and first line indent. You can also use the Character and Paragraph panels, which are located under Type > Character, or Type > Paragraph. For this exercise, you will use the Control panel.

Changing fonts and type styles

You will now change the font and make the type bold using the Control panel.

1 Make sure you have the Type tool (T) selected, then click and drag the *Inside this issue:* text to highlight it.

Type must be selected with the Type tool to make text edits. However, if you are just changing the overall formatting of text in a frame, you can select the frame with the Selection tool and press the Formatting affects text button (T) in the Tools panel.

2 In the Control panel at the top of the workspace, make sure the Character Formatting Controls icon (**A**) is selected.

The Character Formatting Controls.

3 Press the arrow to the right of the font name to see the drop-down menu listing all the fonts InDesign has access to. InDesign has a WYSIWYG (what you see is what you get) font menu, which shows the word *SAMPLE* displayed in the different fonts. Pick any font you'd like, just to see the font change.

This is the WYSIWYG font menu.

You will now change the text to a different font. Instead of scrolling up and down the list to find a font you already know the name of, you can type it in the font name box to get to the font more quickly.

4 Choose Adobe Caslon Pro from the Font drop-down menu in the Control panel. Highlight the text in the Font text field and begin typing **Adobe Garamond Pro**. As soon as you get to the G in Garamond you should see the font name change. Press Enter (Windows) or Return (Mac OS) to see the type now displayed in the newly chosen font.

You will now use the drop-down menu to change the type style to bold.

With type selected, you can simply click next to the name of the font, and use the up and down arrows on the keyboard to preview the highlighted text in all the fonts listed. All the drop-down menus and text fields support this capability.

5   With the text still selected, locate the Font Style drop-down menu
underneath the Font drop-down menu in the Control panel. This drop-
down menu lets you set the style of the font, i.e.: bold, italic, bold italic, etc.
Choose Bold from the Font Style drop-down menu. Your type should now
appear as bold Adobe Garamond Pro. Keep the text selected.

Unlike QuarkXPress and Microsoft Word, which allow you to apply a fake
font style. InDesign requires that you have a font style installed on your
computer in order to apply it. For example, if you have Arial, but you don't
have Arial Bold, Bold will not appear in the Font drop-down menu, when
selecting Arial. This avoids possible problems when printing.

Changing the Type Style to Bold.

Adjusting size

Next you will adjust the size of the selected text.

1   Located to the right of the Font drop-down menu in the Control panel are
the controls for Font Size. Highlight the 12pt in the Font Size text field and
type **20**, then press Enter (Windows) or Return (Mac OS) to increase the
font size of your text to 20 points.

2   Choose File > Save to save your work.

Adjusting line spacing (leading)

Leading is the space between lines in text. It is called leading because historically,
letters were placed by hand in a galley at a press, with bars of lead between the
lines of type to separate them. Look at the list of stories below the text field
where you were just working. You will adjust the leading so that the lines of text
don't sit too closely on top of each other.

1   Using the Type tool (T), highlight the text inside the listed stories frame. Notice that just below Font Size in the Control panel is the Leading drop-down menu and text field. Currently, this is set to 10 pt.

2   In the Control panel, highlight the 10 pt in the Leading text field and type **16**. Press Enter (Windows) or Return (Mac OS) to set the leading of your text to 16 points.

Changing the leading.

Adjusting the kerning and tracking

Tracking is the space between a group of characters, while kerning is the space between any two characters. Next you will see how to control these spaces.

1   With all the text still selected with the Type tool, you will add some space between all the letters, commonly known as tracking. In the Control panel, highlight 0 in the Tracking text field (**AV**), then type **10**. Press Enter (Windows) or Return (Mac OS) to increase the tracking of the text by 10.

Changing the tracking.

You will now make the word *Tech* appear as a logo for the High Tech section you were just editing. You will kern the letters close together first, then use a baseline shift to lift the letter *e* above the *c*.

2   Using the Type tool (T), click between the e and the c in the word *Tech*. The kerning text field (AV) just above the Tracking text field shows a value of 0. To move the letters closer together, highlight the 0 in the Kerning text field in the Control panel, then type **–120**. Press Enter (Windows) or Return (Mac OS) to change the kerning to -120 between the letters.

Changing the kerning.

Using a baseline shift

The baseline is a line that text sits upon. Baseline shift allows you to elevate a character such as a numerator in a fraction or a registered trademark symbol. Here you will use baseline shift to style the type.

1 Select the letters *e* and *c* of the word *Tech* and change the type size to 10 using the Font Size drop-down menu in the Control panel.

2 Now, select the letter *e* and, in the Control panel, highlight 0pt in the Baseline Shift text field (A꜀). Type **6pt** in the text field, then press Enter (Windows) or Return (Mac OS). The *e* is shifted upwards.

Apply the baseline shift to the letter.

3 Choose File > Save to save your work.

Changing paragraph attributes

Now that you have seen some of the character attributes as they are applied to selected text, you will look at paragraph attributes. In this exercise, you will use the Control panel to change paragraph attributes, including text alignment, spacing, and tabs. You can also use the Paragraph panel to set paragraph attributes.

Horizontally aligning text

Aligning allows you to manage the placement of text in your project. By default, text aligns to the left. You can also align text to center, to the right, or use justify to align text evenly to both sides of the frame.

1 Press the Pages button (▯) in the dock on the right side of the workspace to open the Pages panel. Locate page 2 and double-click it to center the page in the workspace.

2 Click anywhere in the line of text that reads *Average Cell Phone Usage.* You don't need to highlight the whole line, because, by default, paragraph attributes affect the entire paragraph.

3   In the Control panel, press the Paragraph Formatting Controls icon (¶) to access the paragraph portion of the Control panel.

The Paragraph Formatting Controls.

4   Press the Align center button (≣) to align the text to the center of the page. The text is now centered. Keep the cursor in this text.

Changing the spacing before and after paragraphs

Adding space before and after paragraphs is a great way to control the spacing between paragraphs without using an extra return, which gives you little control over that space.

In this example, you want all the city names to appear slightly lower than the top line. You need some extra space after Average Cell Phone Usage.

1   In the Control panel, locate the Space After text field (≣). Highlight the text in the text field and type **.0625**.

2   Choose File > Save to save your work.

Using tabs

Tabs are a great way to align text. Tabs are often used to arrange tables of contents, with chapter listings and their respective page numbers separated by a long series of periods known as leaders. Tabs let you align words based on where you insert a tab by pressing the Tab key on the keyboard as a separator. Once you understand how and when to use tabs, you will never have to press the period key many times to create columns of text. In this next exercise, you will set tabs to separate the city name from the average hours used.

1   Using the Type tool (T), select all the text in the *Average Cell Phone Usage* text box. A tab has already been placed between the city name and the hours. If you want to see the difference between a space and a tab, choose Type > Show Hidden Characters.

2   Choose Type > Tabs to open the Tabs panel. The Tabs panel should appear aligned to the top of the selected text frame.

If the Tabs panel is not aligned to the top of the text frame, select the Zoom tool (🔍), and marquee over the text frame to increase the magnification. Reselect the Type tool, then select the text. In the right-hand corner of the Tabs panel is the Position Panel above Text Frame button (⌂). If you move the Tabs panel, press the Position Panel above Text Frame button and the Tabs panel realigns to your text box.

There are four ways to align tabs within the Tabs panel. Located at the top left are the Left-Justified Tab (↓), Center-Justified Tab (↓), Right-Justified Tab (↓), and Align to Decimal (or Other Specified Character) Tab (↓) buttons.

Next to the tab button is the X text field. This value represents where the tab sits relative to the ruler. The Leader text field allows you to insert a period, for example, to have leader dots between your tabbed items. And finally, the Align On text field allows you to set a decimal point for currency or a colon for time, or whatever character you choose to use for alignment on. The place you actually insert and move tabs is directly above the ruler. You should see two triangles to the left and one triangle to the right. This is another way to control your left and right indent as well as your first line indent.

A hanging indent is created when the first line of the paragraph starts at the left margin, but the second and subsequent lines are indented. This is called hanging indentation because the first line hangs out over the rest of the paragraph. To make a hanging indent, make your First line indent a negative value, and the Left indent a positive value.

3   Press the Right-Justified Tab button (↓), then click in the space above the ruler toward the end of the tab area. All the times align to the right of the frame. Highlight the value in the X text field and type **3.25**. Press Enter (Windows) or Return (Mac OS).

4 Create leader dots by typing a period into the Leader text field, then pressing Enter (Windows) or Return (Mac OS).

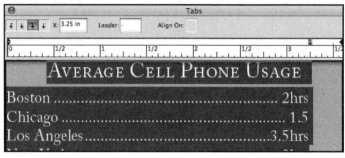

Add leader dots to the listing.

5 Close the Tabs panel, then choose File > Save to save your work.

Adding rules above or below paragraphs

Rules allow you to add a line above or below text. Rules move with the text, so that the rule and the associated text move together. You will add a rule below the words *Average Cell Phone Usage*.

1 Using the Type tool (T), click anywhere inside the text *Average Cell Phone Usage*.

2 Paragraph rules can be found in the panel menu at the far right side of the Control panel. Press the panel menu button (▪≡) in the Control panel and choose Paragraph Rules from the drop-down list.

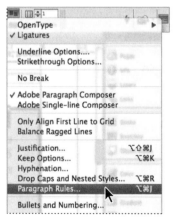

Choose Paragraph Rules from the panel menu in the Control panel.

3 In the Paragraph Rules dialog box, choose Rule Below from the drop-down menu and select the Rule On checkbox, to enable the rule, or line. Select the Preview checkbox in the lower-left corner of the dialog box to see the rule applied.

The line is automatically aligned to the baseline of the text. You will next move it a little lower.

4 In the Offset text field, change the offset value to 0.0625 to shift the line lower than the baseline, if the value shows differently.

5 Choose Text from the Width drop-down menu so that the line only appears below the selected text. Press OK.

The Paragraph Rules dialog box with the correct settings.

Changing text color

When changing text color, you can adjust either the fill or stroke (border) of the text.

1 Using the Type tool (T), highlight the words *Average Cell Phone Usage.*

2 Choose Window > Swatches to open the Swatches panel or press the Swatches button (▦) in the dock.

3 Located in the top left of the Swatches panel are the Fill and Stroke icons. Make sure the Fill icon (**T**) is in the foreground.

This is Fill and Stroke.

4 Locate the color Blue in the Swatches panel, then select it to change the color of the text. Notice that the rule below the text has also turned blue. This is because the rule was set to the same color as the text.

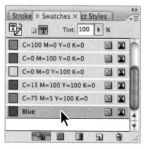

Select the blue swatch in the Swatches panel.

5 Choose File > Save to save your work.

Creating drop caps

Drop caps, or initial caps, are a great way to draw a reader's eye to the beginning of a story. You can create them in the Control panel or from the panel menu. For this example, you will change the *I* in the beginning of the paragraph in the story on page 2.

1 Using the Type tool (T), click anywhere in the first paragraph of the story on page 2. You do not need to highlight the text.

2 In the Paragraph Formatting Controls area of the Control panel, locate the Drop Cap Number of Lines text field (⌶≣) and change the value from 0 to 3. Press Enter (Windows) or Return (Mac OS) to commit the change.

The *I* now appears as a three-line drop cap.

The three-line drop cap.

3 Press the panel menu button (·≣) in the Control panel and choose Drop Caps and Nested Styles.

4 When the Drop Caps and Nested Styles dialog box appears, select the Preview checkbox on the right side to view the changes as they are made. Notice that the *I* is not aligned to the side of the text box. Select the Align Left Edge checkbox to align the *I* to the text box, then press OK. The drop-capped *I* is now aligned against the text frame on the left side.

The drop cap's left edge aligned to the edge of the text box.

Checking and correcting spelling

Checking spelling is an important part of creating a professional-looking document, and InDesign has many features that help you avoid spelling words incorrectly. You can turn on Dynamic Spelling or Autocorrect, which alert you to misspelled words or automatically change them for you. In this exercise, you will take a closer look at some of these options, including the ability to find and change words across an entire document or group of documents.

Finding and changing text and text attributes

Let's say you want to change the name *Tech Magazine* in the top folio of each page to be bold. Instead of going to each page, selecting the text and choosing Bold, the Find/Change feature allows you to change the style of every instance of the word or phrase to bold quickly at once.

1 Choose the Zoom tool (🔍) from the Tools panel and zoom in to the top of page 2 so you can see the words *Tech Magazine*.

2 Choose Edit > Find/Change to open the Find/Change dialog box. In the Find/Change dialog box, type **Tech Magazine** in the Find what text field. Now that InDesign knows what to find, you have to tell it what to change the text to.

Type in the words Tech Magazine.

3 In Change Format text field at the bottom of the Find/Change dialog box, press the Specify attributes to change button (🔍). The Change Format Settings dialog box appears.

4 On the left of the dialog box, choose Basic Character Formats. Select Bold from the Font Style drop-down menu, then press OK.

5 In the Find/Change dialog box, make sure the Search drop-down menu is set to Document. If you have any text selected, the Search dialog box is set to Selection, which would only search, find and change within the text that you have selected.

6 Press Change All. A dialog box appears indicating that the search is complete and that four replacements were made.

7 Press OK to accept the changes, then press Done. All four instances of the words *Tech Magazine* are now bold. You can use your Pages panel to navigate to the other pages to confirm this.

8 Choose File > Save to save your work.

Checking spelling

InDesign looks for misspelled words, along with repeated words, uncapitalized words, and uncapitalized sentences. InDesign also allows you to search a selection, a story, a document, or all open documents at once.

1 Select the Type tool (T) from the Tools panel, then click anywhere in the *What is the next inovation in Cell phones?* headline at the top of page 2.

2 Choose Edit > Spelling > Check Spelling. The Check Spelling dialog box appears.

3 Select Story from the Search drop-down menu at the bottom of the dialog box so that only this text frame is searched.

4 *Inovation* appears at the top as not being in the dictionary. In the Suggested Corrections field, the correct spelling of innovation is listed as the second choice. Select the correct spelling, then press Change.

The Check Spelling dialog box.

The dictionary has found and corrected all the spelling errors for this story or text frame. You can tell that the search is complete because the Start button is available once again, urging you to start another search.

5 Press Done.

Adding words to the dictionary

You can provide InDesign with a list of common terms or proper names that should be ignored when you check spelling. You can add these words to your dictionary so that InDesign does not indicate these words are misspelled.

1 Using the Type tool (T), insert the cursor at the very beginning of the first paragraph on the top of page 2.

2 Choose Edit > Spelling > Check Spelling.

3 In the Not In Dictionary section, *Blippa* appears. This is the name of a new product that appears throughout this document. Pressing Add places *Blippa* to your user dictionary. But you don't have to do this, since Blippa is not a real word, and you don't want to destroy the sanctity of your current dictionary. Press Done.

Adding a word to the Dictionary.

4 Choose File > Save to save your work.

Centralized user dictionary

InDesign allows you to set up a central user dictionary that you can share with your colleagues.

To create and share the edited dictionary, choose Edit > Preferences > Dictionary (Windows), or InDesign > Preferences > Dictionary (Mac OS). Press the New User Dictionary button (🗅). When the New User Dictionary dialog box appears, name the new dictionary and navigate to a server or centralized location so that others may access the file. The location and name of the new dictionary appears listed under the Language drop-down menu.

After adding all your commonly used words to the new dictionary, access the new dictionary file on another user's InDesign program using the Add User Dictionary button (⊕) in the Preferences > Dictionary dialog box.

Checking spelling as you type

InDesign also offers Dynamic Spelling. This feature works as you type, marking words not found in its dictionary with a red underline, just like common word processing applications.

1   Press the Pages button (⊞) in the dock to open the Pages panel. Locate page 3 and double-click the page 3 icon to center the page in the workspace.

2   Using the Type Tool (T), click inside the text frame containing the headline *When is the best time to update equpment?*

3   Choose Edit > Spelling > Dynamic Spelling to activate the Dynamic Spelling feature. A red line appears under the word *equpment.*

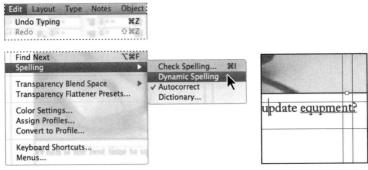

Accessing Dynamic Spelling through the Edit Menu.   *Dynamic Spelling turned on.*

4   Right-click (Windows) or Ctrl+click (Mac OS) the word *equpment.* A list of suggested corrections appears in the contextual menu. Choose the first one, *equipment*, and the word is corrected.

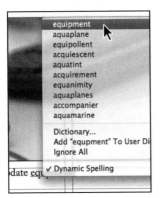

Replacing a word using Dynamic Spelling.

5   You can now shut off Dynamic Spelling by choosing Edit > Spelling > Dynamic Spelling.

Automatically correcting spelling

The Autocorrect feature allows you to add words that you commonly misspell and corrects them automatically as you type. You will now add a word to Autocorrect and see how it works.

1 Using the Pages panel, navigate to page 2 by double-clicking the page 2 icon.

2 Go to Edit > Preferences > Autocorrect (Windows), or InDesign > Preferences > Autocorrect (Mac OS).

3 When the Preferences dialog box appears, select the Enable Autocorrect checkbox if it is not already selected.

The Autocorrect Preferences window.

4 Press the Add button at the bottom of the dialog box to add your own word.

5 When the Add to Autocorrect List dialog box appears, type **useage** in the Misspelled Word text field, and **usage** in the Correction text field.

Add to Autocorrect List	
Misspelled Word: useage	OK
Correction: usage	Cancel

Entering a word into Autocorrect.

6 Press OK, then press OK again to close the Preference dialog box.

7 In the *Average Cell Phone Usage* text frame on page 2, highlight the word *Usage* and delete it from the text frame.

8 Type **Useage**, then press the spacebar on your keyboard. The Autocorrect feature automatically corrects the misspelled word. If necessary, press the Backspace key on your keyboard to delete the extra space.

Editing text using the Story Editor

In some projects, a story might spread to more than one page and it may be hard to concentrate on editing text when you are continually switching pages. In Story Editor, you can view the story apart from the document in its own separate window.

Story Editor also shows you and lets you edit overset text, which is text that does not fit into existing frames. When there is more text than the text frame will accommodate, a red plus sign appears at the bottom right-hand corner of a frame.

1 Using the Type tool (T), click anywhere inside the story text frame on page 2.

2 Choose Edit > Edit in Story Editor or press the keyboard shortcut Ctrl+Y(Windows) or Command+Y (Mac OS) to open the Story Editor window. This allows you to view the entire story, even though the story continues through page 5.

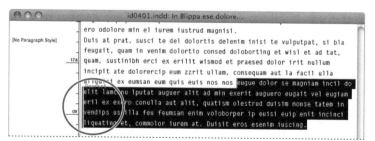

The Story Editor.

3 Use the scroll bar on the right side of the window to navigate to the bottom of the story. The Story Editor allows you to view the overset text starting at the word *eugue*.

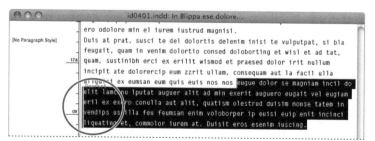

The Story Editor brackets off overset text.

4 Highlight from the word *eugue* to the end of the document and delete the overset text, then close the Story Editor.

5   In the Pages panel, double-click the page 5 icon to navigate to that page. Notice there is no red plus sign at the end of the text frame to indicate overset text. You will be learning how to link text boxes later in this lesson.

6   Choose File > Save to save your work.

Drag and drop text editing

Drag and Drop text editing allows you to highlight words or characters, then drag them to a different location. If you'd like to drag and drop text in layout view, you can turn on this option in the Preferences dialog box, it is enabled in the Story Editor by default.

1   Choose Edit > Preferences > Type (Windows), or InDesign > Preferences > Type (Mac OS).

2   When the Preferences > Type dialog box appears, select the Enable in Layout view checkbox in the Drag and Drop Text Editing section, then press OK.

Turning on the Drag and Drop Text Editing Preference.

3   Click and drag to highlight the words *cell phone* (leave the *s* out) in the headline on page 5.

4   Click, then drag highlighted phrase to before the word *innovation* and release the mouse. The phrase *cell phone* now appears before the word *innovation*.

5 Insert a space between the words *phone* and *innovation*, then delete the word *in* and the letter *s* so that the question mark follows the word *innovation*.

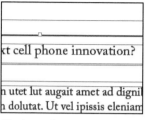

Cleaning up the text.

6 Choose File > Save to save your work.

Glyphs

Have you ever had trouble remembering the shortcut keys for inserting the cents symbol, a bullet, or the registered trademark symbol? Do you ever wish you could just see all of a font's characters, or glyphs in a font family? Well, you're in luck! InDesign has a Glyphs panel that shows you every glyph within a font. You will add a trademark glyph to the words *Tech Magazine* and use the Find/Change feature to add it to all instances throughout the layout.

1 Choose the Zoom tool (🔍) from the Tools panel and zoom in on *Tech Magazine* in the top text frame on page 5.

2 Choose the Type tool (T) from the Tools panel and click after the word *Magazine* to insert the cursor.

3 Choose Type > Glyphs to open the Glyphs panel. From the Show drop-down menu, choose Symbols and locate the trademark glyph (™).

4 Double-click the trademark symbol to place it after the word *Magazine*.

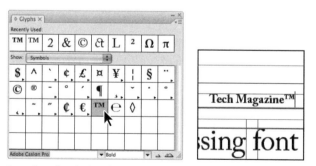

Insert the trademark glyph from the Glyphs panel into the layout.

5 Using the Type tool, highlight the word *Magazine* and the trademark glyph you just added.

6 Choose Edit > Copy, then delete the trademark symbol from the top of the text frame.

7 Choose Edit > Find/Change to open up the Find/Change dialog box.

8 In the Find what text field, type *Magazine*.

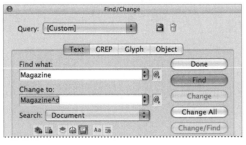

Find Magazine, and change it to Magazine tm.

9 Click inside the Change to text field and choose Edit > Paste.

10 Press Change All. A dialog box appears indicating that the search is complete and five changes have been made. Press OK.

11 Press Done. All instances of the words *Tech Magazine* now have a trademark symbol.

12 Choose File > Save to save your work.

Using the Glyphs panel and glyph sets

The Glyphs panel also allows you to create a custom glyph set, and put the panel in your workspace, then save the workspace. Every time you need a glyph, open the panel and double-click to insert the glyphs you need.

1 Press the panel menu button (⁃≡) in the Glyphs panel, then choose New Glyph Set. In the New Glyph Set dialog box, type Adobe Caslon Pro in the Name text field. Leave the Insert Order drop-down menu at its default and press OK.

Creating a new glyph set.

2 In the Glyphs panel, select the trademark symbol, if it is not selected. Press the panel menu button, choose Add to Glyph Set, then choose Adobe Caslon Pro from the menu that appears.

3 From the Show drop-down menu, choose Adobe Caslon Pro. You can add as many glyphs as you like to the glyph set, but remember that Glyph sets recall the font you were using when you added the glyph to the set. Therefore, you could add different glyphs from different fonts to a given set. It is a good idea to name your Glyph sets the same as the name of the font, then only add from that font to the set. That way you know you have the correct glyph.

The finished Glyph set.

When creating custom Glyph sets, name them according to the font from which you chose them. This way you can be sure the glyph you want is in the right font.

4 Close the Glyphs panel.

Text frame options

Text frame options include the different features of a text frame itself, such as vertical alignment of type, text inset, and the number of columns inside a frame. In this exercise, you will change some of the text frame options for the *Average Cell Phone Usage* text frame on page 2.

Adjusting text inset

Inside the *Average Cell phone Usage* text frame, things are beginning to look better, but there is still the issue of the text touching the side of the text frame. Since there is a border on the box, the text does not look good, as it touches the inside of the frame. You will fix this now.

1   In the Pages panel, double-click the page 2 icon to center the page on the workspace.

2   Using the Type tool (T), click inside the *Average Cell Phone Usage* text frame on page 2.

3   Choose Object > Text Frame Options to access the Text Frame Options dialog box.

The keyboard shortcut to open the Text Frame Options dialog box is Ctrl+B (Windows) or Command+B (Mac OS).

4   When the Text Frame Options dialog box appears, make sure the Make all settings the same button (⦿) in the Inset Spacing section is selected.

5   In the Top text field, highlight the current value, then type **.125**. Press the Tab key on your keyboard and the cursor moves to the next text field. If you select the Preview checkbox, you see changes in the text frame.

6   Press OK. The text has moved and is no longer touching the sides of the frame. Keep the cursor in the same location.

Setting a Text inset.

Vertically aligning text

You can align text inside a frame both horizontally and vertically. With vertical alignment, you tell the frame whether to center the text, align it to the top or bottom of a frame, or justify it to a frame, which will snap the text to the top and bottom of the frame and evenly space the lines.

1 Choose Object > Text Frame Options.

2 In the Vertical Justification section, choose Justify from the Align drop-down menu.

Setting the text to be vertically justified in the text frame.

3 Press OK. Notice that the type now snaps to the top and bottom of the frame. Leading is changed, but text inset is still honored.

4 Choose File > Save to save your work.

Importing text

There are three ways to flow text into an InDesign document: You can flow text manually, and link the text boxes yourself. You can also flow text semi-automatically, which re-loads your cursor with text. And you can automatically flow text into a document that automatically makes new frames and pages for you.

Flowing text manually

In this first exercise, you will manually flow text and practice threading text between frames.

1 In the Pages panel, locate page 3 and double-click the page 3 icon to navigate to that page.

2   Choose File > Place. In the Place dialog box, navigate to the id04lessons folder, select the id0401.doc file, make sure Show Import Options is checked, and press Open. The Microsoft Word Import Options dialog box appears. Confirm the radio button next to Remove Styles and Formatting From Text and Tables is checked, and directly under that, Preserve Local Overrides is not checked. These steps make sure that none of the Word Styles accidentally sneak into your document. You will be changing some of these options later in this lesson.

If you accidentally flow text into your last selected frame, choose Edit > Undo.

3   InDesign CS3 displays a preview of what you are about to place, inside of the loaded cursor. With the cursor loaded with text, you can view a preview of the first few sentences of the text you are about to import. Click just below the headline text frame. Text fills the column.

Flowing text into a column.

You have successfully placed a story in the first column, but there is more type than fits into this frame. You can tell this because of the red plus sign that appears in the bottom-right corner of the text frame. This indicates that there is overset text. In the next exercise, you will thread the text from this text frame to another text frame.

Threading text between frames

Text can be connected through as many text frames as you like. You can connect the frames whether or not they contain text. Text frames include two boxes on the outside edge that let you control how text threads between frames. One is at the top left, called the In Port, and the other is on the bottom right, called the Out Port. You will be using the Out Port of this text frame to thread it to another frame.

1   Choose the Selection tool (⬚) from the Tools panel.

2   Click on the red plus sign in the bottom-right corner of the text frame. This is the Out Port, reminding you that there is overset text. Once you click on the Out Port, your cursor becomes loaded, ready to place or link the overset text into another frame.

The overset text outport.

3   This time, you will create a new text frame in the second column. Click and drag from under the headline frame, starting in the top left of the right-hand column, dragging all the way to the bottom right side of the right-hand column. You have now linked the two text frames together.

4   To see how the Out Port of the first frame is linked to the In Port of the second frame, Choose View > Show Text Threads. Choose View > Hide Text Threads to stop displaying them.

5   Choose File > Save to save your work.

Semi-autoflowing text into frames

Sometimes when you flow text, you don't want to have to go to the added step of clicking on the Out Port every time you make a frame. Holding down Alt (Windows) or Option (Mac OS) when you are flowing text automatically reloads your cursor so you do not need to continue clicking the Out port.

1   In the Pages panel, double-click the page 4 icon to center the page in the workspace.

2   Choose the Selection tool (⬚) from the Tools panel and click anywhere in the pasteboard to make sure that there is nothing selected or choose Edit > Deselect All

3   Choose File > Place. In the Place dialog box, navigate to the id04lessons folder and select the id0402.doc file. Deselect the Show Import Options checkbox and press Open.

4   With the loaded cursor, press and hold down Alt (Windows) or Option (Mac OS), then click in the first column, just below the headline.

5   Notice that your cursor is automatically loaded with the remainder of the text without having to click the Out Port.

6   Click and drag to draw a marquee and flow the text into the second column, just below the image of the Data Center Server.

7   Choose Edit > Undo three times, twice to delete the frames, and once to empty the loaded cursor. You are now going to flow the text automatically onto the page, but first you're going to take a look at how the text is being interpreted from Microsoft Word as it is imported into InDesign.

Importing text from Microsoft Word

When flowing a Microsoft Word document into InDesign, the default setting, Remove all Styles and Formatting from Text and Tables, automatically eliminates all the styles applied to the file in Word. The text comes into your document using the style set in the Paragraph Styles panel.

1   Choose File > Place. In the Place dialog box, navigate to the id04lessons folder and select the id0402.doc file. Select the Show Import Options checkbox, which is toward the bottom of the Place dialog box, then press Open.

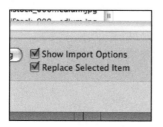

The Show Import Options and Replace Selected Item checkbox.

The Microsoft Word Import Options dialog box opens.

To open the Import Options dialog box automatically when opening a file, hold down the Shift key while you press Open.

2   In the Microsoft Word Import Options dialog box, select the Preserve Styles and Formatting from Text and Tables radio button, and select the Customize Style Import radio button.

The Microsoft Import Options Dialog box.

About Microsoft Word import options

Any Table of Contents text, index text, footnotes and endnotes can be brought into InDesign if they are created in Word. By default, the Use Typographer's Quotes option is checked, which will change all the quotes to typographer's (curly) quotes. This means that every inch and footmark quote will be converted as well.

If the Remove Styles and Formatting from Text and Tables radio button is selected, all the text will be imported in your Basic Paragraph style for that document. If you want to keep all of the character attributes that were applied in Word, select the Preserve Local Overrides checkbox.

If you select the Preserve Styles and Formatting from Text and Tables radio button, the styles created in Word are imported into your document, and the text adopts the imported styles, trying to mimic the styles from Word. However, if you create a template in Word that contains styles named the same as the styles in your InDesign document, there will be paragraph style conflicts upon importing, and by default the imported text will use InDesign's style definition. This means that regardless of how it looked in Word, once imported into InDesign, the text is formatted with InDesign's styles.

3 Press the Style Mapping button at the bottom of the dialog box, next to the Customize Style Import radio button. The Style Mapping dialog box appears.

Microsoft Word Import Options has already mapped the Body and Byline styles from Word to the Body and Byline inside the InDesign document.

4 The dialog box shows that the style *Normal* is mapped to a style inside InDesign. Select the New Paragraph Style next to Normal and choose Basic Paragraph style from the drop-down menu.

Mapping Styles.

5 Press OK to close the Style Mapping dialog box. Press OK again to accept the Microsoft Word Import Options. You now have a cursor loaded with text ready to be placed with already applied paragraph styles.

When you automatically flow text, InDesign creates new frames based on where you click inside the margin guides. To flow text automatically, hold down Shift as you place or flow text. InDesign automatically generates enough frames to flow all the text.

Resizing text frames

You can change the size and shape of a text frame at any time. You will start by making a new text frame, then you will resize it.

1 Select the Type tool (T) from the Tools panel.

2 Click and drag in the first column below the headline down to the bottom margin to create a new text frame.

Instead of building two separate text frames to flow type into, you are going to resize this frame to span two columns, then divide this column into two.

3 Choose the Selection tool (✸) from the Tools panel.

4 Using the Selection tool, click and drag the middle handle on the right side of the text frame to make your frame stretch across both of the columns of the page. The image has a Text Wrap applied to it, so the text flows around the image. See Lesson 6, "Working with Graphics," for more on wrapping text.

Adding or changing columns in a text frame

When a text frame is created, by default it is one column. In the Text Frame Options dialog box you can change a frame to have as many columns as you like.

1 Choose Object > Text Frame Options.

2 In the Text Frame Options dialog box, type **2** in the Number text field in the Columns section.

Adding columns to a text frame in the Text Frame Options dialog box.

3 Press OK. The text frame now has two columns.

Flowing text into existing frames

If you don't have a frame selected when you choose Place, InDesign automatically loads the cursor for you. If you have an existing frame like you do now, you can flow text into this frame.

1 From the Tools panel, select the Type tool (T).

2 Click inside the text frame you just created.

3 Choose File > Place. In the Place dialog box, navigate to the id04lessons folder and select the id0402.doc file. Make sure that the Show Import Options checkbox is selected and press Open.

4 In the Microsoft Word Import Options dialog box, select the Customize Style Import radio button.

5 Press the Style Mapping button. The Style Mapping dialog box appears.

Microsoft Word Import Options has already mapped the Body and Byline styles from Word to the Body and Byline inside the InDesign document. The dialog box also shows that the style Normal is mapped to a style inside InDesign.

6 Select the New Paragraph Style next to Normal and choose Basic Paragraph Style from the drop-down menu. Press OK to exit the Style mapping dialog box, and again to exit the Microsoft Word Import Options dialog box.

Your text now flows into the existing frame, in a single two-column text frame, with all the correct styling applied.

The text frame with two columns and the type stylized.

7 Choose File > Save to save your work.

Baseline grid

Baseline grid allows you to align text in a layout. In this next exercise, you will view the baseline grid, change the grid settings, and align the text to the baseline grid.

Viewing and changing the baseline grid

1 To view the baseline grid, choose View > Grids & Guides > Show Baseline Grid.

Viewing the baseline grid.

It is a good idea to create the baseline grid with an increment or line using the same space as the leading of your body copy. You will now change the increment for the baseline grid.

2 Select the Type tool (T) from the Tools panel.

3 Highlight all the body text except the byline on page 4.

4 In the Control panel, notice that the Leading (⫯A) is set to 14.4 pt. You will enter this value inside the Baseline Grid Preferences.

5 Choose Edit > Preferences > Grids (Windows), or InDesign > Preferences > Grids (Mac OS).

6 In the Preferences > Grids dialog box, highlight the value in the Increment Every text field and type **14.4pt**.

Preferences

Grids

Baseline Grid

Color: ■ Light Blue
Start: 0.5 in
Relative To: Top Margin
Increment Every: 14.4pt
View Threshold: 75%

General
Interface
Type
Advanced Type
Composition
Units & Increments
Grids
Guides & Pasteboard
Dictionary
Spelling
Autocorrect

Changing the Increment Every value is one way to work with the baseline grid.

7 Press OK. Now that the grid has lines in the same increment as the leading, you can align the text to the baseline grid.

8 With the text still selected, press the Paragraph Formatting Controls button (¶) in the Control panel.

9 Located to the left of the Number of Columns text field are the Do not align to baseline grid (≣) and Align to baseline grid (≣) buttons. Press the Align to baseline grid button. Your text on page 4 should now align to the baseline grid.

10 Choose File > Save to save your work.

Adding story jumps

If stories jump from one page to another inside a document, you need to direct the reader to the appropriate page where the story continues. If you were to type in *Please see page*, and then manually enter a page number, there is room for error. Especially if the story jump later gets moved to a different page.

Built into InDesign is a Previous and Next Page marker. If you use these markers correctly, the page numbers will change when story jumps are moved. The story on page 2 inside your document jumps to page 5. There are Please see and From boxes over the text frame that is linked to the other page. The frames with the Previous and Next page marker need to be touching the linked text frames in order for this to work. Since they are already touching, all you will do is enter in the marker.

1 In the Pages panel, navigate to page 2 by double-clicking the page 2 icon.

2 At the bottom right corner of the text frame is another text frame that has the text *Please see page*. Select the Type tool (T) from the Tools panel and place the cursor directly after the word *page*.

3   Press the spacebar on your keyboard once to put a space between the word *page* and the marker.

4   Choose Type > Insert Special Character > Markers > Next Page Number. This automatically comes in as a 5 because the frame knows it is on top of a linked text box that is linking to page 5. Now you will add the Previous page number.

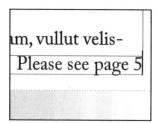

The text box with the Next Page marker.

5   In the Pages panel, navigate to page 5, by double-clicking page 5 in the Pages panel.

6   Using the Type tool, place the cursor after the word *page* in the *From page* text frame.

7   Press the space bar to put a space between the words and the marker.

8   Choose Type > Insert Special Character > Markers > Previous Page Number. The number 2 automatically appears.

9   Choose File > Save to save your work.

Understanding styles

Styles save time when you're working with text that shares the same look and feel across a document. If you decide that your body text should be bigger, or a different font, you don't need to go through the entire document and individually select all the body text and make changes. You can just change the style, and all the text formatted with that style automatically updates. This makes universal changes easy to apply.

Creating a headline and applying a style

In this exercise, you will create a headline style and apply it to another headline.

1   In the Pages panel, double-click the page 2 icon.

2   Select the Type tool (T) from the Tools panel.

3   Highlight the headline *What is the next innovation in cell phones.*

4 Choose Type > Paragraph Styles. The Paragraph Styles panel opens.

5 Press the panel menu button (-≣) in the upper-left side of the Paragraph Styles panel and choose New Paragraph Style. In the Style Name text field, type **Headline**, then press OK.

Naming a new Paragraph Style.

6 Select the Headline style in the Paragraph Styles panel to apply the style to the text. The text looks the same because the headline defined the style. But it is neccessary to apply this style to this text because creating a style does not automatically apply it.

When you make a new style, you can have InDesign apply it to the current selection. In the General section of the new Paragraph style dialog box, select the Apply Style to Selection checkbox for this to occur.

7 Highlight the headline *When is the best time to update equipment?* on page 3 and select the Headline style in the Paragraph Styles panel. The headline is formatted with the paragraph style you created.

Importing styles from other documents

You can import styles from one InDesign document to another. In this exercise, you will import a Drop Cap style from another document and use the style in this document.

1 Press the panel menu button (-≣) in the Paragraph Styles panel and choose Load Paragraph Styles. You will locate a file from which to copy a style.

2 In the Open a File dialog box, navigate to the id04lessons folder and select the id0401_done.indd file. Press Open. The Load Styles dialog box appears.

3 Press the Uncheck All button to deselect all the styles because you only need to bring in one style. Select the Drop Cap checkbox to select only this style.

Loading the Paragraph style Drop Cap.

4 Press OK. Drop Cap is now added to the styles in the Paragraph Styles panel in your document.

Redefining styles

You will now redefine the Body paragraph style to contain a new attribute which will align the text to the Baseline Grid.

1 Select all the text in the story on page 2 by inserting the Type tool (T) anywhere in the text frame and choosing Edit > Select All.

2 Select the Body style in the Paragraph Styles panel to apply it to all the text. If a plus sign appears next to the style name, hold Alt (Windows), or Option (Mac OS) and select the style again. This removes any formatting changes that have been made since the style was applied. Changes made to text after a style had been applied are known as overrides. If you edit a style attribute outside the Paragraph Styles panel, the style is manually overridden. If you hover over the style in the Paragraph Styles panel with your mouse, a tooltip appears, stating which attribute is causing the override. For this example, the tooltip states that the override is Grid Alignment: Baseline.

Applying the Body style.

3 In the Paragraph Formatting Controls section of the Control panel, press the Align to Baseline Grid button (≣).

4 A plus sign next to the style name in the Paragraph Styles panel is displayed. This plus sign indicated the style also has an override, which changed one or more attributes.

5 Press the panel menu button in the Paragraph Styles panel, and choose Redefine Style to add the override attribute to the Body style. All the body text now aligns to the Baseline Grid.

New Paragraph Style...
Duplicate Style...
Delete Style...

Redefine Style   ⌥⇧⌘R

Style Options...

Redefining the Body Style.

By reapplying the Body style, the Drop Cap at the start of the story was erased. Because a Drop Cap style exists in the document, reapplying the drop cap will be easy.

6 Click anywhere in the first paragraph of text. Select the Drop Cap style in the Paragraph Styles panel to apply it. The first paragraph is now formatted with the style Drop Cap, and the rest is set to the Body style.

7 Choose File > Save to save your work.

Type on a path

Your type can be set free from a text frame and placed on a path, following the direction of a line or the outline of a circle.

1 In the Pages panel, double-click page 4 and navigate to the logo at the top of the page.

2 Notice that there is an oval surrounding the word *Tech* in this logo. The logo should read *High Tech Corner*. You need to put the word *High* on the oval. The Type tool (T) allows you to click inside a frame and type, hidden under the Type tool is the Type on a Path tool (⇘) which is what you will use here.

T Type Tool   T
⇘ Type on a Path Tool   Shift+T

The Type on a Path tool.

3 Click and hold the Type tool in the Tools panel until the hidden tools are revealed, then choose the Type on a Path tool.

4 Move your cursor over the top center of the oval until you see a plus sign appear next to your cursor, then click.

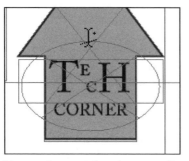

The cursor changes to indicate that you are able to place text on the path.

5 Type **HIGH**, then highlight the text using the Type on a Path tool.

6 In the Paragraph Formatting Controls section of the Control panel, press the Align center button (≣). Notice that the text does not appear to be centered on the line. You will correct this in the next steps.

7 Choose the Selection tool (↖) from the Tools panel. Notice that there are two vertical handles that appear directly to the left of where you clicked on the path. These handles mark where you want text to begin and end. Be careful not to click the boxes when you move them, as these are the In and Out ports, which will load your cursor for flowing text, which you learned about earlier in this lesson.

8 Select the bottom line and drag it to the right center of the oval. Drag down first, then bring the bottom line to the right. You should see your text move. If your text appears inside the box, undo and try it again. This may occur if you click on a third line that appears exactly opposite of where you clicked on the line. It should appear on the bottom center of the circle. Dragging this line inside the frame will flip the text inside the frame. Dragging it out will flip the text back outside the frame.

9 Now take the top line that marks where the text will start, and drag it down to the left center of the oval. Because you had already aligned the text horizontally to center, aligning the start and end points of your text on a path to the opposite sides of the circle let's you know that the text is centered correctly on the path.

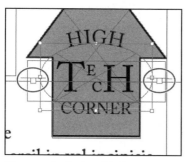

The start and end points of the line.

10 Choose File > Save to save your work.

Missing Fonts

When working on an InDesign document created on another computer, you need the same fonts that were used when creating the document. There are many reasons fonts can go missing. Missing fonts must be dealt with before you attempt to print your document. In this exercise, you will import text from a Microsoft Word document that has missing fonts, and you will fix the font errors.

By default, InDesign highlights missing fonts in pink so that it can warn you about font issues before you print.

Finding and fixing missing fonts

1 In the Pages panel, double-click the page 5 icon to navigate to it.

2 Select the Type tool (T) in the Tools panel.

3 Click inside the empty text frame at the top of page 5.

4 Choose File > Place. In the Place dialog box, navigate to the id04lessons folder and select the id0403.doc file. Select the Show Import Options checkbox if it is not selected, then press Open.

5 Select the Preserve Styles and Formatting from Text and Tables radio button. Press OK. The missing Font dialog box appears because you do not have the font Plantagenet Cherokee Bold Italic installed on your machine.

The missing font dialog box.

6 Press the Find Font button. The Find Font dialog box opens. Highlight Plantagenet Cherokee Bold Italic by clicking on it in the Fonts in Document section. Notice the warning icon (⚠) next to the font name. This indicates that the font is missing.

7 In the Replace with section at the bottom of the dialog box, highlight the text in the Font Family text field and type **Adobe Caslon Pro**. You are going to replace Plantagenet Cherokee Bold Italic with Adobe Caslon Pro Regular.

Replacing a font.

8   Press Change All. To see the missing font replaced, press Done.

9   Choose File > Save to save your work, then choose File > Close. Congratulations! You have completed Lesson 4, " Working with Text and Type."

Self study

1   Start at page 1 and make sure everything has the correct style applied to the text i.e.: body, byline, drop cap, and headline.

2   Change the color of the body text and redefine the style. Watch all your body text turn a different color.

3   Use the Selection tool (￢) to select the story jump, the jump frame, and the frame in which its located. Drag it to page 6. Then go to page 2 and see if the story jump automatically updates.

4   Make a new headline box on page 7 and type in a fictitious headline. Format the headline using the headline style as a starting point. You may need to adjust the size depending on how many words you enter.

5   Make a two-column text box below the headline on page 7 and fill it with placeholder text by choosing Type > Fill with Placeholder Text. Then type **By** and your name at the top of the frame and press Enter (Windows) or Return (Mac OS). Use your Byline and Body Paragraph Styles to stylize the text. Edit the text in Story Editor to get rid of the overset text.

Review

Questions

1 If you have a font that doesn't have the style of italic, can you make it italic?

2 Can you flow text into an existing frame?

3 Can you make a text frame two columns?

4 Where can you find the Previous and Next Page Markers?

5 True or False: You should ignore any Missing Font warnings.

Answers

1 There is no false italic using InDesign. Either you have the italic style of the font or you cannot make it italic.

2 Yes, you can even flow text into frames that already have type in them.

3 Yes, you can have many columns. Make column decisions and settings by choosing Object > Text Frame Options.

4 Under Type > Insert Special Characters > Markers.

5 False—You should always address the missing font dialog box.

Lesson 5

What you'll learn in this lesson:

- Defining and applying paragraph, character, and object styles
- Using nested styles
- Globally updating styles
- Loading styles from another document
- Using Quick Apply
- Organizing styles into groups

Working with Styles

Rather than spending hours repetitively styling text and paragraphs, set up a style to handle the job for you. Styles streamline the formatting of text and can simplify adjustments made later in the layout process. When you change a style definition, InDesign automatically updates all instances of that style in your document.

Starting up

Before starting, make sure that your tools and panels are consistent by resetting your preferences. See "Resetting the InDesign workspace and preferences" on page 3.

You will work with several files from the id05lessons folder in this lesson. Make sure that you have loaded the idlessons folder onto your hard drive. See "Loading lesson files" on page 4.

The project

To demonstrate how using styles can simplify the design process, you will enhance the look of a two-page recipe layout using paragraph, character, and object styles. Although creating the styles adds a bit of prep work, the time you spend will pay off when you need to make changes later. You will learn another time-saver: importing styles. This technique allows you to borrow styles from another document. You will also learn how to organize your styles with the new feature, style sets, and how the Quick Apply technique can speed up the process of applying styles.

Style types

InDesign supports four types of styles:

- Paragraph
- Character
- Object
- Table

Each applies to a different type of page element. Paragraph styles define both the character and paragraph attributes of text, while character styles concentrate only on character formatting. Object styles apply to the graphic elements on your page, enabling you to uniformly format the boxes and lines in layout. New to CS3, table styles format tables, whether they are imported from an Excel spreadsheet or created from scratch in InDesign. This lesson focuses on paragraph, character, and object styles. To learn more about table styles, see Lesson 7, "Creating and Using Tables."

The advantage of using styles is that doing so speeds up the process of both the initial formatting and changes made to formatting, especially in long documents. Since InDesign documents are created with only one basic paragraph, character, object and table style, it is necessary to create the style definitions for each document. But once they are created, you can import styles into any document, thus saving you a great deal of time in the long run.

To apply a style, simply select the text or object you want styled, then select the name of the style you want from the appropriate panel—Paragraph Styles, Character Styles, or Object Styles. You'll use the same basic strategy to create all three, beginning with paragraph styles.

Paragraph styles

Paragraph styles are a way of centralizing the character and paragraph attributes of text under one definition. When you apply a paragraph style to text, all paragraphs you select are formatted according to the style definition. With one click, you can specify a paragraph's font, point size, justification, indentation, and more. Before you can apply it, however, you have to define the style.

Defining a paragraph style

The most effective technique for building styles from scratch is styling by example. Format one portion of your text as desired on the page, then define that formatting as a style using the Paragraph Styles panel. Give it a try by building a paragraph style for the body text of a two-page layout for a cookie recipe.

1 Choose File > Open. In the Open dialog box, navigate to the id05lessons folder and select the gingersnaps_start.indd file. Press Open.

2 Choose Window > Workspace > Default Workspace to reset your panels to the InDesign default position. This ensures that your panels are in position for easy referencing during this lesson.

3 Choose Type > Paragraph Styles to open the panel in the lower-right corner of the screen. All your styles are listed; notice that this document already contains four styles: Basic Paragraph, callout large, rec_steps, and rec_yield.

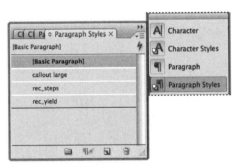

The Paragraph Styles panel lists all available styles for formatting paragraphs.

4 Select the Type tool (T) from the Tools panel.

5 On the left-hand page, page 72, click four times over the first paragraph in the second column (the paragraph beginning with *The smell of fresh baked cookies...*) to highlight the entire paragraph.

6 Because the Type tool is active, the character and paragraph formatting options are available in the Control panel. Click the Character Format Controls button (the letter A) to display the character options. Choose Minion Pro from the font drop-down menu, and Regular from the drop-down menu just below it. Set the point size to 10 pts.

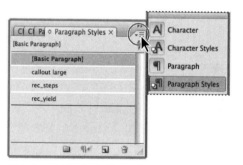

Click the A icon to display the character formatting options in the Control panel.

7 Click the Paragraph Formatting Controls icon (¶) to display the paragraph formatting options, and enter **0.2** in the First Line Left Indent (⁺≣) text field. Press Enter (Windows) or Return (Mac OS) to implement the indentation.

*In the paragraph formatting options section, enter **0.2** in the First Line Left Indent text field.*

8 With the paragraph still selected, click the panel menu (◄≣) in the upper-right corner of the Paragraph Styles panel and choose New Paragraph Style from the resulting panel menu.

Click the arrow icon in the Paragraph Styles panel to open its panel menu.

9 The New Paragraph Style dialog box opens. In the Style Name field, enter **body** to name your newly created paragraph style, then press OK. Notice that the body style is now added to the list of styles in the Paragraph Styles panel.

10 Save the file by choosing File > Save.

Applying a paragraph style

You can now apply the body paragraph style to additional text in your document. The process is simple: highlight the text you want to affect, then click the style name to apply it. Try applying the body style to the rest of the recipe.

1 With the recipe still open, choose Edit > Select All to select all the text in the frame.

2 If you closed the Paragraph Styles panel, press its button in the dock on the right side of the workspace to reopen it.

3 In the Paragraph Styles panel, click the body style to apply that style to all the text in the text frame. The entire recipe should now have the same character and paragraph formatting as the first paragraph.

Character styles

The strategy for building character styles is the same as for paragraph styles: Format a small amount of text, then define it as a style. The main difference between paragraph and character styles is that character styles affect only character attributes, such as font and point size. Character styles are typically used for words that need special treatment, such as bold, italics, or a unique font.

Defining a character style

The text up through the colon at the beginning of each of the recipe's four steps (*Create the cream*, *Mix dry ingredients*, etc.) on page 73 of the document should be bold. You'll format the first two steps, then define a style to apply to the others. Make sure the Type tool is still selected and the character formatting controls in the Control panel are visible (click the A icon if necessary).

1 With the Type tool (T), highlight the word *Create* under the Yield section on page 73 of the recipe layout.

2 In the Control panel, choose Bold for the type style from the font name drop-down menu.

Highlight the text and set the type style to prepare for creating a character style.

3   Choose Type > Character Styles to open the Character Styles panel in the lower-right corner of the screen.

4   With the bold text still highlighted on the page, click the panel menu button (-≡) in the Character Styles panel, and choose New Character Style.

5   In the resulting New Character Style dialog box, enter **rec_stepsBold** in the Style name field. Press OK to create a new style. Its name should now appear in the Character Styles panel.

6   Choose File > Save to save your work.

Applying a character style

Applying character styles is as easy as applying paragraph styles. Simply highlight the text you want to affect, then click the style name to apply the style.

1   On page 73 of the layout, highlight *Create the cream:*.

2   In the Character Styles panel's list, click the name rec_stepsBold to apply that style to the selected phrase.

Apply the character style.

3   Highlight the phrase *Mix dry ingredients:* and once again click rec_stepsBold in the Character Style's panel to apply the style.

Using nested styles

If you need to apply character styles in a consistent way, nested styles can save you time. Nested styles automate the task of applying character styles and dispense with the aggravation of hunting down and highlighting each phrase. The styles are called nested because the character styles reside inside the paragraph styles. For instance, if the first three words of an introductory paragraph need to be bold, nesting a bold character style in the paragraph style would make sense. So, when the introductory paragraph style is applied, the character style for the first three words will also be applied. Because of this arrangement, your document must contain at least one character style for you to use nested styles.

The introductory label of each step should be in the rec_stepsBold style, and each label ends with a colon. Set up rec_stepsBold as a nested style to quickly format the labels of the final steps.

1   With the Type tool (T), click one of the step paragraphs in the document.

2   Choose Type > Paragraph Styles to open the Paragraph Styles panel.

3   In the Paragraph Styles panel, double-click on the rec_steps style to open the Paragraph Style Options dialog box.

4   In the list on the left side of the dialog box, click Drop Caps and Nested Styles. From the resulting options, press the New Nested Style button.

5   In the Nested Styles section's drop-down menu, choose rec_stepsBold. Keep the Through and 1 parameters the same.

6   Select *Words* and, in the text field that appears, type : (the colon symbol).

Creating a nested style automates applying character styles.

If you do not replace Words *with a colon, only the first word of the recipe steps will be bold.*

7   Press OK to close the dialog box. Notice that InDesign automatically updates all the recipe steps to be bold through the first colon.

8   Save the file and keep it open for the next part of the lesson.

Globally updating styles

Styles can speed up formatting a document, but their greatest advantage is the time they save when you need to make changes. By modifying a style definition, you automatically update the entire document. Perhaps you're not happy with the size of the recipe steps; update the rec_steps style to change all the steps at once.

1 With the Type tool (T), click in one of the recipe steps paragraphs.

2 In the Paragraph Styles panel, the rec_steps paragraph style should be highlighted. Double-click on that style to open the Paragraph Style Options dialog box.

3 In the list on the left-hand side of the dialog box, click Basic Character Formats.

4 Choose 11 pt from the Size drop-down menu, then choose Auto from the Leading menu.

Updating attributes in the Paragraph Style Options causes all styled paragraphs to be updated.

5 Click the Preview checkbox in the lower-left corner to see the changes in the document as you make them.

6 Press OK to commit your changes and close the dialog box. All the steps formatted with the rec_steps style are now one point larger. Whether the document is a single spread, as in this example, or a book's worth of spreads, all occurrences of the style will reflect the changes you make to the style definition.

Loading styles from another document

After you create and save a style, you can use it in as many documents as you like, instead of creating new styles for the cookie recipe. For example, you can import styles previously created from another recipe. If you repeatedly use the same formatting across documents, creating a master set of styles and importing them saves a lot of time.

The Paragraph Styles and Character Styles panel menus both include an option to load all text styles from a document. Choose Load All Text Styles to import both character and paragraph styles. If you need just one type of style, open the appropriate panel's panel menu and choose Load Paragraph Styles or Load Character Styles.

In this exercise, you'll import some new styles into the gingersnaps recipe as practice.

1 With the gingersnaps_start.indd document open, choose Load All Text Styles from the Paragraph Styles panel menu.

2 In the resulting Open a File dialog box, choose the file Recipes.indd from the id05lessons folder. This is the document from which you'll import the styles. Press Open, and the Load Styles dialog box appears.

	Load Styles		
Type	Incoming Style	Conflict with Existing Style	
✓ ¶	[Basic Paragraph]	Use Incoming Defini...	OK
✓ ¶	byline		Cancel
✓ ¶	callout		
✓ ¶	rec_head		
✓ ¶	rec_steps	Use Incoming Defini...	
✓ ¶	rec_list		

Check All   Uncheck All

Incoming Style Definition

The import options that appear when choosing Load All Text styles.

To see the entire contents of the Load Styles dialog box, click and drag the lower-right corner until all your options are visible.

If a style you want to import has the same name as an existing style in your document, the Load Styles dialog box lets you choose how to handle the import. Clicking Use Incoming Definition overwrites the existing style with the imported style of the same name, while clicking Auto-Rename gives the imported style a new name so you can use both it and the existing style in your document. The Incoming Style Definition box below each style's name displays the highlighted style's definition for easy comparison.

3 You can import all the styles in a document or only a few. By default, all styles are selected when the Load Styles dialog box opens; to deselect a style, click its checkbox. For the recipe styles, leave byline, rec_head, rec_list, and Head checked; click the other styles' checkboxes to deselect them.

Check these styles to import them into your document.

4 Press OK to close the Load Styles dialog box. The Paragraph Styles panel now includes the imported byline, rec_head, rec_list, and Head styles. You can apply them as you did the styles you created in this document.

5 Choose File > Save to save your work.

Quick Apply

As your list of styles grows, navigating to find a specific one can be tedious. The Quick Apply window offers you a shortcut. Type the first few letters of a style's name in the window's search field, and InDesign displays a short list of possible choices. Highlight the one you want, then press Enter (Windows) or Return (Mac OS) to apply it. Quick Apply is the perfect way to apply two of the new styles that you imported in the previous exercise.

1   Using the Type tool (T), click in the *Molasses Won't Slow Eating These Gingersnaps* text box at the top of page 72. Because paragraph styles format an entire paragraph, you don't have to highlight the text. Simply click in the paragraph, then apply the paragraph style.

2   In the upper-right corner of the Paragraph Styles panel, click the Quick Apply button (*ϟ*) to open the Quick Apply window.

3   Type **hea** in the window's search field. The Head style appears at the top of the list.

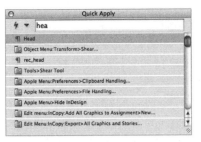

The Quick Apply window makes applying styles faster and easier.

4   Press the Enter (Windows) or Return (Mac OS) key to apply the style to the selected headline text.

5   Click in the box at the top right of page 73 within the phrase *Cookie Color*.

> To make the process even quicker, you can open the Quick Apply window by pressing Ctrl+Enter (Windows) or Command+Return (Mac OS).

6   Click the Quick Apply button again, and enter **rec**. This time the three styles starting with rec appear in the list. Click to select rec_head style at the top (if it isn't highlighted already), and press Enter (Windows) or Return (Mac OS) to apply the style.

7   Click in the paragraph below *Cookie Color*, click Quick Apply, and enter the letter **c** in the field to invoke the callout large style, and press Enter (Windows) or Return (Mac OS) to apply it to the text.

8 Choose File > Save to save your work.

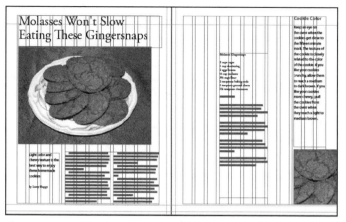

The recipe spread is starting to look more polished.

Organizing styles into groups

Quick Apply makes finding styles easier, but it still requires searching a document's entire collection. Another time-saving approach is to organize your styles using folders. This gives you the ability to show and hide the contents of style groups to help minimize scrolling through a long list of styles. Try organizing the recipe's rec styles into a group.

1 Choose Edit > Deselect All to make sure nothing in the document is selected. If that option is grayed out, you currently have nothing selected; proceed to the next step.

2 In the Paragraph Styles panel, click the rec_steps style to select it. Press and hold the Ctrl (Windows) or Command (Mac OS) key while you click the remainder of the rec paragraph styles. You may need to expand the panel to see all the styles.

3 Click the Paragraph Styles panel menu button. Choose New Group From Styles to create a new group from the selected styles and insert it into the list.

4   For the new style group name, type **rec** and press OK. If you want to rename the group, simply double-click on the group name in the Paragraph styles panel and retype the name. The group folder will be open after it is created.

All rec styles are now grouped within the rec folder.

If you prefer, choose New Style Group from the panel menu from the Paragraph Styles panel and then manually drag styles into a set.

5   Click the arrow next to the set's name to toggle between hiding and displaying its styles. Make sure you leave the arrow toggled down so all styles are visible when you finish.

6   Choose File > Save to save your work.

Object styles

With the recipe's text shaping up nicely, it's time to turn your attention to the rest of the layout and object styles. Object styles are very similar to text styles, except that they apply to frames, lines, and other graphic elements instead of text. The basic methods for defining and applying object styles should be very familiar.

Defining an object style

To practice defining an object style, you'll use the box surrounding the Cookie Color text and paragraph on page 73. As with paragraph and character styles, you'll create the style by example.

1   Choose the Selection tool (◂) from the Tools panel, then click to select the Cookie Color box on the right side of page 73.

2   Choose Object > Text Frame Options. In the resulting dialog box, enter **0.125 in** in the Top text field of the Inset Spacing section. Make sure the Link button (▫) to the right of the Top and Bottom settings is active, so it automatically fills in the Bottom, Left, and Right fields with the same values.

3   In the Vertical Justification section, choose Center from the Align drop-down menu. Press OK to apply the formatting to the object.

The Text Frame Options dialog box lets you format your objects.

4   Choose Window > Object Styles to open the Object Styles panel.

You can click and drag the bottom-right corner of the Object Styles panel to give the list of styles additional space.

5   With the Cookie Color box still selected, press the Object Styles panel
menu button (-≡) and choose New Object Style. Type **callout box** in the
Style Name text field, and press OK.

Name your new object style in the Object Styles Options dialog box.

6   Choose File > Save to save your work. Keep the file open.

Applying an object style

Applying an object style is the same as applying text styles, click to select the
object and click the style name in the Object Styles panel. Two boxes in the
recipe layout need the callout box style. Apply it now.

1   With the Cookie Color box still selected, click on the callout box style in
the Object Styles panel to apply the style.

2   With the Selection tool (⬚), click the box on page 72 that contains the
subhead (*Light color and chewy texture is the best way to enjoy these homemade
cookies*) and byline (*by Larry Happy*).

3   Apply the callout box style to the box by clicking the style in the Object
Styles panel.

4   Choose File > Save, or press Ctrl+S (Windows) or Command+S (Mac OS)
to save your work.

Changing an object style

Modifying an object style is easy. As with text styles, changing an object style's definition automatically updates all elements to which that style is applied. The callout boxes in the layout need some color; try updating the callout box style to add this element to your layout.

1 Make sure the byline box or Cookie Color box is selected, and double-click on the callout box style name in the Object Styles panel to open the Object Styles Options dialog box.

2 In the Basic Attributes section, click on the Fill option to highlight it. The color swatches that were created for this document appear in the Fill section on the right. Most of the colors are named with their CMYK values. Others have custom names. To learn more about working with color see Lesson 8, "Using Color in Your Documents."

3 Choose the swatch named cookie color to add it to the callout box object style. You may need to scroll down through the swatches list to see this color.

Modifications to an object style definition, such as adding a fill color, update all instances of the style.

4 Press OK. Both callout boxes should now be similar to the color of the cookies in the photo.

Finishing up

As a review, apply what you've learned to add some finishing touches to the recipe layout.

1 Import the paragraph styles named callout and byline from recipes.indd into the gingersnap document.

2 Apply the paragraph styles rec_list to the ingredients on page 73 and the rec_head style to the words *Molasses Gingersnaps* located above the ingredients.

3 Using Quick Apply, apply the callout paragraph style to the subhead on page 72 and the byline style to the name listed under the subhead.

4 Choose File > Save to save your work. You've finished your project!

Self study

To practice creating styles, create your own one- or two-page layout for a family recipe, using the styles from this lesson, or your own styles, to format the text and objects. In the next lesson, you'll learn how to work with graphics, which can further enhance your layouts. Combine the lessons to create a digital recipe library.

Review

Questions

1 Which type of style specifies text indenting: character or paragraph?

2 What must exist before you can add a nested style to a paragraph style?

3 What is the keyboard shortcut for Quick Apply?

4 If there are multiple styles in a document and scrolling becomes tedious, what new feature in CS3 should you use to condense the styles?

Answers

1 Paragraph.

2 A character style.

3 Ctrl+Enter (Windows) or Command+Return (Mac OS).

4 Style groups.

Lesson 6

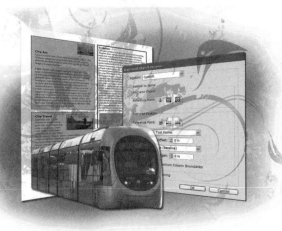

What you'll learn in this lesson:

- Adding graphics to your layout
- Managing links to imported files
- Updating changed graphics
- Using graphics with clipping paths and alpha channels

Working with Graphics

Graphics can add style and substance to your documents, and InDesign offers powerful controls for incorporating them into your layouts. One of InDesign's greatest strengths is its ability to import graphics in a wide range of graphic formats, including Illustrator and Photoshop files and, new to CS3, InDesign files.

Starting up

Before starting, make sure that your tools and panels are consistent by resetting your preferences. See "Resetting the InDesign workspace and preferences" on page 3.

You will work with several files from the id06lessons folder in this lesson. Make sure that you have loaded the idlessons folder onto your hard drive. See "Loading lesson files" on page 4.

See Lesson 6 in action!

Explore more of the features shown in this lesson using the supplemental video tutorial available online at agitraining.com/digitalclassroom.

The project

In this lesson, you'll lay out graphics for a fictional travel magazine called *SoJournal*. You will add graphics to the layout using different techniques. You will learn how to resize graphics, precisely change positioning, change display quality and wrap text around graphics. You will also learn how to handle situations in which graphics have been updated or are missing.

Locating missing images

If an image is renamed or moved from its original location after you import it into an InDesign file, InDesign loses the link to the image. The Links panel can help you find it again. In the Links panel, missing links have a red warning icon (●) next to their names, and modified links have a yellow warning icon (▲) next to their names. In this exercise, you will fix a link that was broken because the associated files were moved, and fix a link to a graphic in the layout that was modified.

1 Choose File > Open. In the Open dialog box, navigate to the id06lessons folder and select id0601.indd. Press Open. When the file opens, InDesign displays a message informing you that the document contains links to missing or modified files. On the right side of the workspace, the Links panel appears automatically, listing the links that are missing or modified. Notice that the citytravel.psd file has a red warning icon—indicating that the link is missing—next to it, while the id0607.psd file has a yellow warning icon—indicating that the link has been modified.

2 Press the Fix Links Automatically button.

> **Adobe InDesign**
>
> ⚠ This document contains links to missing or modified files. Click Fix Links Automatically to have InDesign update this document with the modified files and help you locate missing files. Click Don't Fix to correct the problem yourself using the Links panel.
>
> 1 - Missing Link
> 1 - Modified Link
>
> [Don't Fix] [Fix Links Automatically...]

When you open a file with missing or modified links, choose Fix Links Automatically.

3   In the Locate dialog box, navigate to the links folder in the id06lessons folder and select the citytravel.psd file. Press Open.

A new feature in CS3 is that when you press the Update Links Automatically button to update one broken link, all other broken links that exist in that folder update as well. This saves you the time of fixing each broken link individually.

4   Refer once again to the Links panel. The citytravel.psd, whose link you just fixed, no longer has a warning icon next to it. The other link, id0607.psd, however, still has a modified link that needs to be fixed. In the next part of the lesson you will learn how to do this from the Links panel.

5   Choose File > Save As. In the Save As dialog box, navigate to the id06lessons folder and type **id06_01work.indd** in the File name text field. Press Save and keep the file open.

Working with the Links panel

When you import an image into your layout, InDesign doesn't copy all the file data into your document file. Instead, it saves a reference, or a link, to the location of the original graphic file so it can access the image data when necessary. This lets you import many files into your layout without significantly increasing the file size of the InDesign document. Because graphic files are generally linked, and not embedded within the InDesign file, you need to know how to manage linked graphic files. The Links panel lets you manage these links, find files in the document, find missing files, and update graphics in the document when changes are made to the image file. In this exercise, you will fix a link to an image that has been updated.

1   If the Links panel isn't open, press the Links button (∾) in the dock on the right side of the workspace to open it.

2   Click once on id0607.psd, then press the Go To Link button (⊞) at the bottom of the Links panel.

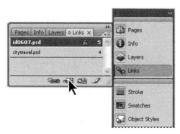

Click the Go To Link button.

3 InDesign takes you to the image that accompanies the *Embrace the Unconventional* article, whose link you selected in the Links panel.

4 With the id0607.psd option still selected, press the Update Link button (⬚) at the bottom of the Links panel. InDesign automatically updates the link.

5 Take a look at the Links panel. Neither of the links listed has a warning icon. You've fixed all your missing and modified links.

6 Choose File > Save, or press Ctrl+S (Windows) or Command+S (Mac OS), to save your work. Keep the file open for the next part of the lesson.

The Relink All Instances button

One of the great new features in InDesign CS3 is the option to relink all instances of missing or modified files. When you click the Links panel's Relink button (⬚), the Relink All Instances checkbox appears at the bottom of the Links dialog box. Click this to select it, and InDesign relinks every instance of the image throughout the document, saving you the task of locating and relinking each one.

Adding graphics to your layout

Adding graphics to your InDesign layouts is a simple process that allows users the flexibility to work with a number of different programs and graphic types. InDesign lets you use native Photoshop, PDF, and Illustrator files in your layouts. You can also use more common file formats, including JPEG, EPS, and TIF. In all, InDesign supports more than a dozen graphic file formats.

The most common way to add these formats to a layout is the Place command. In this exercise, you'll use Place to add an image to the front page of your travel magazine.

You can also import movies and audio in QuickTime, .avi, .wav, and .aif formats, as well as .au sound clips, into InDesign.

1 Navigate to page 1 of id0601_work.indd, which displays the magazine title *SoJournal* at the top of the page.

2 Press Shift+Ctrl+A (Windows) or Shift+Command+A (Mac OS), or choose Edit > Deselect All. If the Deselect All option is grayed out, nothing is currently selected.

3 Choose File > Place, or use the keyboard shortcut Ctrl+D (Windows) or Command+D (Mac OS), and navigate to the id06lessons folder. Select the id0601.psd file.

4   For now, make sure the Show Import Options checkbox in the lower-left corner of the Place dialog box is unchecked, and press Open.

Import id0601.psd with Show Import Options unchecked.

5   Your cursor becomes a paintbrush (🖌) with a thumbnail of the image you are importing. Position the thumbnail image in the upper-left corner of the red bleed guides and click to place the image. InDesign imports the image, the *SoJournal* masthead, at 100% of its original size.

If you accidentally clicked in a different spot on the page and need to reposition the image, use the Selection tool (▶) to drag the image until it snaps to the upper-left corner of the red bleed guides.

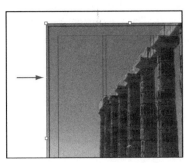

Place the image on page 1 at the edge of the bleed guides.

6   If you don't see a blue bounding box surrounding the image, the image is not selected. Click it once with the Selection tool (▶) to select it.

7 Scroll down to the bottom of your document. The image extends beyond the edge of the bleed; you need to resize it to fit within the bleed lines. Position the Selection tool over the lower-right corner of the image's bounding box. When the pointer becomes a double diagonal arrowhead (↖), click and drag the corner of the frame until it snaps to the lower-right corner of the bleed. The arrowheads turn white when you are positioned over the corner of the bleed.

8 To send the cover image behind the magazine masthead, make sure the image is still selected, then choose Object > Arrange > Send Backward.

9 Choose File > Save to save your work. Keep the file open for the next part of the lesson.

Fitting options

Try choosing Object > Fitting > Fit Content Proportionally. This resizes the image proportionally to fit inside the bounding box. If an image does not fill the box, it is because the proportions of the box do not match the dimensions of the image. To eliminate the empty space in the frame, you can choose Object > Fitting > Fit Frame to Content. The frame snaps to the edges of the image and there is no more unwanted white space.

Avoid using Object > Fitting > Fit Content to Frame, which distorts the image to fit it in the bounding box. Always choose one of the proportional options— Fit Content Proportionally or Fill Frame Proportionally—instead.

Fitting an image in an existing frame

You will now explore a variety of ways to control graphic placement.

1 With id0601_work.indd still open, choose 2 from the page number drop-down menu (to the right of the document percent drop-down menu) in the window's lower-left corner. This takes you to page 2 of the document.

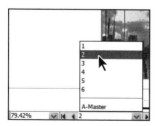

Navigate to page 2.

2   On the page are four image frames for images to accompany the paragraphs about Athens, Austin, Chicago, and Honolulu. To place an image of Athens into the frame at the top of the page, choose the Selection tool (⬚) from the Tools panel and click on the empty frame. Resizing anchors appear around the frame's bounding box.

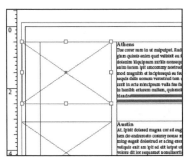

Select an empty frame to make it active.

3   Choose File > Place, or press Ctrl+D (Windows) or Command+D (Mac OS). In the Place dialog box, navigate to the id06lessons folder, select the id0602.psd image and press Open. The image appears in the selected frame.

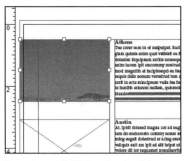

Import image id0602 into the selected frame.

4   Upon placement, all you see is the sky and a small piece of the skyline. Don't worry—you can reposition the graphic in the frame. To do this, you have a few options. First, choose the Direct Selection tool (⬚) from the Tools panel and position your cursor (now in the shape of a small hand) over the image. Click and hold for a moment to allow InDesign to build a preview of the graphic for you to view while repositioning.

5 Drag the image inside the frame until it looks similar to the figure below. While dragging the image, a light brown bounding box appears, indicating the full size of the graphic extending beyond the frame.

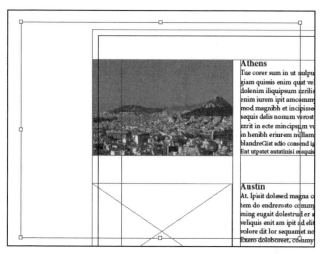

A light brown bounding box appears when you reposition the image, giving you an idea of the image's size.

6 Your other option for repositioning the graphic is to use InDesign's fitting features to center it in the frame. Reactivate the Selection tool and click on the graphic.

7 Right-click (Windows) or Ctrl+click (Mac OS) the graphic and choose Fitting > Center Content. The image, in its entirety, is centered within the frame.

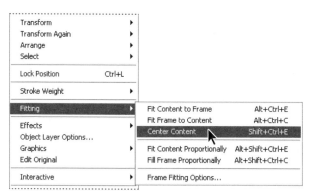

Choose Fitting > Center Content to center the graphic in its frame.

8 Sometimes the graphic works better if you fit it proportionally into an existing frame, even if the graphic and frame dimensions don't match. This is known as filling the frame proportionally. InDesign automatically calculates how to fill the image within the frame. With the Selection tool, right-click (Windows) or Ctrl+click (Mac OS) the graphic, and this time choose Fitting > Fill Frame Proportionally. You will be doing this shortly, but first, you will select the three images to be placed in the frames using Adobe Bridge.

After filling the frame proportionally, only a small part of the graphic extends beyond the edges of the frame. To view this, click on the image with the Direct Selection tool.

Auto Fitting

A new feature in InDesign CS3's Fitting menu is the Frame Fitting Options. This feature allows users to choose settings and create a default for graphic placement inside existing frames. In this section, you are going to set the default fitting option for frames.

1 Choose Edit > Deselect All, or press Shift+Ctrl+A (Windows) or Shift+Command+A (Mac OS), to make sure nothing in your document is selected.

2 Using the Selection tool (↖), Shift+click on the three remaining empty frames on page 2.

3 Choose Object > Fitting > Frame Fitting Options.

Choose Frame Fitting Options to set the defaults for placing graphics in frames.

4 Choose Fill Frame Proportionally from the Fitting drop-down menu toward the bottom of the dialog box, then press OK. Now when you place graphics into the three selected frames, the images will fill their respective frames proportionally.

Set the default frame fitting option to Fill Frame Proportionally.

You can also set the frame fitting defaults as you draw individual frames, if you do not want the same default for every box.

5 Choose File > Save.

Using Adobe Bridge to import graphics

The ability to import graphics using Adobe Bridge is a great workflow feature of the Creative Suite 3. You can preview the thumbnails in Adobe Bridge, then drag and drop one or multiple images onto your InDesign page. This is a more visual approach to importing graphics, especially if you want to first compare images in order to determine which to use in your layout. In this section, you will import the Chicago image to the document by dragging it from the Bridge window directly into the InDesign document.

1 With id0601.indd still open, choose File > Browse, or press the Go to Bridge button (⬚) in the upper-right corner of the Control panel to launch Adobe Bridge CS3.

2 When Adobe Bridge opens, click the Favorites tab in the upper-left corner to bring it forward, then click once on the Desktop listing.

3   If necessary, in the Content tab at the center of the Bridge window, locate the id06lessons folder and double-click to open it.

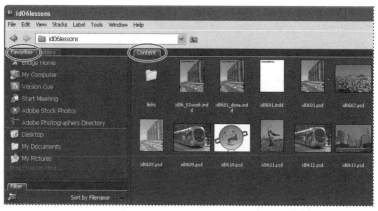

Open the id06lessons folder in Adobe Bridge.

4   In the upper-right corner of the Bridge window press the Switch to Compact Mode button (⊟). This results in a smaller version of Bridge that allows you to work simultaneously with Bridge and your InDesign document.

5   Position the compact Bridge window so you can see the empty Austin frame on page 2.

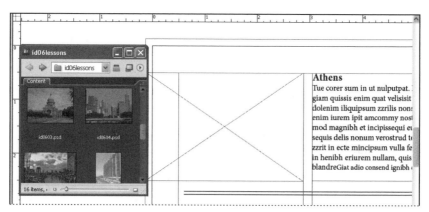

Adobe Bridge in compact mode lets you work directly with an InDesign document.

6 Scroll inside the Bridge window to locate id0603.psd, an image of the Austin Capitol building. Click, hold, and drag the image to the frame on page 2. When your cursor, a black arrow with a small white box with a plus sign in it (☜⊞), is anywhere inside the frame, release the mouse. The photo fills the frame.

7 Close the Bridge window, and with the InDesign document as the active window, choose File > Save.

Placing multiple graphics

Another feature new to InDesign CS3 is the ability to place multiple graphics into multiple existing frames at once. In this section, you will place two graphics, one each in the remaining frames on page 2 of the layout, by choosing two images simultaneously in the Place dialog box.

1 Make sure you are on page 2 of id0601_work.indd and, with nothing selected, choose File > Place, or press Ctrl+D (Windows) or Command+D (Mac OS).

2 Ctrl+click (Windows) or Command+click (Mac OS) to select id0604. psd and id0605.psd, and press Open. The paintbrush icon (🖌) displays the number 2 in parentheses, as well as a thumbnail of the first image (the one that accompanies the Chicago blurb).

3 Click inside the empty frame to the left of the Chicago entry to place the first graphic. The paintbrush's number disappears, and a thumbnail of the Honolulu image appears.

4 Position your cursor over the remaining empty frame and click to place id0605.psd in the frame.

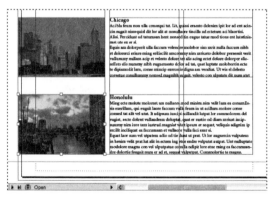

You can sequentially place multiple graphics in multiple frames using Place.

5 Choose File > Save to save your work. Keep the file open for the next part of the lesson.

Adjusting display quality of images

Sometimes users like to see exactly what their images will look like as they position them, and sometimes users just need to work quickly without the image files' sizes slowing them down. InDesign accommodates both working styles with its Display Performance settings.

The default setting is Typical Display, which displays images at a low quality, allowing for faster displays and document response. If your document becomes image-heavy, you can select some or all of the images in the document and choose Object > Display Performance > Fast Display. With this setting in effect, the image is grayed out and you can work much more quickly and efficiently. To change the settings for the entire InDesign document, go to View > Display Performance > Fast Display.

If seeing the image's detail is more important to you than speed, right-click (Windows) or Ctrl+click (Mac OS) the image with the Selection tool. From the contextual menu, choose Display Performance > High Quality Display. The image now displays at a higher resolution.

Remember that high quality is relative; images with different original resolutions will appear differently in High Quality display performance mode, as InDesign can't improve the resolution of the original image.

Using object styles for images

In Lesson 5, "Working with Styles," you learned how to apply object styles to basic boxes and rules. You can also apply them to graphic frames to give your images a more finished look. In this exercise, you'll create and apply an object style that adds a one-point black stroke to all the frames on page 2.

1   Use the Selection tool (k) to select the first image, the one of Athens, on page 2.

2   From the dock on the right side of your workspace, press the Swatches button (▦) to open the Swatches panel. Select the Black swatch.

3 Click on the Stroke tab, which is to the left of the Swatches tab, to bring the Stroke panel forward. Type **1** in the Weight text field and press the Align Stroke to Inside button (▣) to set the stroke to align to the inside of the frame.

Set the stroke weight to 1 pt. and align the stroke.

4 Click on the Stroke panel's tab to collapse it. You can now use the formatting of this first frame to create an object style to apply to the other frames.

5 Choose Window > Object Styles to open the Object Styles panel.

6 With the Athens image on page 2 still selected, Alt+click (Windows) or Option+click (Mac OS) on the Create new style button (▣) at the bottom of the Object Styles panel to create a new object style.

Alt/Option+click the Create new style button.

7 In the resulting New Object Style dialog box, click the checkbox next to Frame Fitting Options, the last option in the list under the Basic Attributes header, then click on this option to highlight it.

8 From the Fitting drop-down menu, choose Fill Frame Proportionally. Name the style Image Frame, and press OK. InDesign saves the attributes of the selected object as a new style.

9 With the first image already selected, Shift+click the remaining three images on page 2.

10 In the Object Styles panel, click the Image Frame style to apply it to all four images simultaneously.

To better view the one-point strokes on the four image frames, you may need to press Ctrl+(plus sign) (Windows) or Command+(plus sign) (Mac OS) to zoom in. This shortcut brings you progressively closer to the page. After you view the final result, choose View > Fit Page in Window to bring you back to a broad view of your file.

11 Press Shift+Ctrl+A (Windows) or Shift+Command+A (Mac OS) to deselect the images. Choose File > Save. Keep the document open.

Text wrapping and images

When placing graphics over text in a layout, the graphic covers the text. In order to force the text away from a graphic without physically resizing the boxes, you can use a technique called text wrap. There are five different options for text wrap: no text wrap (the default), wrap around bounding box, wrap around object shape, jump object, and jump to next column.

Wrapping text around the bounding box

When you place a graphic on a page, you might want the text to wrap around the bounding box that contains the graphic.

1 With the Selection tool (✲), select the image of Athens on page 2. Click, hold, and drag it to the right so the upper-left corner of the image fits into the corner where the top (designated by a pink line) and left (designated by a blue line) margins intersect. Part of the image overlaps the text because the image box is above the text box in the stacking order.

2 Choose Window > Text Wrap. The Text Wrap panel opens.

3 Click the Wrap around bounding box button (▦), which causes the text to wrap around the graphic's bounding box.

Wrap text around the graphic's bounding box.

4 In the middle of the panel are the offset values, which determine how closely the text wraps around the image. The Make all settings the same button (ȸ) in the middle of the offset values (Top, Bottom, Left, and Right) is the default to keep all the values consistent. Make sure it is on, then click the up arrow next to one of the offset options to set the offset to 0.125 inches. Notice the difference in spacing once you change the offset value.

5 Repeat steps 1-4 for the remaining three images on the page, moving them inside the page boundaries and wrapping their respective paragraphs around them.

6 Choose File > Save to save your work. Keep the file open for the next exercise.

Using graphics with clipping paths and alpha channels

Some images contain clipping paths or alpha channels. Clipping paths and alpha channels hide information in an image, typically the background, enabling users to wrap text around part of the image. Clipping paths are stored in the Paths palette in Photoshop, and alpha channels are saved selections stored in the Channels palette in Photoshop. The formats that utilize this option are .psd, .eps and .tif, all of which keep the image information outside the path or channel hidden when importing into another program. You will place into InDesign a graphic that has a prebuilt clipping path from Photoshop, and use the text wrap option to wrap around the object's shape.

1 Press Shift+Ctrl+A (Windows) or Shift+Command+A (Mac OS) to make sure nothing is selected. You will place the next image in the Transportation article on page 3 of the InDesign document.

2 Choose File > Place, and navigate to the id06lessons folder. Select image id0609.psd, click the Show Import Options checkbox at the bottom of the Place dialog box, and press Open. The Image Import Options dialog box appears.

3 Click the Image tab at the top of the dialog box to bring the image options forward. Make sure that the Apply Photoshop Clipping Path checkbox is checked and that Alpha Channel is set to None. Press OK.

Image Import Options (id0609.psd)

Image | Color | Layers

☑ Apply Photoshop Clipping Path

Alpha Channel: None

None
trainOpenWindow

☑ Show Preview

OK   Cancel

Choose import options for id0609.psd.

4 Position the paintbrush-and-thumbnail cursor (🖌) at the top of the leftmost column in the Transportation article and click to place the graphic. The train image, without a background, appears over the text. By selecting the Apply Photoshop Clipping Path option in the Image Import Options dialog box, you set the image to appear without its background.

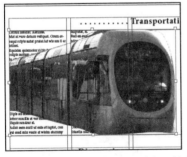

When Apply Photoshop Clipping Path is enabled, the image appears without its background.

5   The train image's lower-left corner is a good anchor point, so now you'll resize the image around that point. With the image still selected, click the lower-left point of the reference point locator (⌗) in the Control panel.

Set the train image's lower-left corner as the reference point.

Choose 50% from the Scale X percentage or Scale Y percentage drop-down menu. Make sure that the Constrain proportions for scaling button (⬤) next to the percentage boxes is chosen to constrain the proportions. The resulting image is a smaller train positioned in the lower-left corner of the Transportation article.

6   Choose Window > Text Wrap to open the Text Wrap panel if it is not already open. Press the Wrap around object shape button (⬛) to wrap the text around the object shape, and change the offset amount to 0.1875.

Wrap text around the object shape.

The text now wraps around the clipping path that was previously defined in Photoshop. The same options are available for alpha channels saved with an image. You will explore this later.

7   Choose File > Save to save your work. Keep the file open for the next part of the lesson.

Removing an image background using InDesign

If you don't have the advantage of an embedded alpha channel or a clipping path in your file, you can still knock out the background without having to go into Photoshop to wrap text around the object. You can do this directly in InDesign using InDesign's own clipping path options.

1 Choose Edit > Deselect All, to make sure no frames are selected. You want to place the next image independently in the *Discoveries* article on page 3.

2 Choose File > Place, or press Crtl+D (Windows) or Command+D (Mac OS). In the Place dialog box, navigate to the id06lessons folder. Select the id0610.psd image. At the bottom of the dialog box, make sure the Show Import Options checkbox is selected, then choose Open.

3 In the resulting Image Import Options dialog box, choose the Image tab. Notice that the Clipping Path options are grayed out, which means that no clipping path exists for this image. Because there is no clipping path, you have to remove the image's background yourself after you place the image. Press OK.

4 Position the paintbrush-and-thumbnail cursor (🐾) anywhere in the *Discoveries* article and click to place the image. With the Selection tool (k), position the image in the middle of the article's text.

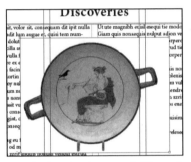

Place the id06_10.psd image in the Discoveries *article.*

5 To remove the image background, choose Object > Clipping Path > Options. Select Detect Edges from the Type drop-down menu, leave the other settings at their defaults, and press OK. You have removed the background.

Remove the image background using Object > Clipping Path > Options.

6   If the Text Wrap panel is not already visible, choose Window > Text Wrap, and click the Wrap around object shape button (▣) to wrap the text around the object shape.

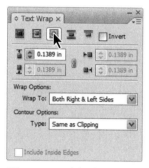

Wrap text around the object's shape.

7   Choose File > Save to save your work.

Anchored (inline) objects

Anchored, or inline, objects allow a graphic to flow with its related text. Consider a dictionary, for example. If you were to add more details to the rhinoceros entry, you would want the drawing of the rhinoceros to move with its definition, rather than hold its position on the page and end up next to the rhinestone entry. Anchoring an object links a graphic with its associated text so that it moves and flows with the text. In this exercise, you will learn how to create anchored objects.

1   With the Selection tool (↖) active, click to select the City Art frame on page 4. Press Ctrl+(plus sign) (Windows) or Command+(plus sign) (Mac OS) twice to zoom in on the selected frame.

2   Select the Type tool (T) from the Tools panel, and click to the immediate left of the word *CHICAGO* on the fifth line. Placing, or anchoring, the text cursor prior to placing a graphic instructs InDesign to insert the graphic into a specific line of text, making it an inline graphic.

3   Choose File > Place, or use the keyboard shortcut Ctrl+D (Windows) or
Command+D (Mac OS). At the bottom of the Place dialog box, uncheck
the Show Import Options checkbox. Navigate to the id06lessons folder,
select id0613.psd, and press Open. InDesign imports the image right where
you placed the text cursor.

Import the image next to the word CHICAGO.

4   Click to position the text cursor at the end of the paragraph above the
image you just imported, and press Enter (Windows) or Return (Mac
OS) once to force the following paragraph down. Notice how the graphic
moves with the text.

The inline image moves with its text.

5 Press Ctrl+Z (Windows) or Command+Z (Mac OS) to undo the paragraph return, bringing the image back to its original position.

6 To manually control the positioning of the anchored image, switch to the Selection tool and click once on the anchored image to select it. Choose Object > Anchored Object > Options.

7 In the resulting Anchored Object Options dialog box, turn on the Preview checkbox in the lower-left corner of the dialog box. Choose Custom from the Position drop-down menu, and click the Relative to Spine checkbox. Activating the Relative to Spine option positions the image outside the text frame. Leave all the other settings to their defaults, and press OK to close the dialog box.

Set the anchored image to Custom and Relative to Spine.

8 With the Selection tool, click and drag the graphic into position in the upper-right corner of the City Art box.

Reposition the anchored image manually.

9 To test the spine-sensitive options, choose View > Fit Spread In Window. Use the Selection tool to select the City Art frame. Drag the frame to the empty column on the right side of the City Music box on page 5. Notice how the graphic automatically adjusts its position within the City Art box relative to the spread's spine.

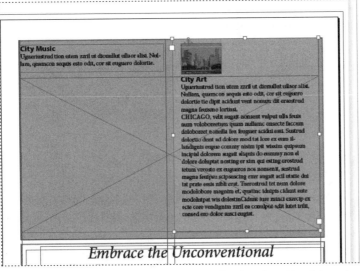

When you reposition the City Art frame to page 5, the graphic adjusts its position relative to the spine.

10 Press Ctrl+Z (Windows) or Command+Z (Mac OS) to undo the repositioning, or simply drag the City Art frame back into position.

11 Save the file by choosing File > Save. Keep the file open for the next part of the lesson.

Applying a text wrap to anchored graphics is the same as applying a text wrap to any object. Click the anchored graphic with the Selection tool, choose the desired option from the Text Wrap panel, and set your offset value accordingly.

Advanced importing

Beyond basic object placement and fitting, InDesign CS3 offers some more powerful import controls. You can import:

- Photoshop files with their separate layers intact
- Complete InDesign documents as single graphics
- Files through Adobe Bridge for a smooth CS3 workflow

Importing layered Photoshop files

A layer comp is a snapshot of the current state of the Photoshop Layers palette. Within Photoshop, you can change the visibility, position, and appearance of the layers to create different versions of a file. When you create a layer comp, it saves those settings by remembering the state of each layer when the layer comp was saved. This allows you to create multiple comps or compositions within a single Photoshop file! When you import a .psd document into InDesign with the Show Import Options checkbox selected, InDesign lets you choose which layer comp to use from that Photoshop file.

One advantage of using layered Photoshop files in an InDesign layout is that you can change the image display using layer visibility directly in the layout. You no longer have to save multiple versions of an image and constantly replace the image; instead you can save time by controlling the layers directly within InDesign. In this exercise, you will display different versions of an image using layer and layer comp visibility.

1 With the Selection tool (⬉), click to select the empty frame under the Sculpture article on page 4 of the InDesign document. Press Ctrl+(plus sign) (Windows) or Command+(plus sign) (Mac OS) twice to zoom in on the selected frame.

2 Choose File > Place, and at the bottom of the Place dialog box, click the Show Import Options checkbox to enable it. Navigate to the id06lessons folder, select id0611.psd, then press Open.

Choose your import options for id06_11.psd.

3   In the resulting Image Import Options dialog box, click the Layers tab to bring the layers options forward. Notice that several layers are listed in the Show Layers section. Make sure the Show Preview checkbox is selected, then click the box next to the hsbGray layer to display that layer's option. Notice how the image preview changes when you select the hsbGray layer.

4   Choose 3w/hsbGray from the Layer Comp drop-down menu to display multiple layer visibility changes as defined by the layer comp determined in Photoshop.

Use the layer comp visibility options to change the visibility of layers.

5   Press OK. The image imports into the InDesign layout based on the Layer Comp options you set in the Image Import Options dialog box.

6   Clearly, this image looks a little strange in your layout. To change layer visibility in an InDesign layout after you place an image, select the image and choose Object > Object Layer Options. Choose Last Document State from the Layer Comp drop-down menu to return the image to its original settings, then press OK.

Return the image to its original state using Object Layer Options.

7 Right-click (Windows) or Ctrl+click (Mac OS) the image and choose Fitting > Fill Frame Proportionally so the image fits nicely inside the frame.

8 Choose File > Save to save your work.

Importing InDesign layouts as graphics

A feature new to InDesign CS3 is the ability to import InDesign layouts as graphics. You may have an ad or a flyer that was created in InDesign that you want to use in another InDesign layout. The advantage to using an InDesign file rather than a PDF file is that you can have changes that you make to the imported InDesign file automatically update in the file in which it was placed. In this exercise, you will import a CD booklet design into the layout.

1 Open the Pages panel from the dock on the right side of the workspace and, in the panel, double-click on page 5 to center it on your screen. Use the Selection tool (**k**) to select the frame beneath the City Music headline.

2 Choose File > Place or press the keyboard shortcut, Ctrl+D (Windows) or Command+D (Mac OS). At the bottom of the Place dialog box, make sure the Show Import Options checkbox is checked, navigate to the id06lessons folder, and select id0614.indd. Press Open.

3 In the Place InDesign Document dialog box, click the General tab to bring it forward, and make sure the Crop to drop-down menu is set to Page bounding box. The other two crop options for bleed and slug would be used if you wanted those additional layout options to be visible. You will not set the Layers tab options. Press OK.

Set the Crop options to Page bounding box in the General section.

4 After InDesign completes the import process, the program displays a warning that the file contains missing or modified links. When you import InDesign files that have links, you need to have those links available for the new layout as well. Press OK to import the file.

If links are missing or have been modified, InDesign warns you when importing the file.

5 The CD booklet design fills the frame. Since it doesn't fit entirely in the frame, right-click (Windows) or Ctrl+click (Mac OS), and from the contextual menu, choose Fitting > Fit Content Proportionally.

6 Choose File > Save. You're finished! At the very bottom of the Tools panel, click and hold the Normal (W) button to reveal more viewing options. Choose Preview, then page through your completed travel magazine. When you're finished, choose File > Close to close the document.

Self study

For a different text wrap option, try placing id0609.psd in a block of text and using the Text Wrap panel to set the wrap to the alpha channel named trainOpenWindow. Make sure to go to the Object menu and choose Clipping Path > Options. Change the Type field to Alpha Channel, and set Alpha to trainOpenWindow.

Also try using Adobe Bridge to add more images to your document. Once you get used to this workflow, you will find that it can speed up the design process.

Review

Questions

1   What menu option allows you to change the way graphics automatically fit inside their frames?

2   To flow text around the shape of a clipping path, which panel should you use?

3   Which tool do you use to reposition a graphic inside its frame?

4   Which graphic format supports the visibility of layer comps?

5   Once a layered graphic is placed in an InDesign document, how do you change the layer visibility?

Answers

1   Object > Fitting.

2   The Text Wrap panel.

3   The Direct Selection tool.

4   Photoshop .psd.

5   With the graphic selected, choose Object > Object Layer Options, or right-click (Windows) or Ctrl+click (Mac OS), and choose Object Layer Options from the contextual menu.

Lesson 7

What you'll learn in this lesson:

- Creating and importing tables
- Pasting text into a table
- Editing tables and table options
- Formatting cells, rows, and text
- Defining a header cell
- Using graphics in tables

Creating and Using Tables

Tables are an extremely effective way to convey a large amount of organized data. Whether you import a table from Microsoft Word or Excel, or build a new one in InDesign, you have at your disposal many powerful ways to design impressive, professional-looking table layouts. Prominent among these is the new, long-awaited feature allowing users to create and apply table and cell styles. After designing a table, you can save all the table's attributes as a style and quickly apply those attributes to another table with just one click!

Starting up

Before starting, make sure that your tools and panels are consistent by resetting your preferences. See "Resetting the InDesign workspace and preferences" on page 3.

You will work with several files from the id07lessons folder in this lesson. Make sure that you have loaded the idlessons folder onto your hard drive. See "Loading lesson files" on page 4.

See Lesson 7 in action!

Explore more of the features shown in this lesson using the supplemental video tutorial available online at agitraining.com/digitalclassroom.

The project

In this lesson, you will add tables to a brochure about Bella's Bakery. The first page of the brochure is complete, but the second page needs tables to list the products for sale. To preview the results you'll be working toward, navigate to the id07lessons folder and open id0701_done.indd. Once you've looked over the layout, you can close the file by choosing File > Close or keep it open for reference as you work.

CAKES			**PIES**			**COOKIES**		

This is what the final layout should look like.

Creating a table

You can create a table from scratch and type in your data, copy and paste information from another table, or convert tabbed text into a table. In this section, you'll start with creating a table from scratch, then explore the other two options as well. Tables exist inside text frames, so to create a table, you must first make a text frame. To select a table, therefore, you must use the Type tool.

Designing a table from scratch

The Bella's Bakery brochure needs multiple tables. For this first one, you'll use the Insert Table control to design your own.

1 From within InDesign, choose File > Browse, or press the Go to Bridge button (🔳) in the upper-right corner of the Control panel to open Adobe Bridge. Navigate to the id07lessons folder and open the file id0701.indd. The file opens in InDesign.

2 Press the Pages button (🔲) in the dock on the right side of the workspace to open the Pages panel. Page 2 should be highlighted blue to indicate it's the current page. If it's not highlighted, click page 2 in the Pages panel to make it the active page.

3 Choose View > Fit Page in Window so you can see all of page 2 of your document.

4 Activate the Type tool (T) from the Tools panel, then click and drag a text frame from the top-left to the bottom-right of page 2's middle column.

5 Choose Table > Insert Table.

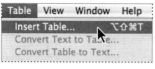

Choose Insert Table from the Table menu.

6 In the resulting Insert Table dialog box, type **7** for the Body Rows, and **4** for the Columns.

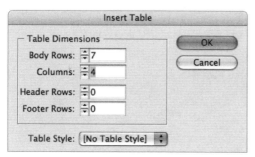

The Insert Table dialog box with the correct settings.

7 Press OK to close the dialog box and insert the table. A table with four columns and seven rows appears in the second column's text frame.

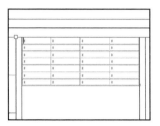

The resulting table has four columns and seven rows.

Copying and pasting table information

You now have a table with no data. You could type the information into the table, but InDesign offers an easier way: cutting and pasting data from another table. InDesign has been able to cut and paste information between resident InDesign tables since CS2, but CS3 gives users more flexibility. You can now cut data from a Microsoft Excel or Word table and paste those entries into a selected table in InDesign. Using the Clipboard Handling section of InDesign's Preferences, you can specify whether the text pasted from another application retains its original formatting or not. If you check Text Only, the information appears as unformatted text, which you can then flow into a selected table. If All Information is selected, the pasted text appears as the table looked in Word or Excel, and InDesign imports the styles from those programs. Whichever your preference, you must select the destination table's cells prior to pasting.

Since you may or may not have Word or Excel, for this exercise you will practice cutting and pasting just between InDesign tables.

1 With the id0701.indd file still open, press the Layers button (👁) in the dock to reveal the Layers panel.

Open the Layers panel.

2 Click on the left-hand gray square to the left of the Pies layer, the visibility icon (👁), to reveal its contents, which appear on the artboard on the right side of the page. Click to select the Pies layer.

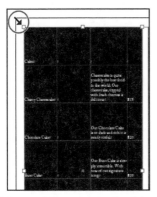

Click the gray square to reveal the layer's contents.

3 Select the Hand tool (✋) from the Tools panel. Click the page with the Hand tool, and drag to reveal the artboard on the right side of the page. Next to the pies images is a table with information on the bakery's pies. Use the Hand tool to position this area so you can see the table and pies images well.

4 Select the Type tool (T) from the Tools panel. You edit tables by selecting either the table or its cells with the Type tool, since they reside in text frames.

5 Hover over the top-left corner of the pies table until you see an arrow that points diagonally toward the lower-right corner. Click to select the entire table.

Click the upper-left corner to select the whole table.

When hovering over a table, the cursor image tells you what you can select. The diagonal arrow means you can select the whole table. An arrow pointing to the right indicates that clicking selects a row. Click when the cursor arrow points straight down, and you select a column.

6 Choose Edit > Copy to copy the selected table to the clipboard.

7 On page 2, you need to select the table you created in the previous exercise, which is the destination table. Select the whole table with the Type tool over the top-left corner of the table; click when you see the diagonal arrow.

8 Choose Edit > Paste to paste the information from the existing pies table into your new table. You have successfully moved table information from an existing table to another new table.

9 Choose File > Save As. In the Save As dialog box, navigate to the id07lessons folder and type **id0701_work.indd** in the File name text field. Press Save.

Converting text to table and table to text

If you prefer, you can bypass the step of creating a table grid, and simply paste data from an existing table into a text frame in your document. The information appears as tab-delineated text, which you can then convert into a table using the Table menu's Convert Text to Table option. You can also perform this process in the opposite direction using Convert Table to Text. When you choose this option, InDesign removes the table lines and inserts the separators you specify at the end of each row and column.

To demonstrate both options, you will convert the table you just created to text and then convert the text back to a table.

1 With the table on page 2 still selected, choose Table > Convert Table to Text.

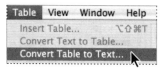

From the Table menu, you can convert a table to text.

2 In the Convert Table to Text dialog box, Tab should be set as the Column Separator and Paragraph should be set as the Row Separator.

Convert Table to Text

Column Separator: Tab

Row Separator: Paragraph

OK

Cancel

Specify your item separators in the Convert Table to Text dialog box.

3 Press OK. InDesign inserts tabs between each column entry, and paragraph returns after each row, removing all table lines.

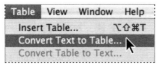

The table is now tab-delineated text.

You will take this mess of text and turn it back into a table.

4 With the Type tool (T), click inside the text frame, then choose Edit > Select All, or press Ctrl+A (Windows) or Command+A (Mac OS), to highlight all the text.

5 Choose Table > Convert Text to Table. In the resulting Convert Text to Table dialog box, keep the default separator settings and press OK to display the selected text as a table again.

Table	View	Window	Help
Insert Table...			⌥⇧⌘T
Convert Text to Table...			
Convert Table to Text...			

Choose Table > Convert Text to Table to display the selected text as a table.

6 Press Shift+Ctrl+A (Windows) or Shift+Command+A (Mac OS) to deselect everything in the document. Choose File > Save to save your work.

Importing a table

For some projects, you may need to incorporate an existing table created in Microsoft Word or Excel into your layout. Instead of simply pasting a table into the document, the better approach is to use the Place option, which gives you more control over formatting. When you place a Word or Excel document, you can edit the resulting table in InDesign using its Microsoft Word Import options to control the formatting.

1   With id0701_work.indd still open, activate the Type tool (T) and choose File > Place to insert the Microsoft Word document with a table onto page 2 of your InDesign file.

2   Click to turn on the Show Import Options checkbox at the bottom of the Place dialog box. Navigate to the id07lessons folder, select id0701.doc, and press Open.

3   The Microsoft Word Import Options dialog box appears. Click the Remove Styles and Formatting from Text and Tables radio button to strip the incoming document of all Word formatting and replace it with InDesign's Basic Paragraph style. This is a good idea if you don't want any of Word's styles, colors, or other formatting in your InDesign document. Later in this lesson, you will format the text and save the results as your own styles.

For more on importing text, see Lesson 4, "Working with Text and Type."

Strip the Word document of its formatting to avoid any inconsistencies once it's in InDesign.

4   Press OK in the Microsoft Word Import Options dialog box. It closes, and to the right of the cursor is a miniature preview of the text.

5   In the left-hand column on page 2, click and drag from the top-left margin to the bottom-right to designate an area in which to place the table. You can also just click in the upper-left corner of the margin area to flow the text into the first column. Notice the red overflow box at the bottom-right corner of the text frame, which indicates that there is more placed text than the column can hold. Don't worry about that right now; you'll fix the proportions of the frame soon.

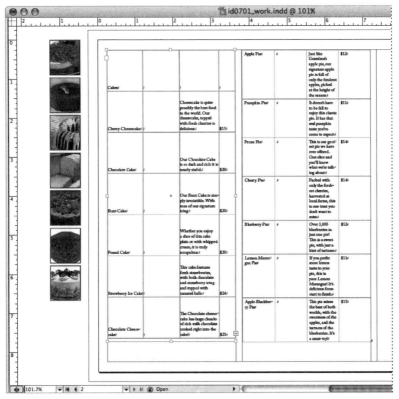

Click to place the table on the InDesign page.

6   Choose File > Save to save your work.

Editing tables and table options

InDesign CS3 has all the same table tools you've come to rely on in CS2 to make your table presentations visually pleasing. In this series of exercises, you will concentrate on ways to adjust the entire Word table you imported. First you'll change the height of the top column to expose the hidden text that is overflowing from the text box, then you will explore Table Options to change the border row strokes, column strokes, and fill of the table.

Changing row width

If your rows are too short to comfortably hold your entries, you can easily expand them.

1 With the Type tool (T) selected, click inside the first table you imported in the left-hand column.

2 Hover between the top row, which holds the word *Cakes*, and the row below it, which contains *Cherry Cheesecake* in its first cell. When the cursor is directly over the row separator it becomes a double arrow.

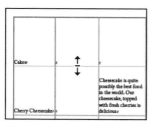

The cursor changes to a double arrow when it is directly over a row separator.

3 Click with the double-arrow cursor, and drag up to resize the top row. Drag up enough that there is no more overset text. If necessary, resize the second row as well until the red overset text disappears.

> *To change just the size of a row or column without affecting the entire table, hold Shift as you drag. You can do this for all rows and columns except the rightmost row and bottommost column, where holding the Shift key alters all the rows at the same time.*

Editing the border

Now you will change the size of the table border.

1 Select the *Cakes* table by choosing Table > Select Table, then choose Table > Table Options > Table Setup. The Table Options dialog box opens.

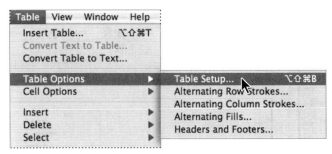

Choose Table Setup in the Table menu to open the Table Options dialog box.

2 In the Table Options dialog box, type **3** in the Weight text field in the Table Border section. Check the Preview box in the bottom-left corner of the dialog box to see the change take effect.

Adjust the weight of the table border in the Table Options dialog box.

Formatting rows and columns

You have changed the border size, and now you will color and change the size of the row and column separators.

1   With the table still selected, and the Table Options dialog box still open, click on the Row Strokes tab at the top of the dialog box.

2   From the Alternating Pattern drop-down menu, choose Every Other Row. This setting allows you to control the appearance of the rows. The options on the left side of the Alternating section are for the first row and the options on the right side are for the next row. It repeats this pattern throughout the rows of the table.

Specify the look and feel of the rows of a table, whether it is every other row, every second row or every third row.

3   In the Alternating section, beneath the First text field, type **3** in the Weight text field, and choose Dark Blue from the Color drop-down menu. These settings affect the first row and every alternating row beneath it.

4 Enter **3** in the Weight text field beneath the Next text field, and choose Light Blue from the Color drop-down menu. This setting affects the second row and every second row beneath it.

Adjust the column settings in the Table Options dialog box as well.

5 Click the Column Strokes tab in the Table Options dialog box.

6 Choose Every Other Column from the Alternating Pattern drop-down menu.

The Alternating Patterns drop-down menu.

7   In the Alternating section, beneath the First text field, enter **3** for Weight, and choose Dark Blue from the Color drop-down menu. These settings will affect the first column and every alternating column after it.

8   Beneath the Next text field, type **3** for Weight, and choose Light Blue from the Color drop-down menu. Press OK to apply the changes. Press the Escape key to deselect the table. Then press W on your keyboard to toggle into the Preview mode and to see how the table will appear when printed. Press W again to return to the normal view.

The settings in the Column Strokes tab determine the look of your column separators.

Using fills

To put the finishing touch on your table, you will fill your table with color.

1   Choose Table > Select Table. Then choose Table Options > Alternating Fills. This opens the Fills section of the Table Options dialog immediately.

2   Choose Every Other Row from the Alternating Pattern drop-down menu.

3   In the Alternating section, beneath the First text field, choose Light Chocolate from the Color drop-down menu and type **20** in the Tint Percentage text field.

4 In the color section beneath the Next text field, choose Light Blue from the Color drop-down menu and type **20** for Tint Percentage. With Preview checked you should see the changes happen instantaneously.

Set the fill color and tint percentage in the Fill tab.

5 Press OK to apply all your fill color. Press the Escape key to deselect the table.

The table now reflects all Table Options changes.

6 Choose File > Save to save your work.

Formatting cells and text

Unlike the Table Options settings that apply to the whole table, your cell styles and Cell Options settings can be different for each cell in the table. You can select and format one cell at a time, an entire row, an entire column, or any other group of cells. You will now format the table on a cell basis. You will start by resetting the cell style of all the cells in the table. You will then change the vertical alignment of type within all cells of the Cakes table. Finally, you will make four paragraph styles, one each for the table's header, name, description, and price sections. In later exercises, you'll use these paragraph styles to create cell styles that will speed the rest of the table's formatting, and ultimately you'll use the cell styles to create a table style with which you'll format the entire Pies table.

Resetting the cell styles within a table

Very soon you will make both cell and table styles so you can quickly apply all the attributes of not only a table but also the cells within a table. This table has mixed cell styles, meaning some of the settings from Microsoft Word have remained with the table.

1   With the Type tool (T) selected, hover over the top-left corner of the frame until you see a diagonal arrow, then click to select the table.

2   Choose Window > Type and Tables > Cell Styles to open the Cell Styles panel. Notice the plus sign next to None in the panel's list of styles. This means that the selected table contains *overrides*, which are Word styles left over from the original document.

Manage the styles used in your table cells from the Manage Styles panel.

3 Hover your cursor over the plus sign to prompt a small yellow box listing all the items on your page that are in a style other than the None style. Alt+click (Windows) or Option+click (Mac OS) the word None to clear the overrides. Each cell's contents are now aligned to the top of their respective cells.

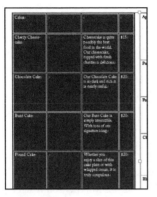

Clear the overrides so the table contents align properly.

4 Choose File > Save.

Text alignment and inset within a cell

Some cell formatting options are similar to the formatting text boxes options you worked with earlier in the lesson. For example, you can use the same alignment options—top, center, bottom, and justified—within a cell as you can in a text box. You also have the same text inset settings that control how far text is inset from the edge of a cell. You will now change these settings for the whole table. You can also change these options one cell at a time, for a range of cells, or for all the cells at once. For the Bella's Bakery table, you will change the alignment and inset settings for all the cells at once.

1   Make sure the whole table is selected (click with the Type tool's diagonal arrow (↘) if it's not), then choose Table > Cell Options > Text to open the Cell Options dialog box.

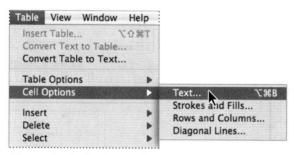

After you select the table, choose Cell Options > Text from the Table menu.

2   In the Cell Insets section of the Cell Options dialog box, type **0.0625** in the Top text field. Press the Tab key to apply the settings to all the insets. If this did not insert 0.0625 automatically in the Bottom, Left, and Right fields, type **0.0625** again and click the Make all settings the same button (⬚) to the immediate right of the top and bottom inset values.

3   In the Vertical Justification section, choose Align Center from the Align drop-down menu.

4   Click the Preview checkbox to see your changes. The text in each cell is centered and inset from each edge. Press OK to apply the settings.

Set the text alignment and inset in the Cell Options dialog box.

Formatting text within a cell and saving paragraph styles

You can also format the text color and font size in your cells. You can also save these settings as a paragraph style for reuse later; applying styles to cells is as easy as applying them to text frames. In this exercise, you'll create several paragraph styles from your cell formatting. In the next section, you'll apply these styles to other cells and see how much time using styles can save.

1 With the Type tool (T), click inside the first cell of the second row, then choose Edit > Select All to highlight the cell's contents (the words *Cherry Cheesecake*).

2 In the Control panel, type **10** in the Font Size field, and click the Small Caps button to apply small caps.

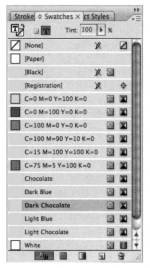

A	Adobe Caslon Pro		T	10 pt		TT	T¹	T
¶	Regular		A	(12 pt)		Tr	T,	T

Set the font size and toggle on Small Caps in the Control panel.

3 Open the Swatches panel. Select the Dark Chocolate swatch to make the text dark brown.

Select Dark Chocolate from the Swatches panel.

4 Press Shift+Ctrl+C (Windows) or Shift+Command+C (Mac OS) to center the type in its box.

5 Press the Paragraph Styles button (⊞) in the dock on the right side of the workspace to open the Paragraph Styles panel. Press the panel menu button (⋅≡) in the Paragraph Styles panel and choose New Paragraph Style from the contextual menu.

Create a new paragraph style in the Paragraph Styles panel.

6 In the resulting New Paragraph Style dialog box, type **Name** in the Style Name text field, then press OK to create a new style. You'll use the Name style to format the names of all the baked goods listed for Bella's Bakery.

Name your style in the New Paragraph style dialog box.

Making a style does not automatically apply that style.

7 Select the Name listing in the Paragraph Styles panel. If a plus sign appears next to it, Alt+click (Windows) or Option+click (Mac OS) it to clear all overrides.

The Paragraph Style panel automatically lists your new style.

You will now make a Paragraph Style for the Description.

8 Repeat steps 1 through 6, using the text in the third cell from the left in the second row, the paragraph that starts with the sentence, *Cheesecake is quite possibly the best food in the world.* Set Font Size to 8 point, however, and leave Small Caps toggled off. Name this new style **Description**.

9 Click Description in the Paragraph Styles panel to apply the style to the selected cell. If a plus sign appears next to the style name, Alt+click (Windows) or Option+click (Mac OS) Description to clear all overrides.

You will now make a paragraph style for the price.

10 With the Type tool, click inside the last cell on the right in the second row (the one containing $15). Choose Edit > Select All, and repeat steps 3 through 6, naming the new style **Price**.

11 Select the Price listing in the Paragraph Styles panel to apply the style to the selected cell. If necessary, clear all overrides.

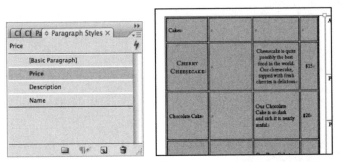

The Paragraph Styles panel now includes three new styles, and the Cakes table is taking shape.

12 Choose File > Save to save your work.

Formatting text in tables by column

You can easily apply paragraph styles to groups of cells, such as a column. The process involves selecting the group and then applying a paragraph style. You will now select the first column of the table and apply one of the paragraph styles created in the last exercise.

1   With the Type tool (T), click in the Cherry Cheesecake cell (second row, first cell), and drag down until all the cells below it in the column are highlighted.

2   Click on the paragraph style Name in the Paragraph Styles panel to apply it to all the selected cells.

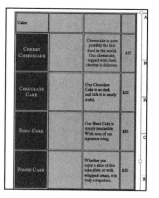

Highlight the first column's cells, and apply the Name paragraph style.

3   Now click in the top cell of the third column (*Cheesecake is quite possibly...*), drag to select all the cells below it, and click Description in the Paragraph Styles panel to apply the Description style.

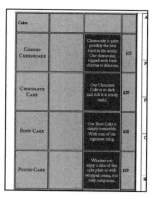

Select the third column, and apply the Description style.

4 Click the $15 cell, drag down until all the price column's cells are highlighted and click the Price style in the Paragraph Styles panel.

Merging cells

You can merge multiple cells in the same row or column into a single cell. To demonstrate, you will merge the top four cells of the example table so that the top row (with the word *Cakes* in it) looks more like a title. In the next section, you'll format it to stand out even more.

1 Select the cells in the first row by hovering your cursor over the left edge of the box until you see an arrow pointing to the right. Click to select the entire row.

2 Choose Table > Merge Cells to make the top four cells into a single cell.

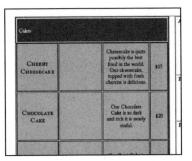

Merge the top four cells into one cell for the Cakes header.

Defining a header cell

For a large table that spans multiple columns, frames, or pages, you can specify a header row or footers to repeat identifying information at the top or bottom of each portion of the divided table. If your table breaks over several pages, headers are vital to orienting readers with the table's data. For instance, if the number of cakes sold by Bella's Bakery increased enough to require two columns, the next linked column would automatically be a header row. This saves you the time of inserting the header on each subsequent page.

Because it treats header cells as special cases, InDesign enables you to color and format them independently, without changing the features of the rest of the table. You can take advantage of this to help the headers stand out from the body of your table. Your header will be instantly identifiable when repeated in a multi-page, -column, or -frame layout, and your readers will be able to more easily decipher the information in the table. In this exercise, you will convert the Cakes cell into a header cell, apply unique formatting, and create a new paragraph style from it. Then you'll create a header for the Pies table.

If you just click in a cell or even highlight its contents, InDesign thinks you want to color the text. Either click with the right-pointing arrow or press Ctrl+/ (Windows) or Command+/ (Mac OS) to select an entire cell.

1 Making sure the top row is still selected, choose Table > Convert Rows > To Header to make the top cell a header cell. Notice how the color dropped out of the cell. It's a header cell now, so InDesign strips the normal cell formatting. You'll now add some header-specific formatting.

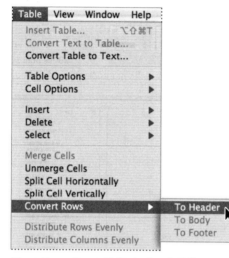

Choose Convert Rows > To Header from the Table menu to transform the selected cell into a header.

2 In the Swatches panel, make sure the Fill icon (⬚) is in the foreground and click the Paper swatch to color the topmost cell.

Choose Paper for the fill in the Swatches panel.

3 With the Type tool (T), click anywhere in the header cell to deselect it, then double-click on the word *Cakes* to select it.

Now you will stylize the type and make a paragraph style.

4 Center the type in the cell by pressing Shift+Ctrl+C (Windows) or Shift+Command+C (Mac OS). In the Control panel, click on the Small Caps button (T) to convert the title to a mix of large and small caps, and type **24** in the Font Size text field. Press Enter (Windows) or Return (Mac OS) to increase the size of the text.

If the type disappears from the cell, the type is bigger than the cell can hold. Hover over the bottom of the header cell until you see the double-arrow cursor, then click and drag down. Make sure you don't lose any of the table at the bottom because of overflow.

5 In the Control panel, type **100** in the Tracking text field and press Enter/Return.

Toggle on Small Caps and set Font Size and Tracking in the Control panel.

6 Press the Swatches button (▦) in the dock to open the Swatches panel. Bring Fill to the foreground and click Light Blue to choose it for the fill color. Click the Stroke icon to bring it to the foreground, then choose Black to add a black stroke around the text.

7 With the formatting finished, you can now save it as a paragraph style. Select the Paragraph styles button from the dock to reveal the Paragraph Styles panel. Alt+click (Windows) or Option+click (Mac OS) the Create new style button (⬛) to open the New Paragraph dialog box. Type **Header** in the Style Name text field, and press OK.

New Paragraph Style	
General	Style Name: Header
Basic Character Formats	Location:
Advanced Character Formats	General
Indents and Spacing	
Tabs	Based On: [No Paragraph Style]
Paragraph Rules	Next Style: [Same style]
Keep Options	Shortcut:
Hyphenation	
Justification	
Drop Caps and Nested Styles	Style Settings: Reset To Base
Bullets and Numbering	[No Paragraph Style] + next: [Same style] + Adobe Caslon Pro + size: 24 pt + tracking: 100 +
Character Color	color: Light Blue + align: centered + small caps + stroke color: [Black]
OpenType Features	
Underline Options	
Strikethrough Options	
	☐ Apply Style to Selection
☐ Preview	Cancel OK

Create a new header style based on the formatting settings you've chosen.

8 In the Paragraph Styles panel's list, click Header to apply the style to the selected text.

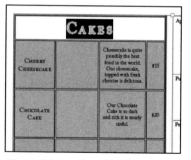

The title Cakes *stands out from the rest of the table thanks to its Header style.*

9 The Pies table in the second column on page 2 needs a header as well. Select it by clicking anywhere in the table with the Type tool.

10 Choose Table > Table Options > Headers and Footers to open the Table
Options dialog box.

11 In the Table Dimensions section, type **1** in the Header Rows text field. Press
OK to create a header row.

Table Options

Table Setup	Row Strokes	Column Strokes	Fills	Headers and Footers

Table Dimensions

Header Rows: 1   Footer Rows: 0

Header

Repeat Header: [Every Text Column]   ☐ Skip First

Footer

Repeat Footer: [Every Text Column]   ☐ Skip Last

☑ Preview   (Cancel)   (OK)

Create a header row for the Pies table.

12 Select the header row in the Pies table, then choose Table > Merge Cells to
convert the row to a single title cell.

13 Click inside the header row with the Type tool, then type **Pies**.

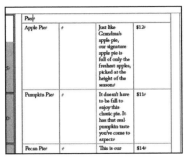

Add the title Pies *to the second table's header cell.*

14 Choose File > Save to save your work.

Setting column and row dimensions

At this point, you've adjusted the contents of rows and columns, but not modified the row height or column width directly. By default, row height is determined by the height of the current font. Tables imported from Microsoft Word or Excel, however, can retain their original, exact row heights. If neither of these options fits your layout, InDesign enables you to change row height and column width in the Cell Options dialog box. Here you can specify whether you want a fixed row height that does not change when you add to or delete from the row, or you prefer a variable height. For a fixed height, choose Exactly from the Row Height drop-down menu, then specify the height you need. Choose At Least to specify a minimum row height; with this setting, rows increase in height as you add text or increase the font size but will not be smaller than the minimum you set. Try out these Cell Options on the Cakes and Pies tables.

Setting a fixed row height

For the Cakes and Pies tables, a fixed row height works best. Because the Cakes table was imported from Word, its row height is already set to Exactly, so you will now fix the row height for the header and the cells beneath. Then you will do the same for the Pies table.

1 With the Type tool (T), click in the Cakes header cell, then press Ctrl+/ (Windows) or Command+/ (Mac OS) to select the cell.

2 Choose Table > Cell Options > Rows and Columns to open the Cell Options dialog box. Notice that Exactly is already selected in the Row Height drop-down menu. You just need to change the row height.

   Type in **0.5** in the Row Height text field, then press OK. The height of the header row changes.

Set Row Height to exactly 0.5 in the Cell Options dialog box.

3 Click and drag from the Cherry Cheesecake cell (top left) to the $24 cell (bottom right) to select the rest of the table.

4   Choose Table > Cell Options > Rows and Columns. Again, the Row Height drop-down is already set to Exactly in the Cell Options dialog box. Type **1.0625** in the Row Height field, and press OK.

5   Using the Type tool, click in the Pies header cell, then press Ctrl+/ (Windows) or Command+/ (Mac OS) to select the cell.

6   Choose Table > Cell Options > Rows and Columns. In the resulting Cell Options dialog box, choose Exactly from the Row Height drop-down menu and type **0.5** in the Row Height field. Press OK.

7   Now you need to select the rest of the table. Click and drag from the Apple Pie cell (top left) to the $15 cell (bottom right) to select the rest of the table.

If the table is overset, use the Selection tool (k) to extend its boundaries down below the page. Setting row height will fit the table into the column.

8   Choose Table > Cell Options > Rows and Columns to open the Cell Options dialog box. If it's not already selected, choose Exactly from the Row Height drop-down menu. Type **1.0625** in the Row Height text field, then press OK.

The Pies table now has a header row height of 0.5 and a body row height of 1.0625.

9   Choose File > Save to save your work.

Setting column width

You will now fix the column width for the Pies table.

1   Activate the Text tool (T), then click inside the $12 cell. Press Shift+Down Arrow to select the current cell, then press Shift+Down Arrow six more times to select the whole column.

2   Choose Window > Type & Tables > Table to open the Table panel and make the same changes you learned earlier in the Cell Options dialog box. Type **0.4215** in the Column Width text field and press Enter (Windows) or Return (Mac OS).

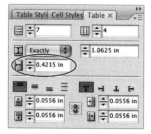

Enter the desired width in the Column Width text field of the Table panel.

3   Click the cell in the top-right part of the table containing the paragraph that starts with *Just like Grandma's* then press Shift+Down Arrow seven times to select the whole column.

4   In the Table panel, type **1.0438** in the Column Width text field, and press Enter/Return.

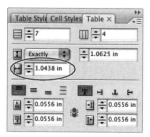

Use the Table panel to adjust the column width for the column containing the pies' descriptions.

5   Click inside the topmost empty cell (the second from the left), then press Shift+Down Arrow seven times to select the whole column.

6   Type **0.9715** in the Column Width text field in the Table panel, and press Enter/Return.

7   Click the Apple Pie cell, then press Shift+Down Arrow seven times to select the whole column.

8 Return to the Table panel and type **0.9382** in the Column Width text field. Press Enter (Windows) or Return (Mac OS). All row and column formatting is now complete for the Pies table.

9 Choose File > Save to save your file.

Using graphics in tables

Images can spice up any table and, perhaps, help sell a few more of Bella's pies and cakes. InDesign offers two ways to insert graphics into tables: select a cell with the Type tool and choose File > Place, or select the graphic with the Selection tool, cut or copy it, then paste it into the table with the Type tool. When you add a graphic that is larger than the cell, the cell height increases to contain the graphic; the width of the cell doesn't change, but the image may extend beyond the right side of the cell. If you place a graphic in a cell of a row set to a fixed height and that image is taller than the row height, InDesign marks the cell as overset and adds a red circle, instead of the image, to the cell. You then need to correct either the height of the table row or the size of the image so the image appears.

Placing graphics in cells

In this exercise, you'll add images to the Bella's Bakery tables. To expedite the process, the document's pasteboard contains appropriately sized graphics that are ready to place. Instead of using the Selection tool to select them, changing to the Type tool, and then back to the Selection tool, you'll use a much more efficient shortcut to manage this task.

1 With the Selection tool (k), click the cherry cheesecake picture in the top-left of the pasteboard to select it.

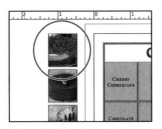

Choose the cherry cheesecake image on the pasteboard to the left of the document.

2   Choose Edit > Cut, or use the keyboard shortcut Ctrl+X (Windows) or Command+X (Mac OS) to cut the image to the clipboard. You will put all the graphics into the empty table cells, in exactly the order they appear on the pasteboard.

3   Double-click the second-from-left cell in the second row. Double-clicking any cell that can contain text automatically turns the Selection tool into the Type tool (T). For the rest of this exercise, you will use another method of placing, without leaving the Type tool.

4   Press Ctrl+V (Windows) or Command+V (Mac OS) to paste the picture into the selected cell.

5   Press and hold Ctrl (Windows) or Command (Mac OS) to change the Type tool to the Selection tool, and click the picture of a chocolate cake.

6   Press Ctrl+X (Windows) or Command+X (Mac OS) to cut the picture.

7   Click the second cell of the third row, then press Ctrl+V (Windows) or Command+V (Mac OS) to paste the picture into the cell.

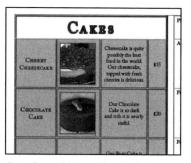

Cut and paste the cheesecake and cake images into the Cakes table.

8   Repeat steps 5–7 for the remaining cake pictures, then repeat them again to paste the pie graphics from the right side of the pasteboard into the Pies table to fit in their respective rows.

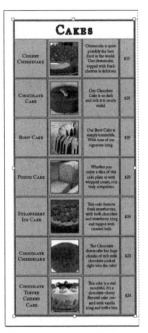

Keyboard shortcuts simplify cutting and pasting graphics into tables.

Cell styles and table styles

In InDesign CS3, you can use cell styles to format cells, and table styles to format tables, in the same way you use paragraph and character styles to format text. Beyond that, you can nest cell styles into a table style in the same way that you can nest character styles. Cell styles contain such information as paragraph styles, cell insets, strokes, and fills, which means that you can apply all these attributes to a cell or range of cells with one click. When you make a cell style, however, it does not automatically include all the selected cell's formatting. From a collection of cell styles, you can build table styles. Table styles contain cell styles as well as Table Options settings, including table borders and row and column strokes. As with all InDesign styles, when you update a table or cell style, all elements to which the style is applied update automatically. These nested styles give you the ability to format an entire table with one click and implement changes throughout a document's tables.

By default, each new document contains a Basic Table style that you can customize to apply automatically to all new tables you create. In addition, each document contains a default cell style called None, which is a quick way to remove all cell attributes (as you saw in the section *Resetting the cell styles within a table*). You cannot modify the None style.

When you use cell styles in a table style, you can specify which cell styles are applied to different sections of the table: header and footer rows, left and right columns, and body rows.

Cell styles

Because you have already formatted the table, formatted the cells, and made paragraph styles, you can now reap the rewards of setting up a table the right way. With all these elements in place, you now can easily create cell styles. In this exercise, you'll create four cell styles—Header, Name, Description, and Price— that contain the paragraph styles you made earlier.

1   Using the Type tool (T), click inside the Cherry Cheesecake cell, then press Ctrl+/ (Windows) or Command+/ (Mac OS) to select it.

2   Press the Cell Styles button (⊞) in the dock to open the Cell Styles panel.

3   Choose New Cell Style from the Cell Styles panel menu.

Choose New Cell Style from the Cell Styles panel menu.

4 In the New Cell Style dialog box that opens, type **Name** in the Style Name
text field, choose Name from the Paragraph Style drop-down menu, and
press OK to create the Name cell style. Now you have created a cell style
that contains a paragraph style.

New Cell Style

General
Text
Strokes and Fills
Diagonal Lines

Style Name: Name
Location:

General

Style Info

Based On: [None]
Shortcut:

Style Settings: [None] + Top Inset: 0.0625 in + Bottom Inset: 0.0625 in + Left Inset: 0.0625 in + Right Inset: 0.0625 in + Vertical Justification: Center

Paragraph Styles

Paragraph Style:

[No Paragraph Style]
[Basic Paragraph]
Header
Price
Description
Name

Preview   Cancel   OK

Choose Name from the Paragraph Style drop-down menu of styles.

5 Click the Cakes header cell using the Type tool, then press Ctrl+/
(Windows) or Command+/ (Mac OS) to select it.

6 Choose New Cell Style from the Cell Styles panel menu, type **Header** in
the Style Name field, choose Header from the Paragraph Styles drop-down
menu, and press OK to create the Header cell style.

7 Click the first description cell (*Cheesecake is quite possibly the best...*), then
press Ctrl+/ (Windows) or Command+/ (Mac OS) to select it.

8 Repeat step 6, naming the new cell style **Description** and choosing
Description for the associated paragraph style.

9 Click the *$15* cell, then press Ctrl+/ (Windows) or Command+/ (Mac OS)
to select it.

10 Repeat step 6, naming the final cell style **Price** and choosing Price for the
associated paragraph style.

Applying cell styles

You can apply cell styles to cells with the usual point-and-click ease. Try it out by applying the styles you just created to the Cakes table.

1 Click inside the Cakes header cell using the Type tool (T), then press Ctrl+/ (Windows) or Command+/ (Mac OS) to select it.

2 Click the Header style in the Cell Styles panel's list to apply that style to the selected cell.

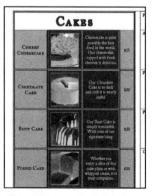

Click a name in the Cell Styles panel's list to select a cell style and apply it to a selected cell.

3 Click the Cherry Cheesecake cell, press Shift+Down Arrow to select it, then press Shift+Down Arrow six more times to select the rest of the column.

4 Click the Name style in the Cell Styles panel's list to apply that style to the selected cells.

5 Click in the first description cell (*Cheesecake is quite possibly the best…*) and drag down and to the left to select both the images and descriptions. This centers the images in the cells for you as well.

Click and drag to select both the images and descriptions.

6 Click Description in the Cell Styles panel to apply the style.

7 Click in the $15 cell, then press Shift+Down Arrow seven times to select it and the rest of the price cells.

8 Click Price in the Cell Styles panel to apply the final style.

Creating table styles

Compared to setting up the initial attributes, making a table style from a group of cell styles is fast and easy. All you have to do is choose which cell styles you want to use and tell InDesign which style to use where. The action takes place in the New Table Style dialog box. Here you can specify which cell styles are applied to different sections of the table: header and footer rows, left and right columns, and body rows.

In this exercise, you'll compile the cell styles from your Cakes table into a table style for use on the Pies table.

1 Using the Type tool (T), select the entire Cakes table by clicking in the top-left of the table frame when you see a diagonal arrow.

2 Click the Table Styles tab next to the Styles panel tab to open the Table Styles panel.

From the Table Styles panel, you can create and apply table styles.

3 Alt+click (Windows) or Option+click (Mac OS) the Create New Style button located at the bottom of the Table Styles panel. The New Table Style dialog box opens. Notice the Cell Styles section, which contains five drop-down menus. This is where you match the cell style to the location where it should be applied. Header and Body Rows are self-explanatory. The Left and Right Column menus, however, let you specify unique styles for the cells, so you could have different paragraph styles within the cell style for each.

4 In the New Table Style dialog box, type **Bella's Bakery** in the Style Name text field.

5 In the Cell Styles section, choose Header from the Header Rows drop-down menu.

6 Choose Description from the Body Rows drop-down menu, Name from the Left Column drop-down menu, and Price for the Right Column drop-down menu. Press OK.

New Table Style	
General	Style Name: Bella's Bakery
Table Setup	Location:
Row Strokes	General
Column Strokes	
Fills	Style Info
	Based On: [No Table Style]
	Shortcut:
	Style Settings: [No Table Style] + Body Region Cell Style: Description + Header Region Cell Style: Header + Left Column Cell Style: Name + Right Column Cell Style: Price Border Stroke Weight: 3 pt + Alternating Strokes First Rows: 1 + Alternating Strokes Next Rows: 1 + Alternating Row Strokes First Weight: 3 pt + Alternating Row Strokes First Color: Dark Blue + Alternating Row Strokes Second Weight: 3 pt + Alternating Row Strokes
	Cell Styles
	Header Rows: Header Left Column: Name
	Footer Rows: [Same as Body R...] Right Column: Price
	Body Rows: Description
Preview	Cancel OK

Assign the cell styles you want to use in the New Table Style dialog box.

7 With the table still selected, choose the Bella's Bakery style to apply it. Choose File > Save.

Applying table styles

Here's where all that hard work pays off: You can format an entire table in one click. In this exercise, you'll style the Pies table and a new Cookies table.

1 Select the entire Pies table using the Type tool (T) by clicking in the top-left of the table's frame when you see the diagonal arrow.

2 From the Table Styles panel, choose Bella's Bakery to apply the style. If there are any plus signs to the right of the table style name, Alt+click (Windows) or Option+click (Mac OS) to clear the overrides. Now you can try it again.

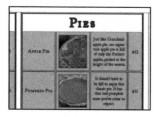

Choosing Bella's Bakery from the Table Styles panel formats the entire Pies table in one click.

3 Press the Layers button (◈) in the dock to open the Layers panel, then click on the left-hand gray box next to the Cookies layer. A table listing different types of cookies appears in the right-hand column of the document.

4 Select the entire Cookie table by clicking in the top left of the table frame when you see a diagonal arrow.

5 Reopen the Table Styles panel and choose Bella's Bakery from the list to apply the style to the Cookies table.

6 Click the left-hand gray box next to the Background layer in the Layers panel. This shows you the intended background color set to the bleed.

7 Select File > Save and you're done!

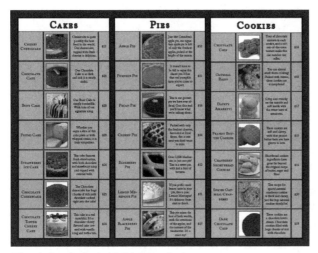

Take a look at the finished Bella's Bakery brochure.

Self study

Save another copy of your document as id0702_work.indd.

1 Because all three of your tables are designed with styles, you can make universal changes. Try changing the paragraph style Description, change the font, turn Hyphenation off, and click the Preview button to see all three tables change as you choose different options.

2 Select a cell and give the cell a stroke, then redefine the style in the drop-down menu of the Cell Styles panel to see the global change.

3 Change all the fonts and colors in the first table. Make new paragraph styles, and apply them. Change the attributes of the four sections of cells you used. Make a new set of cell styles, apply them to the first table, then create a table style from that table. Apply your new table style to the other two tables.

Review

Questions

1 What are three ways to select a cell?

2 Can paragraph styles be included in cell styles?

3 In which five sections of a table style can you apply cell styles?

4 If you needed a reduce a table down to its basic appearance, and remove all formatting, where would you do that?

5 If a plus sign (+) appears next to your table style name, it indicates that some change has happened and there are overrides to some of the cells, tables, or text within the table. How do you clear these overrides?

Answers

1 Click and drag until the whole cell is highlighted; press Ctrl+/ (Windows) or Command+/ (Mac OS); or click in a cell and press Shift+Down Arrow.

2 Yes, but they are not chosen by default; you must pick them in the Cell Style drop-down menu.

3 Cell styles in a table style are in these sections: header rows, footer rows, left columns, right columns, and body rows.

4 In the Table styles panel, click on Basic Table.

5 Alt+click (Windows) or Option+click (Mac OS) the style name to clear overrides.

What you'll learn in this lesson:

- Applying colors and strokes

- Using and saving spot colors

- Updating and editing colors

- Setting up color management

Using Color in Your Documents

Using color for text, frames, and paths is a basic task in InDesign. The more ways you know how to apply, change, and understand color, the faster you can work. Your color choices are not limited to picking from the small selection that appears in the Swatches panel. You can create your own colors, gradients, and tints, as well as choose from a number of swatch libraries, such as Pantone colors, that are supplied for you within InDesign.

Starting up

Before starting, make sure that your tools and panels are consistent by resetting your preferences. See "Resetting the InDesign workspace and preferences" on page 3.

You will work with several files from the id08lessons folder in this lesson. Make sure that you have loaded the idlessons folder onto your hard drive. See "Loading lesson files" on page 4.

See Lesson 8 in action!

Explore more of the features shown in this lesson using the supplemental video tutorial available online at agitraining.com/digitalclassroom.

The project

To explore InDesign's color controls, you will add color to a fictional ad for FiFi's Face Cream. You'll use multiple types of colors, as well as tints and gradients, in the course of the lesson. If you want to review what the finished project will look like, open id0801_done.indd from the id08lessons folder now.

Applying colors to frames and text

InDesign provides many ways to assign color to an object. You can assign color through the Tools panel, the Swatches panel, the Color panel, and the Color Picker. You can also assign color using the Eyedropper tool. No matter which method you choose, however, you must perform the same three steps: select the text or object that you want to color, specify which part of the object you want to color, then apply the swatch color.

Applying color to text

Applying color is a quick, straightforward process. To practice, you will color the text in the FiFi's Face Cream ad.

1 Choose File > Open. Navigate to the id08lessons folder, select the file id0801.indd, then press Open.

2 Choose File > Save As. In the Save As dialog box, navigate to the id08lessons folder and type **id0801_work.indd** in the Name text field. Press Save.

3 Select the Type tool (T) from the Tools panel and click inside the frame containing the text, *It leaves your skin feeling noticeably clean and absolutely radiant!*

4 Choose Edit > Select All to select all the type inside the frame.

5   Select Window > Swatches or press the Swatches button (▦) in the dock on the right side of the workspace to open the Swatches panel.

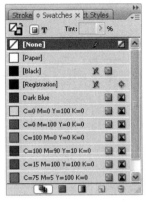

Color the object from the Swatches panel.

The first thing to consider is whether you want to color the border (stroke) or the inside (fill) of the selected text. In the upper-left corner of the Swatches panel are two very small square icons overlapping one another. The icon with the faded T and the red diagonal running through it is the Stroke icon (▧). The icon with the solid T inside it is the Fill icon (▣). You must click the appropriate icon to bring it to the foreground. In this case, you want to fill the text with the color re. If necessary, bring the Fill icon to the foreground.

You can also press the X key on your keyboard to toggle between Fill and Stroke in the Swatches panel, as long as you don't have the Type tool activated.

Choose the fill and stroke colors in the Swatches panel
by bringing their respective icons to the foreground.

6   In the Swatches panel, click on the Dark Blue option. The text turns blue.

Applying color to frames

Next you will color the border, or stroke, of the frame around the text. Follow the same three basic steps that you went through to apply color to the text: Select the frame, specify fill or stroke, and choose the color.

1   Activate the Selection tool (↖) from the Tools panel. Notice that the Stroke and Fill icons no longer have a *T* (for Type), but now appear as a square for a Fill, and a square with a border for the Stroke. Click on the text frame to select it.

2   Click the Stroke icon in the Swatches panel to bring it to the foreground.

3   Click Dark Blue in the Swatches panel to apply the color to the frame.

Choose Dark Blue in the Swatches panel to color the text frame's stroke.

4   To give the frame a little more style, you can round its edges. Choose Object > Corner Options. In the resulting Corner Options dialog box, choose Rounded from the Effect drop-down menu. The size determines how much of a rounded corner effect will actually be applied. The higher the number, the more rounded the corner appears. Click the Preview checkbox to see the frame's rounded corners, then press OK to close the dialog box and apply the effect.

In the Corner Options dialog box, you can apply effects to customize your frames.

5   Choose File > Save.

Creating and saving a new swatch

You can create your own custom color swatches, or use those supplied by InDesign. When you create a color or gradient, InDesign automatically adds it to the Swatches panel, as well as the Fill/Stroke box in the Tools Panel. Because InDesign also automatically applies the color to whatever you have selected, be very careful to select only the items you need colored before you begin. In the next exercises, you will create, name, and apply two new colors.

> *The Swatches panel can contain spot colors, process colors, mixed inks (process colors mixed with spot colors), RGB or Lab colors, gradients, or tints. This exercise concentrates on CMYK colors, but you'll learn more about the specialized color options in later sections.*

1 To make sure nothing on the artboard is selected, press Ctrl+Shift+A (Windows) or Command+Shift+A (Mac OS).

> *If you have the Rectangle tool (or any of the tools hidden below that tool), Line tool, Type tool, Pen tool, or Pencil tool selected, and you select a color swatch, you set the default color for that tool, and every time you go to use it, the tool will have this color as its default. So don't select a tool, and set color with nothing selected unless you want that to be the new default color for the tool.*

2 If, necessary, press the Swatches button (▦) in the dock to open the Swatches panel. From the Swatches panel menu (-≡), choose New Color Swatch.

3 In the resulting New Color Swatch dialog box, uncheck the Name with Color Value checkbox so you can name this color as you make it. Type **Green** in the Swatch Name text field.

4 Increase the Cyan percentage to 80% by moving the slider bar under Cyan or typing **80** into the % text field. Using the sliders or typing the percentages, set Magenta to 10%, Yellow to 100%, and Black to 0%.

To create a new color, adjust the percentages in the New Color Swatch dialog box, then press OK.

5 Press OK to create the new color. Green now appears at the very bottom of your Swatches panel. When you make a new color swatch, it always appears at the bottom of the list of swatches. You can change the order of the swatches by simply clicking and dragging.

6 In the Swatches panel, click and drag the Green swatch upward so it is just below Dark Blue. Release it. You should see a black line indicating where the swatch will appear before you drop it.

Click and drag to rearrange swatches in the Swatches panel.

7 Choose File > Save to save your work.

Applying strokes to text

In the next exercise, you will fill text with your new color, as well as create a contrasting color for the text's stroke. Plus, you'll get your first look at the Stroke panel, which gives you control over the weight and appearance of an element's stroke or border.

1 With the Selection tool (▸) active, double-click the frame containing the words *Face Cream* in the lower-left corner of the document. This automatically converts the Selection tool to the Type tool. Alternately, you can also select the Type tool (T) and click inside the frame. Press Ctrl+A (Windows) or Command+A (Mac OS) to select all the text in the frame.

2 In the Swatches panel, click the Fill icon (🔸) to bring it to the foreground, and click the Green swatch you made in the previous exercise. *Face Cream* is now green.

Turn the Face Cream *text green.*

You will now make a new color for the stroke.

3 Click the Stroke icon (▤) to bring it to the foreground. From the Swatches panel menu (-≡), choose New Color Swatch.

Bring Stroke to the foreground, then choose
New Color Swatch from the panel menu.

4 In the resulting New Color Swatch dialog box, uncheck the Name with Color Value checkbox, and type **Light Blue** in the Swatch Name text field.

5 Increase the Cyan percentage to 32% by moving its slider bar or typing **32** in the % text field. Using the sliders or typing in the percentages, set Magenta to 6%, Yellow to 3%, and Black to 0%.

Create a light blue color by adjusting the CMYK percentages.

6 Press OK. InDesign automatically applies Light Blue to the stroke of the text. The stroke doesn't quite stand out enough, however. In the next steps, you'll use the Stroke panel to increase the stroke's width.

Don't forget to reorganize your swatches for the best workflow. For example, because Green and Light Blue will be used in combination for text in the ad, click and drag the Light Blue swatch just below Green in the Swatches panel. A black line indicates where the swatch will appear before you drop it. Rearranging swatches into logical groups for your project is a good habit to form.

7 Click the Stroke icon (□) in the dock to open the Stroke panel.

8 Type **1.5** in the panel's Weight text field and press Enter (Windows) or Return (Mac OS) to increase the selected stroke's size.

Apply a stroke to the Face Cream *text and increase its size with the Stroke panel.*

9 Select File > Save to save your work.

Creating a tint reduction

A tint, sometimes called a screen, is a lighter shade of a color. Tinting is a great way to put color behind text without subduing the text. Just as you can with regular colors, you can (and should) save tints in the Swatches panel to make editing tints fast and easy. Because colors and tints maintain their relationship in the Swatches panel, a color change to the original swatch updates any tints of that swatch that have been made. In this exercise, you will create a tint for the name FiFi.

1 Using the Selection tool (⟍), click the frame that contains the word *FiFi's*. You use the Selection tool to do this because it is no longer type. It was converted to outlines and is now a path, and therefore no longer editable as type.

2 Click the Swatches icon in the dock to open the Swatches panel, and make sure Fill icon is in the foreground. Select the Light Blue swatch to apply the color to the fill.

3 At the top of the Swatches panel, click the right-facing arrow to expose the Tint slider. Drag the slider to the left to reduce the fill's tint from 100% to 60%. The change is reflected in the document. Now that you have made the tint, you can save the modified version of the Light Blue swatch in the Swatches panel.

The Tint slider changes the tint percentage for the selected swatch.

4 If necessary, open the Swatches panel. Click and drag the Fill icon from the top of the Swatches panel into the list of swatches and drop it below the Light Blue color swatch to add the tint Light Blue at 60% to the list.

This is how the tinted logo should now look.

5 Select File > Save to save your work.

Making a dashed stroke

You've practiced applying, coloring, and widening a basic stroke, but InDesign offers many more ways to customize strokes. To demonstrate, you will make a custom dash around the border of the FiFi ad.

1 Using the Selection tool (k), click the black frame running around the edge of the ad to select it.

2 In the Swatches panel, click the Stroke icon (⧉) to bring it to the foreground.

3   Open the Stoke panel by clicking the Stroke icon in the dock. Use the up arrow to the left of the Weight text field to increase the stroke thickness to 4 points. Notice that the frame, which was aligned to the size of the page, is now bigger than the page. This is because the default alignment of a stroke is always to the center of the frame. In this case, two points of the stroke are inside the frame and two points are outside the frame. You need to change this alignment next.

If every time you make a frame, you notice yourself changing the alignment to the inside so that the frame doesn't break through guides, you can make yourself an Object Style that is aligned to the inside. Or, better yet, change the settings right in the Object Styles panel by changing the Basic Text Frame and the Basic Graphics frame options.

4   In the Stroke panel, click the Align Stroke to Inside button (◘). The border appears to jump inside the frame, because all four corner points are now aligned to the inside of the frame.

5   Still in the Stroke panel, click the Type drop-down menu to reveal all the various styles of lines you can make. Choose Dashed. Dash and Gap options appear at the bottom of the Stroke panel. The dash is the stroke, and the gap is the space between the dashes.

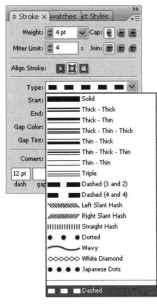

Choose Dashed for the ad's border.

6   Type **12** in the first dash text field. In the first gap text field, type **3**, which sets the length of the gap between dashes. Type **11** in the third text field to give the dash a second dash weight. In the remaining gap and dash text fields type **2** and **10**, respectively.

Set your color, dash, and gap options in the Stroke panel.

7   Press Enter (Windows) or Return (Mac OS) to apply the settings. You have created a custom dash.

Now you can change the color of both the dash (stroke) and gap.

8   Choose Dark Blue from the Stroke panel's Gap Color drop-down menu.

9   In the Swatches panel, click the Stroke icon to bring it to the foreground, and choose Light Blue to apply it to the dash. Make sure you pick the original Light Blue and not the tinted version.

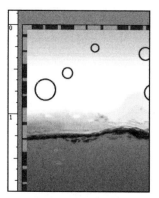

The finished border has light blue dashes separated by dark blue gaps.

10   Choose File > Save to save your work.

Creating and saving gradients

A gradient is a smooth and gradual transition between two or more colors. When you first apply a gradient, the default is set to two color stops. A color stop is the point at which a gradient changes from one color to the next. You can add as many stops as you want to a gradient, and also control how quickly or slowly the colors fade into each other. You can also change the direction of gradients, and even choose whether it is a linear gradient, appearing in linear form, or a radial gradient, which appears in a circular form. In this series of exercises, you will make and save linear and radial gradients, as well as use the Gradient tool to change the direction of the gradient.

Linear gradients

You create gradients in the Gradient panel, then add color to them by dragging and dropping them as color stops on the gradient bar in the Gradient panel. You'll try this here.

1   Using the Selection tool (⬧), click the frame containing the words, *It leaves your skin feeling noticeably clean and absolutely radiant.*

Always select an element before starting your gradient. It's easier to build a gradient when you have something selected because you can preview exactly how the gradient will look.

2   Toward the bottom of the Tools panel are overlapping Fill and Stroke icons, just as in the Swatches panel. Click to bring the Fill to the foreground.

3   Press the Gradient button (▪) in the dock to open the Gradient panel. From the Type drop-down menu in this panel, choose Linear. In the upper-left corner of the panel, click the Gradient color swatch. Your frame now has a white-to-black linear gradient applied by default.

Use the Gradient panel to apply a white-to-black gradient to the frame.

You will now add colors to your gradient.

4 Expand your dock by clicking the double-arrow (◀◀) in the top-right corner. This makes it easier to add color to your gradient. Make sure you can see both the Gradient and Swatches panels, as you will be dragging colors from the Swatches panel into the Gradient panel. Just click on the Gradient tab on top of the Gradient panel to expose it, then do the same for the swatches.

5 Click and hold the Light Blue color in the Swatches panel. Don't just click or you will simply apply the color to the selected frame. Drag the swatch to the right side of the gradient color bar until your cursor becomes a hand with a plus sign (🖑), indicating that it is above the black color stop and that you will replace the black color stop with the light blue one. Even if you're not replacing a color stop, you still get a plus sign when you add a color stop to the gradient.

This cursor indicates you are dragging a color from the Swatches panel to the Gradient panel. Drop the color over a color stop to apply it.

6 Release the mouse to drop the color. The Gradient bar now has a white color stop on the left and a light blue color stop on the right. The frame in your ad should look the same way, with the color fading from white on the left to light blue on the right.

7 Choose File > Save to save your work.

Saving a gradient

You can save gradients in the Swatches panel so that you can apply them later to other objects with just a click. You save a gradient by dragging its preview from the Gradient panel into the Swatches panel. Try it with the white-to–Light Blue gradient.

1   Click and hold the preview of the gradient in the top-left corner of the Gradient panel.

2   Drag your cursor to just below Light Blue 60% in the Swatches panel. A heavy black line appears, indicating where the swatch will appear before you release it. The white box with a plus sign (🖳) that appears next to your cursor as you drag, indicates that you are about to add a gradient to the Swatches panel.

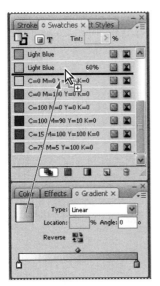

*This cursor indicates that you are adding
a gradient to the Swatches panel.*

3   Release the mouse to drop the gradient into the Swatches panel. InDesign automatically names the gradient New Gradient Swatch. You will now change the name to something more recognizable.

4   Double-click the New Gradient Swatch. The Gradient Options dialog box appears.

5   In the Swatch Name text field, type **Light Blue Linear**, then press OK.

In the Gradient Options dialog box you can name your gradient.

6   Choose File > Save to save your work.

Adjusting fill opacity

As a preview of what's to come in Lesson 9, "Using Effects," you will now turn down the opacity of the fill so you can see through the frame. This is a new feature in CS3 that lets you control fill, stroke, and text opacity separately.

1   Using the Selection tool (🔖), and, with the text frame selected, choose Window > Effects or press the Effects button (*fx*) in the dock to open the Effects panel.

2   Select Fill from the list inside the Effects panel. Double-click inside the Opacity text field and type **70%**, or click the arrow to the right of the text field and move the slider to 70%. Press Enter (Windows) or Return (Mac OS) to apply the settings.

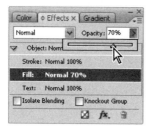

This is the Effects panel with the proper settings.

3   Choose File > Save. You have just changed the opacity of only the fill. You will learn more specifics of this and other effects in Lesson 9, "Using Effects."

Radial gradient

The last gradient you made was a linear gradient, which means it fades from one color to another along vertical lines. This is the default in InDesign. You will now explore radial gradients, which are gradients that don't fade color in the form of lines, but as spheres. If you wanted to make a sphere that looked like light was hitting the top of it, with the shadow at the bottom, you could use the radial gradient to accomplish this. You will use the radial gradient to make bubbles in this next exercise.

1   Using the Selection tool (⬉), click the farthest left circle in the ad.

2   Bring the Swatches panel forward, and click the Stroke icon (▫) to bring it to the foreground. Select None for the stroke.

3   Bring the Fill to the foreground. Select the Light Blue Linear gradient that you saved earlier.

4   If it is not already open, choose Window > Gradient or press the Gradient button (■) in the dock to open the Gradient panel. Here you will change the type of gradient that is applied.

5   Choose Radial from the Gradient panel's Type drop-down menu. The circle now has a radial gradient.

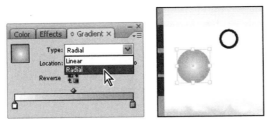

Choose Radial from the Type drop-down menu to change from a linear to a radial gradient.

6   Choose File > Save to save your work.

Adjusting the direction of a radial gradient

The Gradient Swatch tool in the Tools panel allows you to change the direction of both linear and radial gradients. In this case, the radial gradient appears with white in the middle of the circle and blends from the center outward to the Light Blue color. You will change that now using the Gradient Swatch tool.

1 Click the Gradient Swatch tool (■) in the Tools panel to select it.

The Gradient Swatch tool enables you to change a gradient's direction.

2 Click and drag from the top left of the circle to the bottom right to give the sphere the look of a highlight in its top-left part. When you release, the top-left area appears white, then fades radially into Light Blue.

Drag with the Gradient Swatch tool in the direction you desire.

3 From the Gradient panel, drag the gradient color swatch into the Swatches panel to save it. Drop it beneath the Light Blue Linear gradient.

4 Once it is in the Swatches panel, double-click the new swatch to rename it.

5 In the resulting Gradient Options dialog box, type **Light Blue Radial** in the Swatch Name text field. Press OK.

You may notice that saving a Gradient Swatch does not save the angle of the gradient. To save the gradients angle, you must make the gradient an Object Style.

One-click edits

InDesign makes it easy to share attributes among document elements, making global changes with minimal effort.

Using the Eyedropper to copy frame attributes

When you need to copy attributes from one element to another in a document, choose the Eyedropper tool. It can pick up both type and frame attributes, such as fill and stroke settings, and apply those characteristics to other type or frames. By default, the Eyedropper tool picks up all attributes, but you can choose to copy only specific settings using the Eyedropper Options dialog box. You will use the Eyedropper tool to quickly carry the circle attributes from one frame to another.

1   Press Ctrl+Shift+A (Windows) or Command+Shift+A (Mac OS) to make sure nothing is selected.

2   In the Tools panel, select the Eyedropper tool (✐).

3   Click the circle with the radial gradient that you just made. The Eyedropper now appears filled; it is filled with all the fill and stroke attributes of that circle.

When you click an object with the Eyedropper tool, the tool fills with information.

4   Move the cursor to the right, then click in the center of the nearest circle. The gradient fills that circle, and the original stroke disappears.

5   Click a few more of the circles to apply the gradient attributes, but leave some circles as they are for the next exercise.

6   Choose File > Save to save your work.

Applying colors to multiple objects

Although the Eyedropper is quite handy for copying multiple attributes to single objects, sometimes you want to apply changes to multiple objects at once. InDesign makes this simple. When you select a group of objects, you can apply a fill, stroke, or both in one click. Practice this by adding gradients to the ad's remaining circles.

1 Choose the Selection tool (↖) from the Tools panel, then click a circle that still has a black stroke and no fill.

2 Shift+click every circle that does not have the gradient fill.

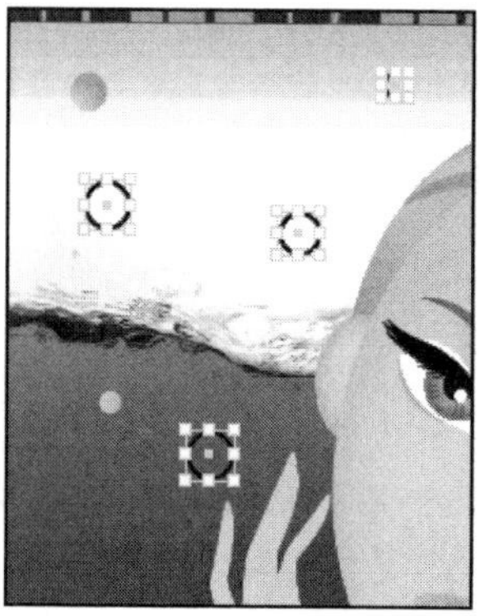

Shift+click to select all the unfilled circles.

3 Click the Fill icon to bring the Fill to the foreground in the Swatches panel, then click the Light Blue Radial swatch for the fill color.

4 Bring the Stroke to the foreground of the Swatches panel, and scroll up to select None for the stroke. All the selected circles now have the Light Blue Radial gradient and no stroke.

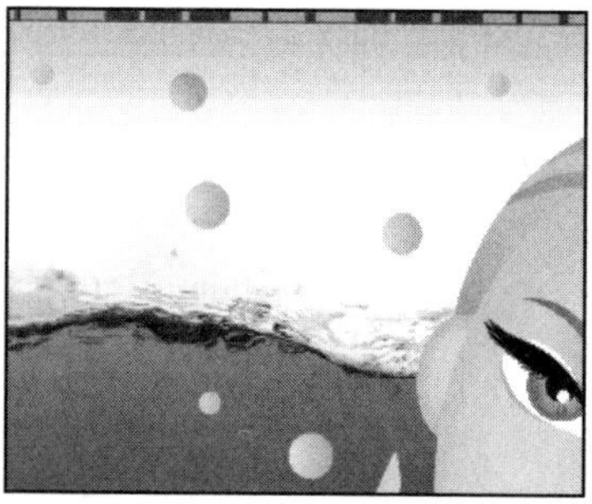

Apply the Light Blue Radial gradient to the selected circles.

5 Select File > Save.

Updating and editing colors

When you apply a color to multiple objects in InDesign, all those objects know they are related to that color in the Swatches panel. If you then change the color of the swatch, all instances of the color throughout the document will change. This makes it quick and easy to apply global color changes. In this exercise, you will change Light Blue to a more purple tone to experiment with a new look for the ad.

1   Press Shift+Ctrl+A (Windows) or Shift+Command+A (Mac OS) to make sure nothing is selected.

2   Double-click Light Blue in the Swatches panel to open the Swatch Options dialog box.

3   In the Swatch Options dialog box, click the Preview checkbox (below the OK and Cancel buttons) so you can see the changes take effect as you apply them.

4   Drag the Magenta slider to the right so that Magenta appears at 38%. All the Light Blues you added to the ad now appear purple.

Increase the Magenta slider to 38% to change all instances of the Light Blue color in the ad to purple.

5   Press OK to implement the changes.

6 Choose File > Save As. In the Save As dialog box, navigate to the id08lessons folder, then type **id0802.indd** in the Name text field. Press Save. You can use this file later for the Self study section.

Save the purple project to use later.

7 Choose File > Close, then reopen id0801_work.indd. It should look as it did before you changed the light blue to purple.

Using and saving spot colors

Spot colors are colors that cannot be produced accurately with CMYK process inks. These colors are considered out of the gamut, or range, of process colors. When printed, spot colors require special premixed ink and their own printing plates on a printing press, which increases the cost of a commercial printing job. The more spot colors you choose, the greater the cost. Use spot colors only when color accuracy is critical. For example, a client might want its logo reproduced using only a specific spot color.

For the most accurate representation of a spot color, certain things must be considered. First, you should pick the spot color from a color-matching system supported by your commercial printer. Several color-matching libraries ship with InDesign. You must also remember that a color's appearance depends on many variables: the gamut limits of your screen and composite printer, as well as the ink your printer mixes, and the paper stock it's printed on.

The good news in all of this is that you can manipulate spot colors in InDesign just as you can ordinary CMYK colors. You can create your own spot colors in the Swatches panel, or place an image that contains a spot color to add that color automatically to the panel. You can adjust and apply spot colors in the Swatches panel, using them for fills, strokes, or gradients. In this exercise, you will create a spot color to apply to the ad.

1   Press Shift+Ctrl+A (Windows) or Shift+Command+A (Mac OS) to make sure nothing is selected.

2   In the Swatches panel, press the panel menu button (-≡) and choose New Color Swatch.

3   In the resulting New Color Swatch dialog box, choose Spot from the Color Type drop-down menu.

New Color Swatch		
Swatch Name: C=32 M=38 Y=3 K=0		OK
☑ Name with Color Value		Cancel
Color Type: Process ▾		Add
Color Mode: Process		
Spot		
Cyan ——△—— 32 %		
Magenta ——△—— 38 %		
Yellow △—— 3 %		
Black △—— 0 %		

Choose Spot from the Color Type drop-down menu to designate a color as a spot color.

4   Choose PANTONE solid coated from the Color Mode drop-down menu to change it from CMYK. PANTONE solid coated, and PANTONE solid uncoated are the two most common color libraries, coated is for a coated or glossy paper, while uncoated is for uncoated stock. Now you need to specify which spot color you want to work with.

5 In the Pantone text field, type **662**. This automatically brings you to that Pantone color, a dark blue color.

Choose PANTONE solid coated from the Color Mode drop-down menu, then search color 662.

6 Press OK to close the dialog box and add the swatch named Pantone 662 C to the Swatches panel. The swatch is automatically named.

7 Drag the Pantone 662 C swatch up in the Swatches panel and drop it directly beneath the Light Blue Radial gradient swatch. You will apply the color in the next exercise.

Colorizing a grayscale image

InDesign can colorize any grayscale image you import as long as it does not contain any spot colors or alpha channels. The two raindrops in the ad are grayscale images that previously had clipping paths applied. Clipping enables you to change the colors of black and gray into whatever color you would like. You will use the Pantone 662 C color you created in the last exercise.

1 To color only the clipping path, choose the Direct Selection tool (⬚) from the Tools panel. If you try to colorize it when it is selected with the Selection tool instead, the whole box will be colored.

2 Select one of the raindrops. A path appears around the edge of the raindrop.

3 In the Swatches panel, make sure the Fill icon is in the foreground. Select the Pantone 662 C swatch to apply the color to the raindrop.

4 Select the other raindrop with the Direct Selection tool.

> *If the active tool changes from the Direct Selection tool to the Selection tool, just double-click to revert to the Direct Selection tool.*

5 In the Swatches panel, select Pantone 662 C to apply it to the second raindrop.

Apply color to the grayscale raindrops.

6 Choose File > Save to save your work.

Setting up color management

Color management essentials: about Color Models CMYK, RGB, and spot

There are three basic color models that you should be aware of: CMYK, RGB, and spot colors. CMYK and Spot colors are used for print, and RGB is used for the Web and on-screen presentations. CMYK, which stands for; Cyan, Magenta, Yellow, and the Key color which is Black, is a measurement of ink or pigment. It is also called a process color, and can be considered a four-color job.

RGB stands for Red, Green, and Blue and is a measurement of light. Digital camera images, images on the Web, and even television, are seen in RGB. RGB is considered an additive color because white is the additive combination of all red, green, and blue, while CMYK is considered subtractive because inks subtract brightness from white.

A spot color is a special premixed ink that requires its own plate at the press. It is used when the CMYK model cannot accurately produce the color you want. A lot of corporate colors easily identified as that company's color are reproduced using spot colors. Spot colors increase the printing cost, but are necessary when a color must be reproduced accurately. The final appearance of the spot color is determined by how the ink was mixed and the paper it was printed on, not by color management.

About the device-independent color space

Color models determine the relationship between color values, and the space the color is in defines the meaning of those values as colors. A color model such as LAB has a fixed color space because it relates directly to the way humans perceive color. These models are described as device-independent. RGB and CMYK can have many different color spaces. Because these models vary with each associated color space or device, they are known as device-dependent.

Because color spaces can shift, color can also shift in the way it looks as you transfer documents between different devices. Color variations can result from the way software applications define color, print media, monitor age, how the monitors are made, and different image sources.

About profiles

It's all about achieving the most accurate color from the images you bring into InDesign, how you view your document on your monitor, and how it looks after it is printed. Precise, consistent color management requires accurate ICC-compliant profiles of all your color devices.

A color management system uses a monitor profile to describe how the monitor produces color, an input device profile to describe what colors an input device is capable of capturing, and an output device profile to describe the color space of a printing press or desktop printer. If your digital camera offers a choice of profiles, Adobe recommends that you select Adobe RGB. Otherwise, use sRGB. The output profile should also take into consideration specific printing conditions, such as the type of paper and ink used. For example, glossy paper is capable of displaying a different range of colors than matte paper.

About color management engines

Adobe InDesign has the Adobe color engine (ACE) built into the program. Its job function is to map the color space of one color gamut to another color gamut. Some devices have a smaller or larger color gamut than others; therefore, colors must be mapped into a different gamut. Changing these options is definitely not recommended unless you are a trained professional, or if your printer instructs you to do so.

Setting up color management

The color settings for InDesign CS3 are located under Edit > Color Settings. The default setting for InDesign CS3 is North America General Purpose. Notice that the default RGB is set to sRGB IEC61966-2.1. You will change this setting to Adobe RGB (1998), which is a larger color gamut for your monitor.

1 Choose Edit > Color Settings to open the Color Settings dialog box.

2 In the RGB drop-down menu, choose Adobe RGB (1998). This changes the way you view RGB on your monitor.

Next you will change your CMYK settings to U.S. Web Uncoated v2. Although, U.S. Web Coated (SWOP) v2 is great for publications printed on coated paper, you are going to change the settings for a web press that does not print on coated paper.

3 In the CMYK drop-down menu, change the CMYK Working Space from U.S. Web Coated (SWOP) v2 to U.S. Web Uncoated v2.

Save your modified color settings.

Saving your color settings

Now you will save this setting and use Adobe Bridge to apply it to all your applications. Adobe Bridge enables you to apply your color settings to all your Creative Suite applications. This way all your images from Photoshop and your illustrations from Illustrator will share the same color settings as InDesign.

1   To save the Color Settings you just made, press Save, and call it Dynamic Learning. Choose Save, then press OK in the Color Settings dialog box. Do not change the folder location when saving.

2   Launch Adobe Bridge by choosing File > Browse or pressing the Go to Bridge button (📷) in the upper-right corner of the Control panel.

3   Once Bridge has launched, choose Edit > Creative Suite Color Settings. Scroll to the bottom of the settings list to choose Dynamic Learning. Press Apply to synchronize the color settings across all your Creative Suite applications.

Synchonize your color settings through Adobe Bridge.

4   To change your settings back to the default color setting across the suite, go to Edit > Creative Suite Color Settings, choose North America General Purpose 2, then press Apply.

5   Choose File > Close to close Adobe Bridge and return to InDeisgn.

Changing a source profile

In this next exercise, you will see why you would change a source profile as you place an image. Generally speaking, you should have the same color management profiles set up in both Photoshop and Illustrator so that when you place an item in InDesign it is already in the correct working space. However, if an image were to come in from an outside source, you would need to change the embedded profile.

Then you would assign a new profile for the overall document.

1 Back in InDesign, press Ctrl+Shift+A (Windows) or Command+Shift+A to deselect all, then choose File > Place. Navigate to the id08lessons folder, and select the id0804.psd file. Check the Show Import Options checkbox, then press Open.

2 In the resulting Image Import Options dialog box, click the Color tab to bring it forward. The Profile should be set to Adobe RGB (1998). If it isn't, change the setting now.

Determine the settings for the face cream file before you import it.

3 Press OK. Your cursor is now a small paintbrush with a thumbnail of the image you are placing.

4 Place the file above the FiFi's Face Cream logo on the left. Click once to place the file, then click and drag it to the correct position over the logo.

This is what the finished document should look like.

Assigning a new source profile

You will now assign a new RGB and CMYK source profile to this document. The only time you should change a profile is if the document you are working on has a different output destination than you normally set in InDesign. Assigning a different profile this way affects only this document, and not your overall document settings.

1 Choose Edit > Assign Profiles.

2 In the RGB Profile section, choose Adobe RGB (1998) from the Assign Profile drop-down menu.

3 In the CMYK Profile section, change the profile from the default of U.S. Web Coated (SWOP) v2, which would be great for a magazine printed on glossy paper, to U.S Sheetfed Uncoated v2, a setting good for printing in a sheet-fed press. Leave the rest of the settings at their defaults and press OK.

Assign your project a new source profile.

4 Choose File > Save, then File > Close.

Congratulation! You have completed Lesson 8, "Using Color in Your Documents."

Self study

Open the id0802.indd file you saved earlier in the id08lessons folder to practice some additional color variations:

1 Try adjusting more colors in the Swatches panel to make universal changes across the ad.

2 Create another spot color and recolor the grayscale raindrops again.

3 Select the text frame with the linear gradient. Experiment by dragging more colors into the gradient, and use the Gradient Swatch tool to change the gradient's direction.

4 Make a new color and put a stroke on the text, *It leaves your skin feeling noticeably clean and absolutely radiant.*

5 Design a new radial gradient for the bubbles, and practice coloring some of them individually with the Eyedropper tool.

Review

Questions

1 How do you change the fill of an object you are trying to color? How do you change the stroke?

2 How do you save a gradient you have already made?

3 If you change a color in the Swatches panel, will it change the color wherever it is applied throughout the document?

4 Can you colorize any grayscale image?

5 True or False: You cannot change the direction of a linear gradient.

Answers

1 In either the Tools panel or the Swatches panel, click the Fill icon to bring it to the foreground, then click the color desired for the Fill. To change the stroke, bring the Stroke icon to the foreground, then click a color.

2 Drag and drop it from the Gradient panel into the Swatches panel.

3 Yes, that is why the Swatches panel is really handy for making universal changes to colors throughout your document.

4 Yes, as long as the image does not contain spot or alpha channels.

5 False—the Gradient Swatch tool lets you change the direction of any gradient.

Lesson 9

What you'll learn in this lesson:

- Applying opacity to objects
- Singling out stroke or fill
- Adjusting effects for objects
- Combining object styles with effects
- Exploring blending modes
- Working with imported files that use transparency

Using Effects

The arrival of InDesign CS3 brings Photoshop-like effects to your documents. You can now apply a new arsenal of effects—Inner Shadow, Outer and Inner Glow, Bevel and Emboss, and Gradient Feather, to name a few—to objects in InDesign. In this lesson, you will discover how to apply interesting changes to your images, objects, and text using a sampling of the effects.

Starting up

Before starting, make sure that your tools and panels are consistent by resetting your preferences. See "Resetting the InDesign workspace and preferences" on page 3.

You will work with several files from the id09lessons folder in this lesson. Make sure that you have loaded the idlessons folder onto your hard drive. See "Loading lesson files" on page 4.

See Lesson 9 in action!

Explore more of the features shown in this lesson using the supplemental video tutorial available online at agitraining.com/digitalclassroom.

The project

In this lesson, you will jazz up a two-page spread using the new Effects panel in InDesign CS3. You can experiment with blending modes, opacity, and other effects without permanently changing your objects. Then you can save effects as an object style so you can easily apply the effects to other objects. If you want to take a look at what the finished project should look like, open the file id0901_done.indd from the id09lessons folder.

This is what the final design should look like.

Creative effects

InDesign CS3's Effects panel offers a brand-new way to use Photoshop-like effects in your documents. In CS2, you could apply feathering and drop shadows, as well as control the opacity and blending modes of objects, text, and photos; but that's just the beginning in CS3. Not only can you apply new effects, but you now have the control to apply the effects to the whole object, or to just the fill, stroke, or text in a frame, and turn those elements on or off without permanently changing your objects.

Open the Effects panel by choosing Window > Effects or by pressing the Effects button in the dock and take a tour of where you'll be working.

For those of you familiar with CS2, the Transparency palette has been replaced by the Effects panel. It still has the blending modes and transparency at the top, but the added ability to apply an effect to the stroke, fill or text now appears below it. It's time to put these controls to work.

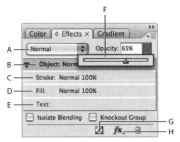

A. Blending mode. *B*. Object. *C*. Stroke. *D*. Fill. *E*. Text.
F. Opacity levels. *G*. Clear effects. *H*. Add an effect button.

Applying opacity to objects

Opacity settings make an object or text appear transparent; to varying degrees you can see through the object to the objects that appear below it. If the opacity is set to 0%, the object is completely invisible. By default, all objects are set to 100%, completely opaque. Some people get confused about the difference between tint and opacity. Tint is a screened (lighter) version of a color, and is not transparent. Opacity is the way you control transparency.

Using these tools, you can implement great-looking effects to images. For example, placing a red frame over a grayscale image and adding a 50% transparency makes the image appear as if it has been colored. This is a task you might think is more suitable for Photoshop, but InDesign now gives you that kind of control. Practice on a few objects now.

1   Choose File > Open. In the Open dialog box, navigate to the id09lessons folder. Select id0901.indd and press Open to begin the lesson.

2   Press the Pages button (⬚) in the dock on the right side of the workspace to open the Pages panel. Notice that the two pages are numbered 6 and 7. You will work on page 7 first. Double-click page 7 to make that the active page.

3   Choose the Selection tool (▶) from the Tools panel, and click the blue rectangle in the lower-right corner of the page to select it. Hidden underneath this blue frame is an image. You will change the opacity settings of the blue frame to see the image.

4 If it is not currently open, choose Window > Effects or press the Effects button (*fx*) in the dock to display the Effects panel.

5 The opacity is set to 100%. Click on the right-facing triangle to the immediate right of the Opacity text field to access the Opacity slider.

6 Drag the slider to the left to adjust the opacity to 65%. You can now see the image—of a pile of record albums—underneath the blue, but you still have the effect of the blue coloring.

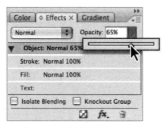

Set the Opacity slider to 65% to see the image beneath the blue frame.

7 Click the blue bar at the very bottom of the page with the Selection tool.

8 Highlight 100% in the Opacity field of the Effects panel and enter **40**. This is yet another way to change the opacity of an object, without using the slider. Press Enter (Windows) or Return (Mac OS) to implement the change in opacity. Notice that the bar, with an opacity of 40%, is more transparent than the frame, whose opacity you set to 65%.

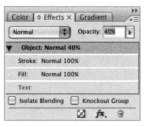

Adjust an object's opacity by entering the number directly in the Opacity text field.

9 Choose File > Save As. In the Save As dialog box, navigate to the id09lessons folder, then type **id0901_work.indd** in the Name text field and press Save. Keep the file open, as you'll need it for the rest of the lesson.

Apply effects to stroke or fill only

Remember that in CS3 you can apply an effect to a whole object, or to an object's stroke, fill, or text individually.

1   With id0901_work.indd still open, use the Selection tool (⬉) to select the white box containing a quote in the top-left corner of page 7.

2   In the Effects panel, click the right-facing triangle next to Opacity to reveal the slider, then drag the slider left to 50%. Notice that both the text and the fill are now fairly transparent. The effect makes the text difficult to read, something you don't want. The text needs to stand out and remain legible.

Apply the opacity change to both the fill and text.

3   Before you can apply the opacity change to the fill only, you must undo the last step. Either highlight 50% in the Opacity text field in the Effects panel and type **100**, or press Ctrl+Z (Windows) or Command+Z (Mac OS) to undo the previous action.

4   In the Effects panel, click to select the Fill listing. Selecting the Fill property ensures that the opacity will change only to the Fill inside the frame and not to the text.

5   Click to reveal the Opacity slider, and drag it to the left to an 80% setting. The fill is more transparent, but the text still has an opacity of 100%.

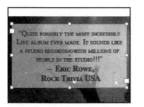

Adjust the opacity of the box's fill only.

Drop shadow

As with opacity, you can apply the drop shadow effect to a whole object or just the stroke, fill, or text of an object. Drop shadow creates a three-dimensional shadow on whatever you have chosen in the Effects panel. You can also change such parameters as the drop shadow's color, offset, and blending mode, to name a few. This exercise demonstrates the effect and provides you with your first look inside the Effects dialog box.

1 Click on the Pages button (⊞) in the dock on the right side of the workspace to reveal the Pages panel. Double-click page 6 to select it.

2 With the Selection tool (↖), click the box containing the words, *Johnny Guitar rocks again!* at the top of the page.

3 In the Effects panel, click the Add an object effect to the selected target button (*fx*) at the bottom of the panel. From the contextual menu that appears, choose Drop Shadow.

4 When the Effects dialog box opens, check the Preview checkbox in the bottom-left corner. Look at the change: InDesign applied a drop shadow to the frame because it has a fill of paper. If there were no fill color or stroke color, it would have applied a Drop Shadow to the text. Since InDesign CS3 lets you apply an effect to either the fill, stroke, or text individually, you will change the settings in the Effects dialog box in the next step so that only the text gets the drop shadow.

Apply effects in the Effects dialog box specifically to the object, stroke, fill, or text.

5 Still in the Effects dialog box, click the Drop Shadow checkbox in the list on the left side of the dialog box to turn it off. A drop shadow is no longer applied to the whole object.

Turn off the drop shadow.

6 In the Settings for drop-down menu at the top of the dialog box, choose Text to affect only text with the drop shadow.

The Settings for drop-down menu enables you to specify which portion of an object receives the effect.

7 Click the Drop Shadow checkbox to turn it on and apply the drop shadow to the text only. Press OK to close the dialog box and apply the effect.

8 Choose File > Save to save your work. Keep the file open.

Adjusting effects for objects

All InDesign's effects are nondestructive. In other words, when you implement an effect, you always have the option of turning it on or off, as well as re-editing it. You can, for example, change the Drop Shadow effect you applied to the text in the previous exercise. In this exercise, you will change the position of the drop shadow and add the Use Global Light effect, which makes the lighting effect global. In other words, all drop shadows appear as if they have the same light source. When Use Global Light is on and you alter the drop shadow's position, all instances of the effect change. Think of a light shining in a room: if the light source changes positions, all the shadows in the room change positions.

1   Continuing from where you left off in the previous exercise, double-click the new *fx* symbol (*fx*) that appears next to the Text listing inside the Effects panel to open the Effects dialog box. Once you apply an effect, this symbol appears in the Effects panel next to the component of the document to which the effect was applied. By double-clicking the symbol, you can edit the effects you applied.

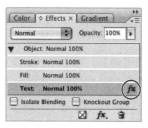

Double-click the fx symbol next to the Text listing in the Effects panel.

2   In the Position section, click the Use Global Light checkbox to turn it on.

3   Type **0p7** (7 picas) in the Distance text field. The Distance parameter controls how far from an object the drop shadow appears.

Turn on Use Global Light and set the Drop Shadow's Distance parameter in the Effects panel.

If you are not familiar with working in picas and would rather work in inches, simply right-click (Windows) or Ctrl+click (Mac OS) the ruler and change your unit of measurement. The Distance field should then be set to 0.0972 inches.

4 Press OK to apply the changes and close the Effects dialog box. The Drop Shadow moved up from, and to the left, of its former position.

5 Choose File > Save.

Bevel and Emboss

The Bevel and Emboss effect, new in InDesign CS3, gives an object a three-dimensional look. In this exercise, you will apply Bevel and Emboss to one of the stars, then apply the given effects to another star more quickly by dragging and dropping the effect from the Effects panel.

1 Using the Selection tool (▶), select the leftmost star beneath the *Johnny Guitar rocks again!* article on page 6.

2 Press the Add an object effect to the selected target button (*fx*) at the bottom of the Effects panel. From the resulting contextual menu, choose Bevel and Emboss.

3 When the Effects dialog box appears, leave the settings at their defaults and press OK to apply a Bevel and Emboss lighting effect to the star. Press Ctrl+(plus sign) (Windows) or Command+(plus sign) (Mac OS) to zoom in on stars and compare the first star with the others. Now you'll apply the same effect to the second star using a little drag-and-drop trick in the Effects panel.

Apply the Bevel and Emboss effect to the star.

4 With the first star still selected, take a look at the Effects panel. To the right of the Objects entry is the same symbol (*fx*) that appeared next to the Text entry when you applied the drop shadow. Click and drag the symbol from the Effects panel into the layout and over the second-from-left star. When the cursor, which now looks like a small hand with a plus sign over it (⊞), is positioned over the star, release to apply the Bevel and Emboss effect. Dragging and dropping is an easy way to reapply an effect without having to work within the Effects dialog box. InDesign offers still more ways to apply effects. In the next exercise, you will apply Bevel and Emboss using object styles.

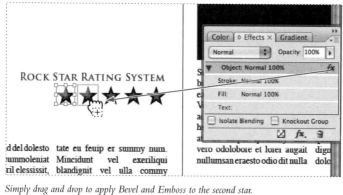

Simply drag and drop to apply Bevel and Emboss to the second star.

5 Choose File > Save and keep the document open.

Object styles with effects

In Lesson 5, "Working with Styles," and Lesson 6, "Working with Graphics," you explored using object styles to record stroke, fill, and paragraph styles. With CS3, you can also use object styles to record and apply effects. As with other style attributes, a change to an effect is reflected wherever you applied the style. In the next exercise, you will record an object style for the Bevel and Emboss effect and apply it to the rest of the stars.

1 On page 6, select the first star using the Selection tool (↖).

2 Choose Window > Object Styles to open the Object Styles panel. From the Object Styles panel menu, choose New Object Style.

3   In the New Object Style dialog box, type **Embossed** in the Style Name text field to name the new style. Although the style automatically inherits all effects applied to the selected object, you can choose which of them you want to save with the style. Notice the new section in the bottom-left corner of the dialog box that details all the effects currently applied to the selected object, in this case Transparency as well as Bevel and Emboss. Before you save the style, you can turn these on and off individually by clicking the checkbox next to each attribute. For now, leave them as they are.

4   Check the Apply Style to Selection checkbox to automatically apply the new object style to the image. Press OK.

Note the listing of applied effects in the New Object Style dialog box when you create a new object style.

5   Shift+click all the stars on page 6, be sure to include the 4 stars on the bottom-left of the page. Click on the object style named Embossed in the Object Styles panel to apply it to all the stars.

6   Choose Window > Pages or press the Pages button (▣) in the dock to open the Pages panel. In the Pages panel, double-click page 7. The stars on this page are grouped, but you can apply object styles to groups of objects as well.

7 Select the first group with the Selection tool and return to the Object Styles panel. Select the Embossed object style to apply it. Repeat this with the second group of stars.

If you would like to see how changing the style effects all the stars, open the Embossed object style by double-clicking it the stars on page 7. Make sure Preview is checked in the lower-left corner of the dialog box, and try adding a few different effects on your own, like Inner Shadow for example. Notice that the stars, all of which have the embossed style applied to them, update as you make changes to the object style. Once you've experimented a little bit, press Cancel to revert back to the Embossed style you've been working with.

You can apply object styles to single objects or groups. Here all the stars have the Embossed object style applied.

Basic Feather

Feathering fades the transparency of an object's border at a distance that you determine. Instead of using Photoshop to feather an image's border, you can use InDesign to fade the image borders. You can produce some pleasing effects by softening the edge of an image to make it appear as if the image fades into the page. A new feature of CS3 is Directional Feathering, which allows you to control which side of an image or a colored frame receives the feather. The Basic Feather effect's settings include Corners, which determines how the corners of the feather appear; Noise, which sets how smooth or spotted the feather appears; and Choke, which controls how much of the feather is opaque or transparent.

In this exercise, you will apply a Basic Feather effect to the image on page 6, then use CS3's new Gradient Feather tool to apply a one-sided feather to the image on page 7.

1   If you didn't change the unit of measurement earlier, do so now by right-clicking (Windows) or Ctrl+clicking (Mac OS) the ruler guide and selecting inches.

2   Choose Window > Pages, then double-click page 6.

3   Use the Selection tool (⬀) to select the image of Tommy Acustomas.

4   If necessary, choose Window > Effects to open the Effects panel, then click the Add an object effect to the selected target button (*fx*). From the resulting contextual menu, choose Basic Feather.

Choose Basic Feather to open the Effects dialog box
and apply the Basic Feather effect to the photo.

5   Click the Preview checkbox to see what the feather looks like. The edges of the image are diffused and quickly blend into the background.

6   In the Effect dialog box's Options section, click in the Feather Width text field, which currently reads 0.125 inches.

7   To change the Feather Width, which is the distance the feather will be
applied, press the Up Arrow key on your keyboard twice to increase the
amount in the Feather Width text field to 0.25 inches.

	Effects	

Settings for: [Object ▲▼]   Basic Feather

Transparency
☐ Drop Shadow
☐ Inner Shadow
☐ Outer Glow
☐ Inner Glow
☐ Bevel and Emboss
☐ Satin
☑ Basic Feather
☐ Directional Feather
☐ Gradient Feather

┌ Options ─────────────────────┐
│   Feather Width [0.25 in]   │
│   Choke: [0%]   ▸   │
│   Corners: [Diffused ▲▼]   │
│   Noise: [0%]   ▸   │
└─────────────────────────────┘

OBJECT: Normal 100%; Basic Feather
STROKE: Normal 100%; (no effects)
FILL: Normal 100%; (no effects)

☑ Preview   (Cancel)   (OK)

Adjust the Basic Feather settings to tweak the effect.

8   Press OK to close the Effects dialog box and apply the Basic Feather effect.
Next, you will apply the same feather settings to the quote box on page 7.

This is how the image looks after Basic Feather is applied.
Notice how edge of the image appears to fade out.

9   Double-click the Hand tool (✋) in the Tools panel to fit your InDesign
spread in the window.

10 Make sure you still have the Tommy Acustomas image on page 6 selected; if not, do so using the Selection tool.

You will now apply the same effect to the quote box on page 7, using a different method.

11 From the Effects panel, drag the symbol (*fx*) that appears just to the right of *Object* and drop it over the quote box on page 7. Now the quote box also has the feather; it is very easy to add and share effects this way.

12 Choose File > Save to save your work.

The Gradient Feather tool

The Gradient Feather tool is a brand-new tool in CS3. In this section, you will use the tool to fade the bottom of the Garage Band image on page 7 to transparency. In the previous exercise, Basic Feather applied the feather to all sides equally. You can use the new Gradient Feather tool to fade one side of an image to transparency without affecting the other sides. You also have control over the angle at which the gradient is applied. By using this new tool, you can click and drag as many times as you like, adjusting the gradient feather to whichever angle you want, live, without a dialog box.

1 Use the Selection tool (k) to select the Garage Band image at the top of page 7.

2 Click and hold on the Gradient Swatch tool (■) in the Tools panel to reveal a submenu listing hidden tools. Select the Gradient Feather tool.

Click and hold the Gradient Swatch tool to access the Gradient Feather tool.

3 Click just below the baseline of the phrase *Summer of '88*, and drag down so the cursor touches the bottom of the image, then release. The bottom of the image fades to transparency. The longer you click and drag, the larger the area the fade is applied to, and the more dramatic the effect. Try holding Shift as you drag to keep the gradient effect horizontally straight.

Drag down from the lower middle of the image.

4 Choose File > Save to save your work.

Gradient Feather fades the selected edge to transparency.

Converting text to a path

Here you'll learn how to modify your text so that instead of filling it with a standard color, you fill it with a photo, producing a cool effect that's actually fairly simple to implement. You cannot place an image directly into text while it is still editable. You can only place an image into text if you first convert the text to outlines.

You can use the Type menu's Create Outlines command to convert the original font outline information into a set of compound paths. Compound paths are separate paths combined into a single object. In this exercise, you will convert the letters *GB* on page 7 to compound paths and place a photo inside them.

1 Using the Selection tool (▶), click the box on page 7 that contains *GB*.

Make sure you did not accidentally select the type with the Type tool; if you did, the Create Outlines option is not available.

2 Choose Type > Create Outlines to convert the font information to paths.

Type	Notes	Object	Table	View
Font				▶
Size				▶
Character				⌘T
Paragraph				⌥⌘T
Tabs				⇧⌘T
Glyphs				⌥⇧F11
Story				
Character Styles				⇧⌘F11
Paragraph Styles				⌘F11
Create Outlines				⇧⌘O
Find Font...				
Change Case				▶

Choose Type > Create Outlines to convert text to paths.

3 Choose the Direct Selection tool (▶) in the Tools panel to view the paths you created. Because these are compound paths, you can now place a picture inside them.

View the new paths around the type.

4   Choose File > Place. In the Place dialog box, navigate to Links folder inside the id09lessons folder, select id0907.psd, and press Open. The GB compound paths fill with the photo.

Choose File > Place to position an image inside the paths.

5   Choose the Direct Selection tool, then click and hold on the photo for a second. You should see the image ghosted where it does not fall inside the path area. The photo you imported is the same as the image over which it appears, only cropped. Drag to fit the photo in the box however you like.

When repositioning an image inside a path, do not click and drag until you see the hand cursor. If you click and drag when it appears as the Direct Selection tool, you could accidentally select and move a point on the path.

Click and drag an image to see the ghosted portions of the image outside the path area.

6   Choose File > Save to save your work.

Applying blending modes to objects

Did you ever place a black logo with a white background on a colored page and wonder how to get rid of the white so the logo itself rests on the page? There are many potential solutions in InDesign to this particular problem, you will now learn how to use a blending mode to achieve the effect with the logo on page 6.

Blending modes affect how color pixels in one layer blend with color pixels in the layers below it. The two most common blending modes are Multiply and Screen. You can remember what they do in the following way: Multiply blends out the white; Screen blends out the black. If you're interested in the more advanced explanation: Multiply looks at the color information for the items and multiplies the base color by the blend color. The outcome is always a darker color. Screen examines each item's color information and multiplies the inverse of the blend and base colors. The outcome is always a lighter color.

In the next two exercises, you will practice applying Screen and Multiply to examine how blending modes work.

The Screen blending mode

The Screen blending mode is useful for colorizing the black within an image. You will apply a Screen blending mode to the blue box that's part of the records image on page 7 to give the records below the box a blue tint.

1   With the Selection tool (↖), click the blue box in the lower-right corner of page 7. This box is the one you tweaked in the first opacity exercise. Because InDesign effects are editable, you will remove the opacity.

2   Open the Effects panel from the dock, reveal the Opacity slider (click on the right-facing triangle next to the settings), and drag it to 100%. The blue box covering the records image should be solid blue again.

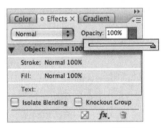

Return the box's opacity to 100% in the Effects panel.

3 To the left of the Opacity setting in the Effects panel is the Blending Modes drop-down menu. It is currently set to Normal. Click Normal to reveal the other options, and choose Screen. The blue box is now blending with the image of the records.

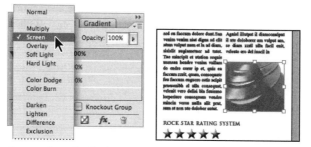

Once you change the Blending Mode to Screen, the records look blue where they were formerly black.

Remember that the Screen effect drops the black out of an image, so if you put a blending mode of Screen on the blue box, the black parts of the image beneath the box appear blue.

The Multiply blending mode

You will now work with an image that has been hidden on a layer up to this point. You will use the Multiply blending mode visually remove the white areas of a logo, while leaving the black areas untouched.

1 Press the Layers button (⊙) in the dock. There is a hidden layer called Johnny that you will need for this exercise and the next one.

2 Click in the lefthand gray box to the left of the Johnny layer to make that layer visible. An image of Johnny Guitar appears on page 6. On his T-shirt, in the upper-right corner, is a swirly *J* and *G*—his signature and logo.

When the visibility eye icon is turned on next to a layer, the layer is visible.

3 Select the signature using the Selection tool (↖).

4 Open the effects panel, if necessary, and from the Blending Mode drop-down menu at the top of panel, choose Multiply. The white box around the logo disappears and the logo appears directly on Johnny's T-shirt.

Applying the Multiply effect blends Johnny
Guitar's logo in with his shirt.

Because Multiply blends away the white, applying it is a handy trick to get rid of the white only in black-and-white images. This blending mode does not work with full-color images that have white around them, because it tries to blend white throughout the image and your image will appear transparent, or blended into the colors beneath them.

As you'll learn in the next section, there are alternative ways to achieve this same effect such as using a clipping path or alpha channel selection.

5 Choose File > Save to save your work. Keep the file open.

Working with imported files that use transparency

If you have walked through the previous lessons in this book you probably have noticed that incorporating images created and/or modified in Photoshop into InDesign is a well-established part of the print production workflow. In this exercise we look at the ways that InDesign supports transparency in images edited in Photoshop.

Photoshop has a number of ways to define areas of transparency in an image. While Photoshop is not required for this lesson, there are concepts such as alpha channels, clipping paths and selections which would be worth investigating in Photoshop and would help you get the most out of this chapter.

The choice of using alpha channels or clipping paths depends on which tools you are more comfortable using. As a rule, pen paths are cleaner because they are created using vectors, which give you nice clean curves, while an Alpha Channel selection is based on pixels and give you a choppier edge. The Pen tool takes some time to master, but it is clearly the better choice.

In this next exercise, you will place two images with different types of transparency. The first image simply has a transparent background, the second has an alpha channel and a clipping path that were created in Photoshop. After learning how to control these transparent areas in InDesign, you will examine how transparency interacts with text wrap.

1 Press Shift+Ctrl+A (Windows) or Shift+Command+A (Mac OS) to deselect all objects in your document. In the Layers panel, select Layer 1, if necessary.

2 Open the Pages panel from the dock and double-click page 7 to select it. You will be placing a photo on this page. Double-click the Zoom tool, if necessary, to view the page at 100%.

3 Choose File > Place, navigate to the Links folder within the id09lessons folder, select the id0902.psd file, and press Open.

4 Your cursor should now contain a thumbnail image of the file within it. In the second column of page 7's Allison Copper story, click in the white space to place the image. Click and drag to move the picture into position.

Use the Selection tool to position the image on page 7.

Move the image over some text, notice that it does not have a white background. Instead the file has a transparent layer. InDesign automatically recognized the .psd file's transparency. Move the image to match our example above.

Applying an alpha channel selection

The photo of the band members (id0902.psd) contains an alpha channel selection that was saved in Photoshop. An alpha channel is a way to save a selection you made in Photoshop so you can later access that selection in InDesign to make the parts outside the selection transparent. Alpha channels are stored inside the channels of an RGB or CMYK image. In this exercise, you will access that selection using the Clipping Paths option. A clipping path is InDesign's generic term for the path that exists with this type of transparent object. Consider the outline of the two band members, this outline represents the clipping path, all areas inside the path are non-transparent, all areas outside the path are transparent. Without a clipping path applied, InDesign would only be able to apply the text wrap around the image's bounding box, but not to the band members themselves.

You could use InDesign's Detect Edges feature, which would build a path for you around the two band members based on the transparency, but an even more accurate way is to access the saved alpha channel selection already made for you.

1   Make sure you still have the band photo selected. If it is not selected, select the image using the Selection tool (k), then choose Object > Clipping Path > Options.

Choose Clipping Path Options in the Object menu.

2 In the Clipping Path dialog box, choose Alpha Channel from the Type drop-down menu and rockers from the Alpha drop-down menu. Notice that the Alpha setting default is Transparency, based on the transparent pixels of the file. Click to turn on the Preview checkbox to see the path you created from the alpha channel. You need this clipping path for the text wrap to work correctly.

Clipping Path	
Type: Alpha Channel ⬍	OK
Alpha: rockers ⬍	Cancel
Threshold: 25	☑ Preview
Tolerance: 2	
Inset Frame: 0 in	

☐ Invert
☐ Include Inside Edges
☐ Restrict to Frame
☑ Use High Resolution Image

Choose Alpha Channel and rockers in the Clipping Path dialog box.

3 Press OK to accept the path shown in the preview and close the dialog box. Now you can apply a text wrap around the alpha channel selection.

4 Choose Window > Text Wrap to access the Text Wrap panel.

5 In the panel, click on the Wrap around object shape button (⊞) to wrap the text around the object's shape rather than its bounding box. You should choose this option because the text wrap is based on the clipping path.

Notice that in the Contour Options section of the Text Wrap panel, the default Type setting is Same as Clipping.

Wrap the text around the object shape.

6   Choose the Selection tool (▶), then click and drag the image slightly to the left to allow the text to wrap slightly around the guitarist's leg.

7   Choose File > Save to save your work.

Applying a path selection

A path selection is a selection made and saved in Photoshop using the Pen tool. You can access these selections in InDesign the same way you select a .psd file's alpha channel. Pen tool selections are cleaner than alpha channels in InDesign because they are vector selections. Alpha channel selections are based on pixels, and InDesign makes the path for you. To see the difference, you will now apply a pre-made path to Johnny Guitar and apply text wrap again.

1   Open the Pages panel from the dock and double-click page 6 to bring it into view.

2   Select the image of Johnny Guitar using the Selection tool (▶).

3   Choose Object > Clipping Path > Options.

4   In the Clipping Path dialog box, check the Preview checkbox, then choose Photoshop Path from the Type drop-down menu. *Guitarist* should automatically appear as the Path name.

5   Press OK. Notice how the black around the image disappears based on the saved Pen tool selection. Now you can apply the text wrap.

With the path applied, you're ready to wrap text around Johnny.

6 Choose Window > Text Wrap to open the Text Wrap panel, then click the panel's Wrap around object shape button (⬛). Again, the text wraps around the object's shape and not its box, just as it did in the previous exercise with alpha channels.

Here is the final design with all your effects applied.

7 Choose File > Save to save your work. Take a look at your *rock 'n' roll journal* spread. You're finished working with imported files and transparency.

Self study

Here are some projects you can create on your own:

1 Apply a drop-shadow to Johnny Guitar and choose Use Global Lights. Then adjust the direction of the drop shadow and watch the headline drop shadow update as well.

2 Select the top photo on page 7, and remove the Gradient Feather effect. Try to accomplish the same effect with directional feathering.

3 Apply more effects to Johnny Guitar, save the result as an object style, then apply that style to the images of Johnny and Allison Copper. Change the object style so that both images update simultaneously.

4 Experiment with blending modes by making a colored frame over Tommy Acustomas, then changing the Blending Modes and Opacity settings to get different effects.

Review

Questions

1 After you apply an Effect, can you adjust it?

2 What is the difference between opacity and tint?

3 If you apply Create Outlines to type, can you still edit the text with the Type tool?

4 Can you feather only one edge of a photograph?

Answers

1 Yes, you can always return to the Effect panel, select the effect again, and make adjustments.

2 Tint is a screened (lighter) version of a color, and is not transparent. Opacity is the way you control transparency.

3 No, if Create Outlines is applied, the text is made into paths and is no longer related to the font information.

4 Yes, with the Gradient Feather tool, you can control the angle and direction of a feather.

What you'll learn in this lesson:

- Adding dynamic text variables to your document

- Managing multiple InDesign documents using the Book feature

- Generating a table of contents

- Generating an index

Advanced Document Features

Although the lessons so far have used single, small documents as examples. InDesign can manage complex, book-length documents, and maintain consistency across multiple files. The software's advanced document features enable you to add dynamic text that changes based on specified criteria.

Starting up

Before starting, make sure that your tools and panels are consistent by resetting your preferences. See "Resetting the InDesign workspace and preferences" on page 3.

You will work with several files from the id10lessons folder in this lesson. Make sure that you have loaded the idlessons folder onto your hard drive. See "Loading lesson files" on page 4.

See Lesson 10 in action!

Explore more of the features shown in this lesson using the supplemental video tutorial available online at agitraining.com/digitalclassroom.

The project

In this lesson, you will work with several chapters of a book to see for yourself the capabilities of InDesign's book feature. You will add the chapters to a book file and update the page number of each page based on its position in the book. Using text variables, you will automate the generation of elements on each page that can save hours of manual work. The master page of each chapter will then be synchronized to give the book a consistent appearance.

Adding text variables

InDesign CS3 enables you to add dynamic text called *variables* to your documents. In a general sense, a variable is a way to store information that is not necessarily permanent. In InDesign, a variable is text-based content that dynamically changes when certain criteria are met or specific changes occur in your document. For example, you might want a running footer in your document that contains the title of the chapter. Traditionally, you would type the static text on a master page for the content to appear properly. In InDesign CS3, inserting a variable provides a more powerful option. In the example above, for example, using a variable would automatically update all footer text when the chapter title is modified.

When you place a text variable on a page, you must place it within a text frame, just like normal text. That frame can be in the live, printable area of your documents or in the non-printing portion. In this exercise, you will use text variables in a non-printing area to display the filename and modification date of the documents, which can be helpful in a collaborative environment.

1 Choose File > Open. Navigate to the id10lessons folder, choose TOC.indd, and press Open.

Notice the light blue outline that extends beyond the edge of the page on the right side. This area is called the *slug*, and information entered here doesn't automatically print on the final page. You will use the slug area to house the filename and modification date variable, displaying the name of the file and the date it was modified. This is useful for you when viewing a printout of a document or when viewing onscreen to determine when the file's most recent edit or modification was made.

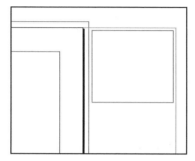

The slug area can hold information that will not show up in the final printed project.

What is a slug?

Defined within the Document Setup dialog box (File > Document Setup), a slug is an area that can be located on any side of a page. Information you place in this area does not print automatically. Common uses for slugs are for holding a company logo for ownership purposes, signoff information, or a list of the colors used in the document. A slug prints only when you choose Include Slug Area from the Print dialog's Marks and Bleed section. When printing using this option, you'll notice that the slug area's information prints on the outside area of the page where the slug has been defined.

2 Select the Type tool (T) from the Tools panel and drag to create a text frame within the top of the slug area on your page. Be careful to keep your frame within the slug's bounds.

3 Click on the Paragraph Styles button (🖺) in the dock on the right side of the workspace to open the panel. Choose the Variable Text style from the Paragraph Styles panel. This assigns the Variable Text style to the text you type in the frame and gives the text a standard appearance.

4 With the cursor inside the text frame, choose Type > Text Variables > Insert Variable > File Name to insert the value of the File Name variable in the slug area's text frame. Because you're working in the file TOC.indd, InDesign inserts *TOC* in the frame. Choose File > Save to save this addition to your document.

5 Press Enter (Windows) or Return (Mac OS) to create a second line in the text frame, then choose Type > Text Variables > Insert Variable > Modification Date. InDesign inserts the value of the second variable, Modification Date, beneath TOC in the text frame. The Modification Date's value reflects the time and date of the file's most recent save, and since you saved the document in the last step, the current date and time appear.

Later in the lesson, you will see how the File Name and Modification Date variables can be useful in a production environment. A quick look at the variable text tells which file you're working in and if the file has been updated recently.

6 Choose File > Save, then close the document.

Creating a book from multiple files

Any job that contains numerous pages, whether it's a book, magazine, or other long document, can be large and cumbersome. Not only is the file's size—especially if it contains a lot of graphics—an issue, but the more pages your document contains, the more challenging it is to navigate through your document. InDesign's Book feature offers some help. Book enables you to break up your document into smaller, more manageable sections or chapters. It also boasts a number of document management capabilities that allow for easy navigation between sections and maintains consistency from one file to the next.

To demonstrate the Book feature, you will work with five files that represent the different chapters of a work in progress. The first task in managing a large job like this is to create a book file.

1 In InDesign, choose File > Open and navigate to the id10lessons folder. Open each of the lesson files named 1_Trees.indd, 2_Flowers.indd and 3_Plants.indd. Press OK to accept any missing links or missing fonts, you will fix these later. Scroll quickly through each of the documents and note that the page numbers begin at 1 and continue until the last page. In this exercise, you'll create a book file that numbers the pages consecutively across the chapters. Close each file by choosing File > Close.

2 Choose File > New > Book. When the new dialog box opens, navigate to the id10lessons folder, type **Book** in the Name text field, then press Save. The Book panel appears and gives you access to your book file of the same name.

3 Press the Add documents button (✦) at the bottom of the Book panel.

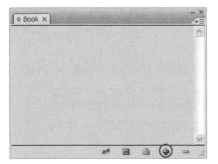

Add the documents in the id10lessons folder to the Book panel.

4 In the resulting Add Documents dialog box, Press Ctrl (Windows) or
Command (Mac OS) to select the TOC.indd, 1_Trees.indd, 2_Flowers.
indd, 3_Plants.indd, and Index.indd. Press Open. You will receive a warning
that a document has missing fonts. Press OK, you will solve this later in
the exercise. InDesign automatically lists the documents in the Book panel.
Although the documents in the Book panel are still separate files, they are
now being managed by the Book panel and are related to each other.

Defining pagination and document order

When you choose files from the Add Document dialog box, InDesign adds
them to the Book panel and adjusts the page numbers within each document so
they are sequentially numbered. Unfortunately, this does not always match the
logical sequence for your documents. For example, in your book, the TOC and
Index files should be first and last, respectively, in the panel. Because InDesign
adds files to the Book panel in numerical, then alphabetical order, based on each
document's file name, they are currently fourth and fifth in the list. Rearranging
the file order is a simple matter of clicking and dragging.

Once a book's pages are in order, you can turn your attention to the pagination
within the files. Do you need your book documents to open on left pages,
for example? InDesign's Book Page Numbering Options help you tweak the
document flow.

In this exercise, you will resolve some typical pagination issues, rearrange files
and explore the Book Page Numbering Options dialog box.

1 Within the Book panel, click and drag the TOC document to the top of the list (a bold divider rule will indicate the destination of the selected document), and release the mouse button at the top of the list. The TOC file is now the first document of the book; the page numbers to the right of the list adjust to accommodate the change.

2 Rearrange the documents within the Book panel so they are ordered: TOC, 1_Trees, 2_Flowers, 3_Plants, Index. Notice that every time you rearrange the documents, the Book panel updates the page numbering based on the new page order.

The documents in the Book panel after arranging them in the correct order.

3 Double-click the 2_Flowers file in the Book panel. You may receive a message indicating that there are missing fonts in this document as well as other documents. Press OK, you'll fix this in the following section by synchronizing the styles across all the book documents so they all use the same fonts.

The document opens just like it would if you opened it from the Open dialog box. The difference here is that the Book panel performs some automated management tasks, such as pagination, available only when you use the Book feature. Notice that the chapter starts on a right-hand page, though it should start on the left. Close the document.

4 Deselect all files in the Book panel by clicking in the empty area below the panel's list. Press the panel menu button (·≡), and from the resulting menu, choose Book Page Numbering Options. Again, you will receive a missing fonts warning, press OK for now.

5 In the Book Page Numbering Options dialog box that appears, click the Continue on Next Even Page radio button. In books and magazines the left page is usually even and the right page is odd, so this option forces each chapter to begin on a left-hand page.

6   Click the Insert Blank Page checkbox to instruct InDesign to add a blank page when needed, so the book can be numbered properly. In this case, InDesign adds a page to any chapter that does not end on an odd page so that the following chapter can begin on an even page.

7   Make sure that the Automatically Update Page & Section Numbers checkbox is checked as well. This tells InDesign to update page and section numbers automatically. Press OK. A progress bar pops up while InDesign CS3 rearranges and adds pages to your document as needed. The page numbers in the Book panel adjust to reflect the changes. Press OK each time you encounter the missing fonts warning, this will be fixed in the next exercise.

8   Double-click to open 1_Trees and 3_Plants to see the results. Scroll down the document and note that the pages are numbered consecutively at this point, unlike they were before added to the Book file. Your book now flows correctly from one chapter to the next.

9   Close all the open files.

Synchronizing attributes across a book file

When multiple people collaborate on files for a large job, inconsistencies sometimes sneak in no matter how well coworkers try to keep each other informed. The Book feature solves these hard-to-trace problems by synchronizing elements of your documents to maintain consistency across the documents within your book file. You can synchronize:

- Paragraph styles
- Character styles
- Object styles
- Table styles
- Cell styles
- Swatches
- Lists
- Variables
- Trap presets
- Master pages

In the design process, it isn't always feasible to start from a template with established master pages and styles. You can, however, create a base set of styles, such as body, subhead, etc., then synchronize all your documents to these styles and any other attributes agreed upon later.

The book files suffer from their own inconsistencies: The body text in 1_Trees is different, for example, from in 2_Flowers and 3_Plants. Page 3 of 1_Trees establishes a chapter intro master page for the chapter but the intro pages of 2_Flowers and the 3_Plants are different. The missing font warnings you have been ignoring up to this point could have been the result of multiple designers using fonts unique to their system. This in turn would create discrepancies in the chapters that need to be resolved. In this exercise, you will fix these discrepancies to establish cross-document consistency in the book.

1   If the 1_Trees document isn't open, double-click its name in the Book panel to open it. Go to page 3 and notice the word *Chapter* at the top of the page. You want the chapter number to appear next to the word for all the interior chapters in the book. To do this, you will use a variable.

You will add another variable so that each chapter's respective number appears.

2   Open the Pages panel by clicking on its button in the dock. Double-click on the right page icon of the A-Chapter Intro master page in your Pages panel. This displays the contents of the right-hand master page for the chapter.

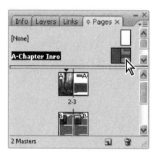

Double-click on the Right Page icon of the A-Chapter Intro master page.

3   Select the Type tool (T) from the Tools panel, and click to the immediate right of the word *Chapter* on the master page.

4   Type a space, then choose Type > Text Variables > Insert Variable > Chapter Number. The number 1 appears where you inserted your variable text. Choose File > Save and close the document.

5 Now you're ready to synchronize attributes across multiple chapters. If necessary, click in the Style Source box to the left of the 1_Trees document name in the Book panel. The style source is the document to which all other documents in your book synchronize.

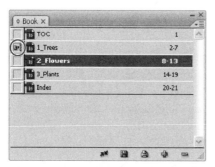

The style source icon indicates the document to which all other documents synchronize.

6 Before you synchronize documents, you must specify your synchronize options. Choose Synchronize Options from the Book panel menu. In the resulting Synchronize Options dialog box, you can specify which styles or elements to synchronize. For this project, make sure all options are selected. Press OK.

7 In the Book panel, click 1_Trees, then Shift+click 3_Plants to select all three of the interior chapters. (You won't use Select All, because you don't want to synchronize TOC or Index.)

8 Click the Synchronize styles and swatches with the Synchronize styles and swatches with the Style Source button (✸) at the bottom of the Book panel to initiate the synchronization of the selected chapters.

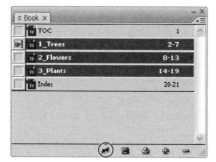

Select the documents and click the Synchronize styles button to begin synchronization.

When finished, InDesign displays a message to convey that synchronization completed successfully and some documents may have changed. InDesign changes the styles, master pages, and so on, in the selected documents to match those of the style source document. Here synchronization changed the definition of the paragraph styles to match the style source.

9 Click OK to accept the synchronization. To confirm the changes, double-click to open the 2_Flowers document. Notice that the chapter intro pages feature the appropriate chapter number because you included master pages in the synchronization options. In both 2_Flowers and 3_Plants, the body text matches that of the style source document and you will no longer see the missing fonts dialog box when opening these files. To add the finishing touch, you'll change the names of the chapters to reflect the actual name of each chapter.

10 Go to page 9 of the 2_Flowers document and press Shift+Ctrl (Windows) or Shift+Command (Mac OS) while you click the green title bar at the top of the page. This detaches the item from the master page so you can edit it. For information on master pages, refer to Lesson 3, "Building Documents and Master Pages."

11 Select the Type tool, highlight the word *Trees* in the green bar and type **Flowers**.

12 Choose File > Save then close the file.

13 Double-click 3_Plants in the Book panel, then repeat steps 10 and 11 on the title page, changing the word *Trees* to *Plants*. Choose File > Save to save your changes and close the file by choosing File > Close.

14 Double-click to open 1_Trees, and Shift+Ctrl+click (Windows) or Shift+Command+click (Mac OS) on the green bar at the top of the page to detach it from the master page. This is the Trees chapter, so don't change any of the text. The chapter title must be detached from the master page in preparation for the next exercise.

Now that your document has been synchronized, you have established consistency throughout the pages of your book. As the book grows, and documents are added, you can synchronize your book again to ensure consistency of styles and pages in those new documents.

Creating a table of contents

A book needs a table of contents, and InDesign helps you build one by automating its creation and formatting. For the Table of Contents feature to work, however, you must prepare the files correctly. For example, you must use paragraph styles throughout your document or book, and you must also create styles for the text in the table of contents itself. The TOC document in the example book already contains these styles. In this exercise, you'll use these styles and the Table of Contents feature to generate and format a table of contents for the example book.

1 Double-click the TOC document in your Book panel to open it.

2 Click on the Paragraph Styles button in the dock on the right side of the workspace. In the Paragraph Styles panel, notice that several styles begin with the prefix TOC. You will use these to style your table of contents copy. The styles you used to style the text of the chapters is missing, however. To create a table of contents, you'll load those styles into the TOC document by performing another synchronization.

3 Press the Book panel menu button (-≣) and choose Synchronize Options to open the Synchronize Options dialog box.

4 Uncheck all the options except for Paragraph Styles and Character Styles to instruct InDesign to synchronize only the Paragraph and Character styles. Press OK to close the dialog box.

Tell InDesign CS3 exactly which attributes you would like to synchronize.

5 Make sure that the Style Source is set to the 1_Trees document in the Book panel (by clicking in the gray box to the left of the document name), then Shift+click TOC and 1_Trees to select them for synchronizing.

6 Press the Synchronize styles and swatches with the Style Source button (⚲) at the bottom of the Book panel. When the dialog box appears, announcing that the synchronization completed successfully (and that documents may have changed), press OK. Look in the Paragraph Styles panel; paragraph styles were added to the list. Now you are ready to generate the table of contents for your book.

7 Choose Layout > Table of Contents. The Table of Contents dialog box appears.

Control every aspect of how your table of contents will be styled and generated in your document.

8 In the dialog box's Title text field, type **Contents**. This is the name that appears at the top of the Table of Contents of your book.

9 From the Style drop-down menu, choose TOC_Contents. This paragraph style defines how the title is formatted.

The top portion of the Table of Contents dialog box controls the title and title style of the table of contents.

10 The Styles in Table of Contents section is where you choose which styles in your document or book will appear in the table of contents. In the Other Styles list, click Chapter_Number to highlight it. Press the Add button to move the Chapter_Number style into the Include Paragraph Styles list. Highlight and click to add the Chapter_Hed and Sub_Hed styles as well, in that order.

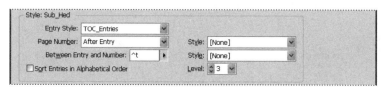

In the Styles in Table of Contents section, specify which styles InDesign uses to pull content from your document or book.

11 Now you need to define the attributes of each style's appearance. Click the More Options button at the right side of the Table of Contents dialog box to expand the Style section. (If you see a Fewer Options button, you don't need to do anything, as you can already see the additional options.)

12 Click the Chapter_Number Style in the Include Paragraph Styles list. The Style section below it is now called Style: Chapter_Number. Choose TOC_ ChapterNumber from the Entry Style drop-down menu, and No Page Number from the Page Number drop-down menu.

13 Click the Chapter_Hed style in the Include Paragraph Styles list and in the Style section, set Entry Style to TOC_ChapterHed. Leave all other fields in this section at their defaults. Click the Sub_Hed style next, and set Entry Style to TOC_Entries.

Determine how to format the table of contents' elements in the Style section of the Table of Contents dialog box.

14 Click the Include Book Documents checkbox at the bottom of the dialog box to tell InDesign it should search all book document files when it generates the table of contents. It uses elements formatted with the styles you added to the Include Paragraph Styles list.

15 Press the Save Style button in the upper-right corner of the dialog box. In the resulting Save Style dialog box, type **Book TOC** in the Save Style text field, and press Save to save the settings that define how your table of contents is created. This saves time if you ever have to generate another table of contents in the future.

Pressing the Save Style button inside the Table of Contents dialog box saves the settings that you painstakingly configured for your table of contents. This can be useful if you have several versions of a document that all need their own table of contents, or if you made a mistake and later need to modify your settings. The load button inside the Table of Contents dialog box allows you to load a Table of Contents style from another document for use in the open document.

16 Press OK in the Table of Contents dialog box to generate the table of contents for your book. A dialog may appear asking if you want to include items in overset text. Press Yes. This ensures that if any of the text in the other documents is overset, it will still be included in the Table of Contents.

Overset text is text that appears in a frame that isn't big enough to display it. This can happen for several reasons; often when text is added or adjusted, it will make the text within a frame longer than the frame itself. For this reason, you generally want to include items in overset text when creating a Table of Contents to make sure that the overset text is included.

17 Your cursor changes to a loaded text cursor (📰) which indicates that InDesign has text to place in your document. Click in the upper-left corner of your document where the margins meet. InDesign automatically creates a text frame within the boundaries of your margins and places the table of contents text within the frame.

Contents

Chapter 1

Trees of the World... 3
Beech (Fagus sylvatica) 4
Red Oak (Quercus rubra) 5
Sugar Maple (Acer saccharum) 6

Chapter 2

Flowers of the World 9
Sunflower (Helianthus annuus).................................... 10
Rose (Quercus rubra) 11

Chapter 3

Plants of the World 13
Fountain Grass (Pennisetum alopecuroides)........................ 14
Aloe (Aloe succotrina) 15
Golden Ball Cacti (Notocactus leninghausii) 16

The table of contents.

18 Choose File > Save, then File > Close to save and close the document.

> *Whether you add or delete pages and documents to your book while you work, you can easily update the table of contents to reflect these changes. Click the text frame that contains the table of contents text, and choose Layout > Update Table of Contents.*

Building an index

Indexes are very complex components of a book. A good index is based on specific topics and can quickly direct you to the exact location of the information you need; a poorly created index is one that is confusing or unhelpful. InDesign CS3 doesn't know what you want indexed, so it can't automatically create an index for you. It can however, make the process a lot easier. Using the Index panel, you can assemble an index with topics, references, and cross-references.

To demonstrate what's possible, two chapters of the example book have been indexed already. In this series of exercises, you'll tackle the third chapter, adding index topics to categorize your references, supplementing these with cross-references to help direct your reader to the correct topic, and finally, generating the index.

Adding topics

The most basic component of an index is its topics. Although InDesign can't help you with what to index, it makes adding the topics you choose a simple matter of point and click. Think of topics as categories into which entries will be categorized.

1   In the Book panel, double-click to open 3_Plants, the file you need to index.

2   Choose Window > Type & Tables > Index to open the Index panel.

3   Make sure the Book checkbox in the upper-right corner of the Index panel is checked. This tells InDesign to look in all the documents within a book for references when generating the index.

4 Click the Topic radio button at the top of the Index panel to switch to Topic view, then click the New button (⊡) at the bottom of the panel. The New Topic dialog box opens so you can add your first topic.

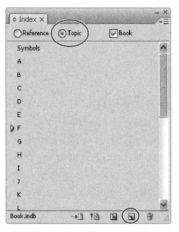

Click the Topic button then the New button to begin building a topic list.

5 In the New Topic dialog box, type **Plants** in text field 1 under Topic Levels and press the Add button on the right side of the dialog box to add *Plants* to the topic list. Each letter of the alphabet appears at the bottom of the New Topic dialog box and there is now a triangle next to *P*. If you click the triangle, the list expands and you see the word *Plants* has been added to the list of topics. In text field 1 under Topic Levels, type **Genus**, then press Add. Press the Done button. You have now added *Plants* and *Genus* to the topic list of the index.

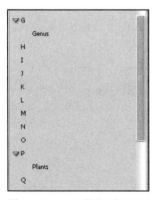

The new topics are added to the topic list of the index.

6   Click the Reference radio button at the top of the Index panel to switch to the Reference view, which shows each entry's page number and any cross-references that you add.

7   If the Pages panel isn't open, click on the Pages button in the dock to open it. Double-click on page 14 in the Pages panel to display page 14 and, using the Text tool (T), select the phrase *Fountain Grass* at the top of the page.

8   Press the Create a new index entry button (⊟) at the bottom of the Index panel. The New Page Reference dialog box appears with the Fountain Grass entered in the Topic Level 1 field. Press the Add button to add the reference to Fountain Grass to the index. In order to accommodate a range of searching styles, you will add Fountain Grass as a subtopic beneath the Plants entry.

9   With the New Page Reference dialog box still open, click the Down Arrow icon to move Fountain Grass to the Topic Level 2 field. Click to insert your cursor in the Topic Level 1 text field, then scroll down to the P topics in the list at the bottom of the New Page Reference dialog box. Click on the triangle next to P to expand its entries, and then double-click Plants to insert it in the Topic Level 1 text field. Press the Add button, and then press OK or Done to close the New Page Reference dialog box.

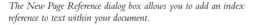

The New Page Reference dialog box allows you to add an index reference to text within your document.

10 Repeat steps 6 through 9 for the word *Aloe* on page 15 and the phrase *Golden Ball Cacti* on page 16.

Now, in addition to the plant's name, you need to add each plant's scientific name to its Genus topic.

11 Double-click on page 14 in the Pages panel to go to that page. Highlight the scientific name (*Pennisetum alopecuroides*) and click the Create a new index entry button at the bottom of the Index panel. Click the Down Arrow icon to move the entry to the Topic Level 2 text field. Click to select the Topic Level 1 text field then scroll down to the G topics in the list at the bottom of the New Page Reference dialog box. Click on the triangle next to G to expand its entries, and then double-click Genus to insert it in the Topic Level 1 text field. Press the add button, then press OK or Done.

12 Highlight the scientific name for the remaining plant names on pages 15 through 16 and add their references to the topic Genus. Press OK or Done to close the New Page Reference dialog box. Save the 3_Plants.indd document and keep the file open for the next exercise.

Adding cross-references

Now that you've added all the necessary references to your index for the 3_Plants document, it's time to think about adding cross-references to your index. Cross-references refer a reader to a similar topic if there are no entries for the topic being looked up. For example, someone may look up the topic *grass* in your index. It does not contain a topic for grass, but the index can refer the reader to the closest thing, which would be fountain grass. Try adding the cross-reference now.

1 With the 3_Plants.indd document still open, choose New Cross-reference from the Index panel menu. The New Cross-reference dialog box appears.

Enter the referenced word, as well as the related topic to which you will direct the reader.

2 In the list at the bottom of the New Cross-reference panel, scroll to the letter F and expand the topic by clicking on the triangle to its left. Double-click *Fountain Grass* to add it to the Topic Level 1 text field.

3 In the Referenced text field, type **Grass**. This tells InDesign to direct the reader to the Fountain Grass topic when the word *grass* is referenced. This will put an entry in the index under the topic *Fountain Grass* that says, *See also* Grass.

4 Press the Add button to add the cross-reference to the index, then press OK or Done to close the New Cross-reference dialog box.

5 Choose File > Save to save your work, then close it by choosing File > Close.

Generating the index

With all the pieces in place, you're ready to generate the index and place it within the book.

1 Open the Index.indd file from the Book panel.

2 If the Index panel is not open, choose Window > Type & Tables > Index to open it.

3 Make sure that the Book checkbox in the upper-right corner of the panel is checked.

4 Choose Generate Index from the Index panel menu.

5 In the resulting Generate Index dialog box, leave the settings at their defaults. It's important that the Include Book Documents option is checked. Press OK to close the dialog box and generate the index.

In the Generate Index dialog box, you can name your index and format it with a paragraph style.

6 Your cursor changes to a loaded text cursor containing all the text that makes up your index copy. Click in the upper-left corner of page 19 of the Index document to place the text. InDesign creates a text frame on your page with the index text inside it.

> *If all your index does not fit on the page you choose, simply flow the extra text onto the second page of the document. For more on flowing text from one frame to another, see Lesson 4, "Working with Text and Type."*

7 Save and close the Index.indd file.

> *When you make changes to an index and need to update the existing index with new content, simply choose the Generate Index option from the Index panel menu to display the Generate Index dialog box. Within that dialog box is a checkbox called Replace Existing Index. When that checkbox is turned on, InDesign replaces your current index with the new index content.*

Creating PDFs and printing from the Book panel

Now that you are finished working on your book, you may want to send the document to a coworker or client as proof of progress or for review. Because not everyone has InDesign, you want to convert your InDesign file to a file type that can be easily shared. InDesign's Book panel simplifies the process of creating PDF files and printing so you can easily share your file.

Creating PDFs

Creating a PDF from a book file is quick and easy in InDesign, and the results can be read by anyone with Adobe Acrobat Reader (Free download available at *www.adobe.com*). You will now export your book as a PDF.

1 Click in the beige area below the list of documents in the Book panel to ensure that no documents are selected. From the Book panel menu (-≡), choose Export Book to PDF.

2 In the resulting Export dialog box, name the file **id10book.pdf**, navigate to your desktop, and press Save.

3 In the Export Adobe PDF dialog box, choose High Quality Print from the Adobe PDF Preset drop-down menu. Press Export. A Generating PDF dialog box appears with status bars showing the progress of the PDF file.

> *The High Quality Print preset generates a PDF file of approximately 12MB. If you need a smaller PDF, choose the Smallest File Size setting from the Adobe PDF Preset drop-down menu. This setting presents an additional dialog box indicating that the transparency blend space is different from the document's blend space. Simply press OK and proceed as usual.*

Printing

The Book panel also simplifies the process of printing your book, should you want a hard copy. Although the steps are few, keep in mind that printing the entire book—six files—will take some time.

1 Click in the beige area below the list of documents in the Book panel to ensure that no documents are selected.

2 From the Book panel menu, choose Print Book. InDesign opens the standard print dialog box from which you can print all the pages of your book.

> *For more on printing from InDesign CS3, see Lesson 11, "Document Delivery: Printing, PDFs, and XHTML."*

3 Choose File > Save to save your book file, then File > Close to close the project. Congratulations! You've just finished working in your first InDesign book file.

Self study

Work with other text variables available in InDesign CS3 to find out other ways in which they can be used. The Running Header variable, for instance, allows you to define a Paragraph Style within your document, whose content will appear where the Running Header variable is placed, saving considerable time when working with long documents.

Create your own paragraph styles for the table of contents to change its appearance. Get creative by changing the fonts and paragraph spacing, then choose Update Table of Contents to see your changes.

Add additional references to the index. Practice creating index references and cross-references and then regenerate the index to apply your recent entries. With index copy, you can customize the appearance of the text by using paragraph styles. You can change these settings by clicking on the More Options button in the Generate Index dialog box.

Review

Questions

1 What feature in InDesign allows you to ensure that Paragraph and Character styles have a consistent appearance throughout multiple files in a book?

2 What is the key requirement for creating a table of contents in InDesign?

3 How do you update an existing index within InDesign?

4 How can you make a PDF file of all pages within a Book file?

Answers

1 The synchronize options.

2 Paragraph Styles must be used to format text throughout the document.

3 Choose Generate Index from the Index panel menu and make sure that the Replace Existing Index checkbox is checked.

4 Choose Export Book to PDF from the Book panel menu.

What you'll learn in this lesson:

- Preflighting your document
- Collecting for distribution
- Creating and customizing a PDF file
- Exporting an XHTML file
- Printing a proof

Document Delivery: Printing, PDFs, and XHTML

Designing your document is only half the job. You still need to deliver it, whether to a commercial printer, the Web, or just your coworkers for review. To help you, InDesign offers multiple methods for proofing and packaging your files, as well as flexible export controls for a variety of formats, including PDF and HTML.

Starting up

Before starting, make sure that your tools and panels are consistent by resetting your preferences. See "Resetting the InDesign workspace and preferences" on page 3.

You will work with several files from the id11lessons folder in this lesson. Make sure that you have loaded the idlessons folder onto your hard drive. See "Loading lesson files" on page 4.

For this lesson, you need either Adobe Acrobat or Adobe Reader to view the PDF files you will create. If necessary, you can download the free Adobe Reader at *adobe.com*.

See Lesson 11 in action!

Explore more of the features shown in this lesson using the supplemental video tutorial available online at agitraining.com/digitalclassroom.

The project

To sample InDesign's PDF, XHTML, and print-related controls, you will prepare a car ad for delivery to multiple customers. You'll package it using InDesign's Preflight and Package feature, match it to a printer's specifications, and convert it to XHTML for posting to a web site using the new Cross-Media Export feature.

Preflight checks

Before you send your files to a printer, or other service provider, in order to print your job professionally it's important that you check the file for common errors that can occur during the design phase of your project. If your files aren't prepared to the required specifications, your job could be delayed or, even worse, reproduced incorrectly. InDesign's Preflight feature enables you to check all the mechanics of your file to ensure that everything is in working order, like a pilot checking over his plane prior to takeoff. Preflight assesses your document, then reports potential problems—missing fonts, missing images, RGB (Red, Green, Blue) images, and more—that could prevent a printer from outputting your job properly, or hinder a customer's ability to view your file accurately.

For example, you're planning to submit an ad for the new IDCS3 sports car to a newspaper. In this exercise, you'll use Preflight to see how well your ad complies with the newspaper's specifications.

1   Choose File > Open, navigate to the id11lessons folder, and select CarAd.indd. Press Open.

2   Choose File > Preflight. InDesign analyzes the document, and displays a
        summary of its findings in the Preflight dialog box. For more information
        on a specific category, click its name in the list on the left side of the
        dialog box.

*The Preflight dialog box displays detailed information about your file and flags
potential errors that could cause problems.*

3   From the list on the left side of the dialog box, choose Fonts. The right
        side of the dialog box now lists all the fonts used in your document as well
        as their format and status. If the status is OK, the font is loaded onto your
        system and recognized by InDesign. A status of Missing indicates that the
        font cannot be found. Because this lesson file was created using fonts that
        load with InDesign, all your fonts should say *OK*.

4   Choose Links and Images from the list. This section displays information
        about the images that are used within your document. At the top of this
        dialog box is a caution icon (⚠), indicating that InDesign found a potential
        problem, specifically that one of the images uses the RGB color space. Most
        printing companies require images to be submitted in the CMYK color
        space; ask your printer for its specifications prior to sending your files.

*Since you won't be printing this, you don't need to worry about this message. If
you were working on a piece for printing, however, and this warning appeared, you
would have to open the RGB file in Adobe Photoshop and convert it to CMYK.*

The Links and Images section also indicates the state of your images, linked
or unlinked, as well as the actual versus effective resolutions of your images.

Actual vs. effective resolution

The resolution of an image is indicated by the number of pixels per inch (ppi) that make up the image—a seemingly simple concept that can be a bit complicated. As a general rule, the higher its resolution, the higher the quality of an image. Most images that you see when browsing the Internet are 72 ppi or 96 ppi, which is the standard screen resolution of most monitors. For high-quality printing, however, image resolution should generally be around 300 ppi.

To further complicate things, the Preflight window's Links and Images section lists two different numbers at the bottom: actual ppi and effective ppi. Actual ppi is the actual resolution of the file that you are placing into InDesign. The effective ppi is the resolution of the image after it has been scaled in InDesign. For example, if you place a 300-ppi image in your document then scale it 200%, the effective resolution becomes 150 ppi. As you increase the size of images in InDesign, the effective resolution decreases. The effective resolution is the number that you should pay most careful attention to, as it determines the quality at which the image is output.

5   Select Colors and Inks in the Preflight list to see which ink colors the document uses. This file uses a color called Pantone 187 C. Any color besides cyan, magenta, yellow, or black is considered a spot color or plate. You'll learn more about these later in the "Separations Preview" section. Press the Cancel button to close the Preflight dialog box.

For more information on Pantone colors, see Lesson 8, "Using Color in Your Documents."

Keep the file open, as you'll need it for the next part of the lesson. Now you're ready to package it to send to the newspaper running the ad.

6   Choose File > Save As. Navigate to the id11lessons folder and type **CarAd_work.indd** in the Name text field. Press Save.

Packaging your document

When you need to send your InDesign document out for review, alterations, or printing, you must be sure you're sending all the necessary pieces. Without the font and image files used by the document, your coworker or service provider can't accurately see and reproduce the file as you intended. To avoid this frustrating scenario, turn to InDesign's Package feature. Package gathers all the document elements the recipient needs into one folder and even enables you to include an instructions file. In this exercise, you will use Package to collect the car ad's fonts and graphics.

1 Choose File > Package. InDesign automatically runs Preflight and displays a warning if it finds problems. Pressing the warning's View Info button opens the Preflight dialog box. Because in this case the Preflight dialog box displays the same information you saw in the last exercise, press Continue instead.

You can access the Package feature from the Preflight dialog box as well.

2 For this exercise, press Continue when the Printing Instructions dialog box opens. For a real project, you would enter your contact information as well as any detailed instructions that the printer might need to output your file properly.

3 The Package Publication (Windows) or Create Package Folder (Mac OS) dialog box opens next; here you choose what to include in the file package, what to call it, and where to save it. Make sure the first three options are checked: Copy Fonts, Copy Linked Graphics and Update Graphic Links in Package. All others should be unchecked. Type **CarAd Folder** in the Folder Name (Windows) or Save As (Mac OS) text field, choose Desktop from the Save in (Windows) or Where (Mac OS) drop-down menu, and press Package (Windows) or Save (Mac OS).

Use the Create Package Folder dialog box to tell InDesign which files to gather and where to save them.

4 In response to the Font Alert dialog box that details the legalities of giving your fonts to a printer or service provider, press OK to begin packaging the files. (If you don't want to see this alert in the future, click the Don't show again checkbox before you press OK.)

5 When the dialog box closes, a small progress window appears, displaying the status of the packaging process. Once it has finished, close your CarAd_work.indd file.

6 Choose File > Open, navigate to the Desktop and double-click the CarAd folder. Inside you'll find a copy of the document file, an instructions file, a Fonts folder with all the fonts used in the job, and a Links folder that contains all the graphics—all in one easy-to-send package. Press Cancel to close the dialog box.

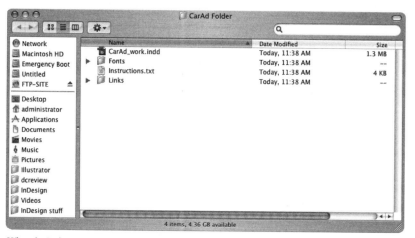

When the Package process is complete, all the project's elements are grouped together in the CarAd folder.

Now that all the files required to reproduce your job have been copied to the location you specified and are contained within their own folder, you can send this folder to another person to review, or to your printer or service provider to output your job. To ensure the integrity of the files and speed the transfer, compress the packaged folder before sending the files via e-mail or uploading them to an FTP server.

Creating an Adobe PDF

The Package feature collects all your data files, but the recipients still must have InDesign to read the document. What if they don't?

The answer is to send a PDF file. PDF (Portable Document Format) is a common format that can be viewed and printed from any computer platform—Mac, Windows, Linux, etc.—that has the free Adobe Reader program installed. A PDF file is an excellent way to make your project available for a wide range of users, and InDesign CS3 makes the process of creating a PDF file of your project very easy. In the following steps, you will create a PDF file of your CarAd_work.indd file so that other people can see your progress and provide feedback on changes that might need to be made before this project is sent to a printer for production.

1 If it's not still open, choose File > Open Recent to open the CarAd_work.indd file.

2 Choose File > Export. In the resulting Export dialog box, name the file CarAd.pdf, choose Desktop from the Save in (Windows) or Where (Mac OS) drop-down menu, and select Adobe PDF from the Save as type (Windows) or Format (Mac OS) drop-down menu. Press Save.

Choose the destination for your PDF file in the Export dialog box.

3 The Export Adobe PDF dialog box appears. From the Adobe PDF Preset
drop-down menu at the top of the dialog box, you can choose settings
that control the PDF file's size and quality, among other options. Because
you will send the car ad to several people for general review, choose the
[Smallest File Size] option from the Adobe PDF Preset drop-down menu.

*PDF presets are a way of saving favorite settings for the final generated PDF file.
If you own Adobe Acrobat 7.0 or a more recent version, InDesign CS3 shares
these settings with Acrobat Distiller, which is included with Acrobat. Likewise,
if you create a custom setting within Distiller, you'll see those settings in the
Adobe PDF Preset drop-down menu when you export a PDF file from within
InDesign CS3.*

*The Export Adobe PDF dialog box allows you to customize the PDF you create
from your InDesign file.*

4 Click the Hyperlinks checkbox, near the bottom. Activating the Hyperlinks
option makes any hyperlinks created in the InDesign document clickable
hyperlinks in the resulting PDF document.

5 Press the Export button. InDesign displays a warning that your document's
transparency blend space doesn't match the destination color space. Because
your PDF file is for viewing purposes only, this is not a concern. Press OK
to begin generating the PDF.

6 When the PDF is finished, double-click the CarAd.pdf file on your Desktop to open it. Hover your cursor over the www.idcs3.com link, and the cursor should change to a hand. Click on the link to go to the web site specified in the ad. If you receive a message warning you that the document is trying to connect to a web site, choose Allow.

The exported PDF file can contain interactive elements that are included in your InDesign file.

7 Choose File > Close to close the PDF file.

Generating XHTML

That takes care of the print side of the ad campaign, but what about the Web? Your client wants all the used cars listed in the ad to be published on the company web site. Although InDesign is a page-layout program, it can help you generate XHTML files from your document. XHTML is a markup language used for formatting pages on the Web. In this exercise, you'll use InDesign's Cross-media Export controls to publish your content in XHTML format. Greatly improved from previous versions of InDesign, InDesign CS3's Cross-media Export function allows you to repurpose the content of your document to an XHTML file that is easily opened in an XHTML editor such as Adobe Dreamweaver. In several of Adobe's Creative Suite packages, Dreamweaver is included, making it easier to move content from print to the Web.

HTML vs. XHTML

HTML (HyperText Markup Language) has been the standard markup language on the Web since the inception of the World Wide Web as we know it today. HTML allows you to describe how a page is formatted and displayed in a web browser. XHTML (Extensible HyperText Markup Language) expands on traditional HTML by separating the presentation of a page from its structure, allowing you to describe the content of a page in addition to its formatting. XHTML incorporates the power of XML in HTML, so basically an XHTML document is both a hypertext document and an XML document, making pages easier to maintain and more flexible at the same time. Some very powerful tools developed for use with XML can now also be utilized on an XHTML document. For more on XML, see Chapter 12 "Using XML."

1 With the CarAd_work.indd file open, choose File > Cross-media Export > XHTML/Dreamweaver.

2 In the Save As dialog box, name the file CarAd.html, choose the Desktop for its location, and press Save.

When using the Cross-media Export feature, make sure that you don't have any objects or text selected in your document. If an element is selected, InDesign exports only that text or object.

3 In the XHTML Export Options dialog box that opens, leave the General settings at their defaults, since there aren't any lists in the ad, and click Images in the list at left.

4   In the image-related settings that appear at right, choose Optimized from the Copy Images drop-down menu. For Image Conversion, choose JPEG, and for Image Quality, choose High.

Control the quality of the images exported from your InDesign layout.

5   Click Advanced in the list on the left of the dialog box. At right, click the Empty CSS Declarations radio button. This option inserts cascading style sheet (CSS) tags in the resulting XHTML file so you can later add CSS definitions to format the copy. (See the next section for more on CSS.) Make sure that all other options are unselected, then press Export to save the XHTML file.

Customize the formatting of the exported XHTML file to change the appearance of the resulting file.

6   On the Desktop, double-click on the CarAd.html file to view it in your default web browser. (Try File > Open in your browser if double-clicking doesn't work.)

Adding CSS formatting

The web page you exported has fairly rudimentary formatting, because formatting in XHTML isn't nearly as flexible as in a page-layout application such as InDesign CS3. You can, however, improve the formatting of your web page by using cascading style sheets. Just as styles control element formatting in InDesign, cascading style sheets specify which elements of an XHTML file should be formatted in which way. By linking your exported XHTML file to an external CSS file, you can mimic the formatting of your InDesign styles with cascading style sheets. For your text to be properly identified in the resulting XHTML file, however, you must use InDesign's Character and Paragraph Styles to format the text and code (or have someone else code) a separate CSS file. If you format your copy manually (without styles), the CSS file cannot interpret what needs to be formatted. Try exporting the car ad again, this time linking it to a ready-made CSS file.

1   Choose File > Cross-media Export > XHTML/Dreamweaver and name the file CarAdFormat.html. Save it to your Desktop.

2   In the XHTML Export Options dialog box, leave the General settings at their defaults.

3   Click Images in the list at left, and choose Optimized for Copy Images, JPEG for Image Conversion, and High for Image Quality. This generates a separate folder called CarAdFormat-web-images containing all the images formatted for the Web.

4   Click Advanced in the list, then click the External CSS radio button and type **CarAd.css** in the text field if it's not already entered. This is the CSS file that contains the document's formatting instructions. Now you need to reorganize a few files so that the XHTML file can find it.

Point the XHTML file to an external CSS file for improved formatting.

5 Press Export. Once the process is completed, navigate to the desktop. On your desktop, create a folder called XHTML. Move the CarAdFormat. html file and CarAdFormat-web-images folder from your desktop into the XHTML folder. Copy the CarAd.css file from your id11lessons folder to the XHTML folder.

6 Open the XHTML folder and double-click the CarAdFormat.html file. You should see that the text for the used cars is now formatted similarly to the text in the print ad design.

CSS and XHTML

Traditionally, formatting in HTML was limited to a predefined list of tags that changed the appearance of text and objects on a web page. These tags provided general formatting and were often inconsistent because different browsers' preference settings made it difficult for a designer to ensure the accurate appearance of a web page. CSS (Cascading Style Sheets), as the name implies, are similar to Styles in Adobe InDesign CS3. This feature allows you to be more specific when formatting text, images, and layout in an XHTML file and streamlines the process of applying formatting to a page. CSS can be used to apply consistent formatting to a number of pages because multiple pages can be linked to a single CSS file. This also makes formatting adjustments quick and easy, because modifications to a CSS file are automatically translated to all pages that are linked to that CSS file.

Separation preview

Designed primarily to produce print layouts, InDesign supports both traditional methods of printing color: the CMYK model and spot colors. In the four-color process model cyan, magenta, yellow, and black inks (C, M, and Y, with black as the K) combine in various values to reproduce numerous colors. A printing press uses a separate plate for each of these four colors, laying the ink down on the substrate in separate layers. Spot colors are pre-mixed inks that match standard color values. To ensure the green in your company's logo matches across all your print jobs, for example, you could choose a specific green spot color to use consistently.

Probably the most widely used spot color system is the Pantone Matching System, which is also called PMS, or simply Pantone colors. As a companion to the system it developed, Pantone Inc. also offers a swatch book so you can see how the colors reproduce on paper. All the Creative Suite applications have the Pantone library built in, so you can add spot colors to your document easily. Spot colors each require their own plates as well.

All Pantone colors have CMYK equivalents that enable you to reproduce the color using the standard process colors, as well, should you need to conform to CMYK-only printing requirements, or reduce the number of plates.

Keep in mind, however, that printing a Pantone color as a CMYK color may cause it to look drastically different from the spot version of that Pantone color. This is because of the limited gamut, or color range, that process colors are able to reproduce. Pantone offers a Process Color Simulator guide that compares the printed spot color against the printed process color and is indispensable when you reproduce spot colors as four-color process.

In the printing industry, printers charge customers for each plate that has to be produced for the printing job. You want to be sure that unnecessary colors aren't mistakenly sent to the printer, as extra colors increase your cost and can cause confusion. To prevent this added expense and frustration, InDesign's Separation Preview panel lets you view the separate plates, or separations, as the printer would see them before you send your file. Take a tour of the panel as you check the car ad's separations.

1   Choose Window > Output > Separations Preview or press Shift+F6 to open the Separations Preview panel.

2   Click on the Separations Preview panel menu button (-≡) and choose Show Single Plates in Black to turn off that option and see each plate in its actual color.

3   Choose Separations from the View drop-down menu in the Separations Preview panel.

See where certain colors are used in your document.

4 Click on the eye icon (👁) to the left of the CMYK entry to turn off the visibility of the Cyan, Magenta, Yellow, and Black plates in your document. InDesign now displays only the elements in Pantone 187 C.

You can tell that Pantone 187 C is a spot color because it is still visible after all the other separations have been hidden. Another way to identify a spot color in your document is to look at your Swatches panel. If any color has this icon (◉) to the right of the color name, it indicates that the color is a spot color and outputs on its own plate. Because the newspaper's specifications forbid spot colors, you must replace them in the car ad.

5 Click on the panel menu button in your Separations Preview panel, and choose Ink Manager from the list. The Ink Manager lists all the plates or inks that are currently in your document.

6 In the Ink Manager, click the spot icon to the left of the Pantone 187 C plate to change it from a spot color to a process color. You now see a process color icon (✖) to the left of the Pantone 187 C plate, indicating that the color will output as process instead of spot. Click OK. Because you mapped the Pantone 187 C plate to process and you turned off display of your process colors in step 4, no colors are currently visible.

7 Click on the eye icon to the left of CMYK to see all the colors in your document again. The red color that was Pantone 187 C is now a red made of the four process colors. If you hover your cursor over different areas of your document, the Separations Preview panel shows you the ink percentages to the right of each color in the Separations Preview panel.

Hover your cursor over areas of your document to see the ink percentages.

8 Toggle the visibility of various separations in your Separations Preview panel to see how the colors in your document are combined to achieve other colors, called builds.

9 Choose Off from the View drop-down menu in the Separations Preview panel to get back to your normal viewing mode, and close the Separations Preview panel. Now your ad is properly prepared for printing in the newspaper.

Printing a proof

The best way to avoid surprises at press time is to print a proof of your document on your desktop printer. Seeing your project on paper sometimes reveals design flaws or mistakes you missed when viewing your document on screen. Printing out a version of your document on a printer is referred to as printing a proof. The term *proof* is used to describe any type of output that is generated prior to making plates for a printing press. In this exercise, you'll use InDesign to print a proof to your desktop printer.

1 With CarAd_work.indd open, choose File > Print to open the Print dialog box.

2 From the Printer drop-down menu at the top of the Print dialog box, choose a printer that is available to your computer.

3 Because there is only one page in your CarAd_work.indd file, leave Pages set to All. For multi-page documents, however, you could specify a limited range of pages to print.

4 Click Setup in the list at left. On the right side, choose Letter[8.5 x 11] from the Paper Size drop-down menu and click on the Landscape Orientation icon (⊞) to print your document in landscape orientation on standard letter-sized paper. The preview in the lower-left corner shows your page orientation and selected printer.

5   Your ad is larger than the letter-sized paper you specified in step 4, so click
on the Scale to Fit radio button to scale your document to fit the available
space. This automatically centers your document on the printed page. (If
you have a large format printer, of course, you can adjust the paper size as
needed and print at full scale.)

*The Print dialog box enables you to control all aspects of how your page is
oriented to the paper and printer.*

6   In the list at left, click Marks and Bleed. Click the All Printer's Marks checkbox to tell InDesign to add the appropriate trim, bleed, and color marks to your page as you would see on a printer's proof. Leave the other settings at their defaults.

The Marks and Bleed section allows you to control the marks that are placed on your page when it is printed.

7   Click Output in the list at left. If you are printing to a color printer that prints CMYK colors, choose Composite CMYK (or Composite RGB, if your printer doesn't print CMYK colors) from the Color drop-down menu at right. If you are printing to a black-and-white printer, choose Composite Gray instead.

8   Click Graphics in the list at left. In the Send Data drop-down menu of the Images section, choose the output quality of the graphics. For the best quality possible, choose All, or choose Optimized Subsampling to let InDesign reduce the quality of your images slightly so the document prints faster. The higher the quality of the graphics, the more data InDesign needs to send to the printer and the longer it takes.

9   Press Print.

10   Choose File > Save to save your file, then File > Close to close it.

If you use the same set of print settings frequently, click the Save Preset button in the Print dialog box to save a preset of the current settings. The next time you need them, choose the preset from the dialog box's Print Preset drop-down menu. This streamlines the process of printing, especially when you are printing to the same printer with the same settings on a frequent basis.

Self study

Try the Find Font feature by choosing Type > Find Font to replace the fonts that Preflight or Package identifies as missing, with fonts you have loaded on your machine. Likewise, use the Links panel by choosing Window > Links to fix images that are missing or modified in your document.

Investigate InDesign CS3's numerous tools that enable you to add interactivity to a PDF document when it is exported. For example, you can use the Button tool to add navigation to your exported PDF document, or you can add hyperlinks that are clickable links in the final PDF file.

Using the Separation Preview panel's Ink Manager, you can create an Ink Alias that maps one spot color to another. For instance if you have two spot plates, you can map one ink to output on the same plate as the other ink. This feature is great when you realize at the last minute that you have too many spot colors in your document and need to minimize them. Practice this by creating a new document and adding at least two spot colors to your document.

Review

Questions

1 What command groups the active document and all the fonts and graphics used in the document into a single folder on your computer?

2 When creating a PDF file from InDesign, what's the easiest way to make sure that the settings for the PDF are consistent every time?

3 What web technology is used to automatically format text in an XHTML file exported from InDesign?

4 InDesign's Preflight dialog box tells you that there is a spot color used in your document. What's the easiest way to see where that spot color is used?

Answers

1 Package.

2 Save the settings as a PDF Preset.

3 CSS (Cascading Style Sheets).

4 Use the Separations Preview panel to view only the spot color plate.

Lesson 12

What you'll learn in this lesson:

- Importing and exporting XML

- Applying tags to your InDesign layout

- Validating XML

- Understanding the XML structure

- Using data merge to automatically generate documents

Using XML

Through its XML support, InDesign CS3 connects the worlds of print and the Web. You can, for example, apply tags to your existing print layout and export its content (text and images) as an XML file for reuse on a web site. InDesign can also import an XML file, complete with formatting, from a database or the Web, into a layout. Another great feature is InDesign's ability to export the content of an existing layout and then import that XML file into a layout of a different size, with the formatting intact.

Starting up

Before starting, make sure that your tools and panels are consistent by resetting your preferences. See "Resetting the InDesign workspace and preferences" on page 3.

You will work with several files from the id12lessons folder in this lesson. Make sure that you have loaded the id12lessons folder onto your hard drive. See "Loading lesson files" on page 4.

See Lesson 12 in action!

Explore more of the features shown in this lesson using the supplemental video tutorial available online at agitraining.com/digitalclassroom.

The project

In this lesson, you'll work with content for a fictitious ski slope called Feather Ridge. You'll begin with a flyer that has already been created and then you will tag the content of the flyer using XML tags and a variety of XML tools, then repurpose that content for a large poster for display in local stores and other venues. To finish up, you will use the Data Merge feature in InDesign CS3 to generate business cards for employees of Feather Ridge to hand out to potential clients.

XML basics

Before you can effectively work with XML in InDesign, you should understand a bit about the language itself. XML, which stands for Extensible Markup Language, allows for the repurposing and distribution of content to multiple destinations. XML does nothing to describe how its content is formatted—that is left to the destination program where the XML will be used or to the source program that creates it. XML does, however, describe data. Since XML encloses content in tags, other programs can interpret the data in a variety of ways. Consider this simple XML file:

```
<application>

    <name>Adobe Indesign</name>

    <version>5.0</version>

    <vendor>Adobe Systems, Inc.</vendor>

</application>
```

In the example on the previous page, you can see that the tags or elements define and describe the content. Each tag resides within opening (<) and closing (>) angle brackets, and elements appear in opening and closing pairs (*<name>* and *</name>*, for example) that tell any program reading the file when the element starts and stops. The *<application>* element (at top) is called the root, or document, element because it contains all other elements. Every XML file must have a root element, but doesn't necessarily need to be named as such. By looking at the example, you can determine that the application is Adobe InDesign version 5.0 and is manufactured by Adobe Systems, Inc.

You don't need a XML-specific program to write XML; a basic text editor suffices. In fact, to work with XML in InDesign, you don't even need to know how to write XML code; just select and click.

XML tags in InDesign

Tags in InDesign are used to represent and specify the occurrences of elements within an InDesign layout. InDesign uses the Tags panel and a list of tags to specify the type of content that is, or will be, contained within a frame. A frame can be tagged as text or an image, and the text within a frame can be tagged as well. These tags are used whenever you import or export XML in InDesign.

1   In InDesign, press the Go to Bridge button (🔲) in the Control panel at the top of your screen. This opens the Adobe Bridge application

Adobe Bridge is a separate application that ships with the Adobe CS3 package. Bridge is an excellent tool for browsing through files on your computer, allowing you to preview files before opening them.

2   In Adobe Bridge, click the Favorites tab in the upper-left corner of the screen and select Desktop from the list. This displays all the items located on your computer's desktop.

3   Double-click on the id12lessons folder in the Content area of Bridge to display the items within that folder.

Notice that when you view items using Bridge, you can preview many different file types. There is a slider at the bottom of the Bridge window that allows you to change the size of the thumbnails within Bridge. Bridge is extremely useful when you are searching through a folder with many InDesign files or images.

4   Double-click the file named id001.indd to open it in InDesign.

5 Back in InDesign, choose Window > Tags to open the Tags panel, which displays an alphabetical list of the tags available in your document. Currently, the panel lists two: Root and slopename. Root is always in the Tags panel because every XML file needs a root element. The slopename tag was added to the document manually.

The Tags panel displays all the tags available in your active document.

The root element doesn't need to be named Root. You can rename it whatever you like by double-clicking on that tag within the Tags panel. In fact, any element can be renamed this way, provided you follow the rules for naming XML elements. To learn more about the rules of XML, visit w3schools.com.

6 Choose View > Structure > Show Tag Markers, then choose View > Structure > Show Tagged Frames. Turning on these options enables you to see tagged items in your document.

7 Activate the Selection tool (k) from the Tools panel, then select the frame that contains the phrase *Feather Ridge* to make the frame active.

8 Click on the slopename tag in the Tags panel to apply the slopename tag to the Feather Ridge frame. Notice that the frame changes color to indicate it was tagged, and that the associated tag is highlighted in the Tags panel. Because the Tags panel assigned orange to slopename, the frame turns orange. The color of each tag is simply a visual aid and does not affect the actual XML content. If you don't like orange, you can easily change it.

A tagged frame takes on the color assigned to its tag.

9 Double-click the slopename tag in the Tags panel to open the Tag Options dialog box. Choose Magenta from the Color drop-down menu, and press OK. The Feather Ridge frame and its tag are now magenta.

10 Choose File > Save As. In the Save As dialog box, navigate to the id12lessons folder, type **id001_done.indd** in the Name text field, then press Save.

If you don't see the color on your frame after you've tagged it, you may not have turned on your Show Tag Markers and Show Tagged Frames options in the View > Structure menu. If those options are on and you still don't see the markers, you may be in Preview mode. Turn this off by clicking on the view button (◼) at the bottom of your Tools panel and making sure Normal is selected from the view options.

Importing and applying XML Tags

You can create XML tags directly within InDesign CS3, but most often you'll be given a list of tags to use. For instance, if you're repurposing the content of your layout for the Web, your client or IT department may supply an XML document containing all the tags required in the final XML output. Import it into InDesign, then click to apply the tags as necessary. If at any time you are not provided with tags and need to create them manually in InDesign, you can do so by simply pressing the New tag button (⊡) at the bottom of the Tags panel.

1 From the Tags panel menu (-≣), choose Load Tags. In the Open a File dialog box, navigate to the id12lessons folder, select the file named id001tags.xml, then press Open. The tags contained in the XML file now appear in the Tags panel; it's that simple.

Import tag names from an external file into InDesign.

2 If the tagged frames are not activated from the beginning of the lesson, choose View > Structure > Show Tagged Frames so you can see the tags you're about to apply.

3 Using the Selection tool (➤), click the image of the snowboarder in the page's lower-right corner, then click the image tag in the Tags panel. The image changes color slightly, indicating it is tagged with an image tag.

4 Select the Type tool (T) from the Tools panel and triple-click on the phrase *A Seasonal Paradise!* to select the entire line. Click on the subhead tag in the Tags panel. Three things happen: pale blue brackets appear around the tagged phrase, InDesign automatically adds the Story tag to your Tags panel and applies it to the frame that contains the phrase and the corresponding text below it, and that frame changes to the Story tag's color. When you apply multiple tags to text within a frame instead of using the same tag for the entire block of text, InDesign tags that frame using the Story tag. InDesign does this to create an element that contains the various tags within the text, giving them the logical structure of a paragraph. The Story is the default element that InDesign uses, but can be changed in the Tagging Preset Options found in the Tags panel menu.

To more easily see what is tagged, you may prefer to turn off your guides and frame edges. Press Ctrl+; (Windows) or Command+; (Mac OS) to hide guides, and press Ctrl+H (Windows) or Command+H (Mac OS) to hide your frame edges. You can also hide tagged frames by choosing View > Structure > Hide Tagged Frames.

The tagging.

Guides, frame edges, and tagged frames are hidden to reveal the text that was tagged.

5 Highlight the two paragraphs below the subhead using the Type tool; take care to include the paragraph return after the second paragraph. Click the body tag in the Tags panel to tag the paragraphs.

To be sure you include a paragraph return in a selection, turn on Show Hidden Characters by pressing Ctrl+Alt+I (Windows) or Command+Option+I (Mac OS).

6 Highlight the next subhead *A Snowboarder's Dream!* and apply the subhead tag to it. Highlight the remainder of the text in the current frame and the frame to its right, and apply the body and subhead tags to the remainder of the text.

You have just finished tagging this InDesign document. Now every item that you want to export as XML has been tagged so that it's included in the final XML file. In the Exporting XML section later in this chapter, you'll export all the tagged elements in your InDesign file to an XML file and reuse the content in another project. Remember that untagged content in your InDesign document does not appear in the final XML file, and it is therefore very important to be thorough during the tagging process to ensure that all the information you wish to repurpose is tagged. Without the proper tagging, elements in your InDesign layout do not appear in the resulting XML file.

Using a DTD

XML is incredibly flexible: You can create a language that meets your needs by customizing element names to match what you are trying to accomplish. Unlike other markup languages, such as HTML, XML doesn't have standard, predefined elements that are required for proper interpretation of the file. In XML, you create your own element names or tags to apply to content within the XML file. Although XML is flexible, there is the potential for errors and miscommunication. The safety net is the DTD or Document Type Definition. A DTD is basically a set of rules that dictates how an XML file can be structured. For instance, a DTD could specify that the *<person>* element can have a *<firstname>* and *<lastname>* element but not a *<middlename>* element. The DTD's job is to govern the structure of any XML file that is validated against it.

More than likely, you will receive a DTD from the same source that supplies the tags you must use. Validating the structure of your document to a DTD is not required, but it is often helpful. In this exercise, you'll validate your newly tagged file to a DTD to check compliance.

1 Press the Show Structure button (◄►) in the bottom-left corner of the document window to open the Structure pane.

2 Click the triangle to the left of the word *Root* in the Structure pane. The Root element expands to display the elements contained within it.

3 Click the Story and Image elements' triangles to expand them.

Alt+clicking (Windows) or Option+clicking (Mac OS) on the triangle to the right of the Root element expands it and every other element with it.

Alt/Option+click the triangle next to Root to expand all elements.

4 Press the panel menu button (-≡) in the upper-right corner of the Structure pane. Choose Load DTD from the menu. In the Load DTD dialog box, navigate to the id12lessons folder, select the id001.dtd file, then press Open to load the associated DTD into your document.

Choosing Load DTD from the Structure panel menu enables you to load a DTD file to validate your XML file.

5 Simply loading the DTD file doesn't do anything by itself. You need to perform a validation to see if the XML structure of your InDesign document complies with the DTD. Press the Validate structure using current DTD button (⚡) in the upper-left corner of the Structure pane to validate your XML file to the DTD. Several elements in the Structure pane turn red; these elements did not validate to the DTD. In the next exercise, you will fix those problems.

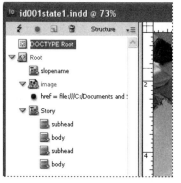

Items that fail to validate to the DTD show up red.

Viewing and organizing structure

As you tag elements in a layout, InDesign lists each tag in the Structure pane in the order that you use it. The tagging process, however, doesn't always happen in a logical order that matches what a DTD might be expecting. Fortunately, InDesign CS3 provides a means of fixing these structural problems.

1 Continuing from where you left off in the previous exercise, click on the image element in the Structure pane. A window at the bottom of the pane displays possible solutions to eliminate the error for the selected element. Two of the three suggestions in this case are unacceptable. Retagging the element would incorrectly identify the content, and deleting the element would remove it from the XML output. The remaining option is to insert the Story element before the image element. We'll try that in the next step.

2 Click the Story element to highlight it and then drag straight up until the black dragging bar appears above the image element.

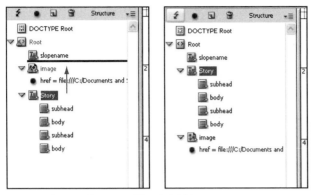

Reposition the Story element to validate the DTD.

3 Click the Validate structure using current DTD button (⚡) again to refresh the DTD validation.

You can see that now there are no reported errors during the validation process and that the existing XML structure of your InDesign layout validates to the current DTD loaded into your document.

Viewing and applying attributes

Another component of an XML file is the attribute. An attribute defines a property of an element and comprises two parts: a name and a value. Attributes do not show up as content of an element; rather, they are generally interpreted by other programs and can add descriptive information about the element itself and are generally interpreted by other programs. A DTD often dictates that an attribute is applied to an element to more accurately describe information about the content of an element. For example, when an image is tagged in InDesign, the program automatically creates an attribute that points to the location of the file on a server or hard drive. That pointer information doesn't show up in the content of the element, but it is necessary for the interpreting program to display or locate the image. InDesign CS3 makes it easy to both view and apply attributes within your current layout.

1   In the Structure pane, make sure that the image element is still expanded. Notice the entry within the image element that has a bullet in front of it followed by *href = file://...* This is an attribute.

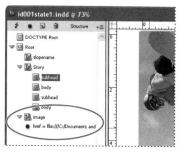

Use attributes to add additional information about a tag.

2   Double-click the image element's attribute to open the Edit Attribute dialog box. Here you see the components of the attribute, including the Name and Value. By default, when you tag an image in InDesign, it applies an attribute named href (or Hypertext Reference); its value is the path to the image location on your computer. You don't need to change anything at the moment, so press Cancel.

3   In this layout, you want to add some attributes that indicate the location of the ski slope. In the Structure pane, click on the slopename element to select it.

4   Press the Add an Attribute button (•) to open the New Attribute dialog box.

5   In the Name text field, type **slopecity**, and in the Value text field, type **Killington**. Press OK.

Add an attribute with information about the slope's location to the slopename element.

6   Repeat steps 3 through 5, typing **slopestate** in the Name text field, and **Vermont** in the Value text field.

7   Now that you have the attributes applied, press the Validate structure using current DTD button (✦) to determine if your document structure validates to the DTD. There shouldn't be any problems.

If your document structure doesn't validate to the DTD, verify that the attribute names are spelled exactly as shown in steps 5 and 6. Attribute names, just like element names, are case sensitive and cannot contain spaces. The value, however, can contain any characters you desire. In the exercise, the attributes validated to the DTD because you used the names given to you. When you are creating your own projects, you can find out which attributes are valid by asking your IT department or by opening the DTD file in a text editor.

8   Choose File > Save to save your work.

Exporting XML

The document is tagged, the structure validates to a DTD, and you added attributes about key elements in your document—you're now ready to export the XML to a separate .xml file. From there, the content can be repurposed to a web site, intranet, RSS feed, content aggregator, or another InDesign document. You are now beginning to experience the power of XML. The fact that it only describes content and not formatting makes it extremely versatile. Give it a try.

1   Choose File > Export. In the Export dialog box, choose XML from the Save as type (Windows) or Format (Mac OS) drop-down menu.

2   In the Name text field, type **id001_done.xml**, then in the Save in text field at the top of the window, navigate to the id12lessons folder. Press the Save button to save the XML file and open the Export XML dialog box.

Use the Export XML dialog box to control how your XML file is exported.

3 Leave the settings at their defaults, and press the Export button. InDesign exports all the tagged content in your layout as an .xml file. Choose File > Close and Save if necessary.

4 Launch any text or XML editor on your computer. For Windows users, common text editors are Notepad and Wordpad. Mac OS users can open a text editor like TextEdit or BBEdit and open the id001_done.xml file to see what the finished XML file looks like. When you are finished, close the document.

Importing XML

Because XML describes content as opposed to formatting, you can easily repurpose XML content multiple ways. For example, imagine you need to create an advertising poster for the Feather Ridge ski resort. Why start from scratch when you have the content in XML format? Simply set up a poster template and import the XML content into it. XML also gives you the flexibility to reproduce the same poster design quickly with details from different resorts.

Prepare the document template

In this exercise, you will prepare the poster template to receive the content, and in the next, you will import the XML content that you exported from the first project to create the advertising poster.

1 Using File > Open or Adobe Bridge, open id002.indd from the id12lessons folder.

2 Choose File > Save As. In the Save As dialog box, navigate to the id12lessons folder and type **id002_done.indd** in the File name text field, then press Save. This file is a poster that you will populate with XML data. Currently it is simply an InDesign document with frames placed where content should go. If you were to import XML data now, you would end up with elements in the Structure pane but no content on the page. You must first tag the document so the XML flows into the tagged frames when you import the file.

3 If the Tags panel is not open, choose Window > Tags to open it. The only tag available in the document is the Root tag. You need to load more, and your client supplied you with an XML file of the necessary poster tags, as well as usage instructions to make it easier for you to tag the layout.

4 From the Tags panel menu (-≡), choose Load Tags. Navigate to the id12lessons folder, choose id002Tags.xml, and press Open. The Tags panel should now list a few more choices.

5 Using the Selection tool (↖), click on the empty frame that partially overlaps the image of the snowboarder at the top of the document. Click the facility tag in the Tags panel to apply it to the selected frame.

6 Click the empty frame in the middle of the poster, then click the article tag in the Tags panel.

7 Click the empty frame at the bottom of document, and apply the photo tag.

8 If your Structure pane is no longer open, click the Show Structure button (↔) in the bottom-left corner of the document window to open it. Click the Root element in the Structure pane to select it, then click poster in the Tags panel to change the Root element's name to poster, as required by the client's usage instructions.

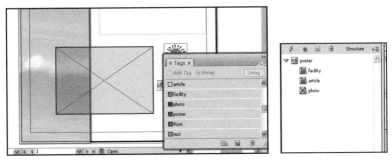

Tag the poster's empty frames and rename the Root element in the Structure pane.

9 Choose File > Save.

Applying XSLT on import

You have now prepared your empty poster layout to receive XML data, but you have run into a common dilemma: The tag names in the template file are different from those used in the XML file you're about to import. The solution is to apply an XSLT to the XML file to transform it into the format necessary for the poster layout. An XSLT (eXtensible Style Language Transformation) transforms an input XML file into an output XML file that is formatted or altered in some way. In this lesson, you'll apply the XSLT to the XML file you created in the previous exercise. The XSLT looks for any image element, for example, in the input XML file and changes it to a photo element in the output XML file, keeping its attributes while applying other transformations.

XSLT is extremely powerful because it can do so much more than a text editor's basic find and change. It can reorganize the structure of the incoming XML file in any way that is necessary, renaming elements, making some elements children (subelements) of others, and so on. XSLT is written in the same format that an XML file is written, which makes it easier for someone familiar with XML to write. Now it's time to put this theory into practice.

1 Choose File > Import XML to open the Import XML dialog box.

2 In the resulting Import XML dialog box, navigate to the id12lessons folder and choose the id001_done.xml file. Click the Show XML Import Options checkbox at the bottom of the dialog box to turn it on (if it's checked already, don't click it). Press Open.

Click the Show XML Import Options checkbox to access additional features that affect how an XML file is imported.

3   In the XML Import Options dialog box, click to turn on the Apply
XSLT option. From the Apply XSLT drop-down menu, choose Browse
(Windows) or Choose (Mac OS) and open id001.xsl from the id12lessons
folder. You should now see the file path to the XSL file in the field next to
Apply XSLT. Leave all other settings at their defaults, and press OK.

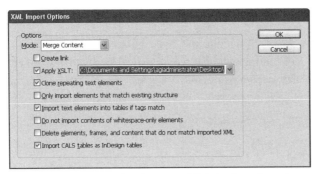

Choose an XSLT file to transform the incoming XML data into a format that you need.

4   After you import the XML file, several things happen:

- InDesign applies the XSLT to the incoming XML, which changes the
names of the elements in the original XML file to the names of the
elements that the poster layout was expecting.

- The XML file imports into your InDesign layout.

- Because the structure of the incoming XML data matched the structure
of pre-tagged poster layout, the text and images automatically flowed into
their respective pre-tagged frames.

5   Choose File > Save to save your work.

Where to get an XSLT

An XSLT can be created directly on your computer using a basic text editor. It
uses an XML-like structure that makes it fairly easy for somebody with a basic
programming background to get up-and-running quickly. Writing XSLT is
beyond the scope of this book and some people may find that they do not have
the background or the desire to learn XSLT. A quick search on the Internet
provides you with many resources that can create an XSLT quickly and
affordably for your project.

Mapping tags to styles

Importing the XML file did a considerable amount of the work for you, but the poster isn't quite finished. When InDesign imports XML data into tagged frames, it formats the text in the receiving document's default font. You need to map the tags to InDesign styles to automatically format the text to match the poster's design concept. This exercise explores how to do just that and puts the finishing touches on your poster.

1   Click on the Paragraph Styles button (¶) in the dock on the right side of the workspace to open the Paragraph Styles panel. Notice that it contains several styles with the same names as the elements in the Structure pane. You'll use these in the next steps to apply to the text.

2   From the Structure pane panel menu (-≡), choose Map Tags to Styles.

Choose Map Tags to Styles to automatically match tags with the paragraph styles of the same name.

The Map Styles to Tags option takes a pre-styled layout that uses paragraph styles to format the copy and automates the tagging process by tagging elements based on the name of the paragraph style.

3   In the resulting Map Tags to Styles dialog box, make sure the preview checkbox is checked and click the Map by Name button at the bottom of the dialog box. This tells InDesign to map paragraph styles to their matching tag names.

You can see two paragraph styles match exactly. Content whose tag matches the name of a paragraph style now has that style applied, automatically formatting that copy. If the paragraph style names do not match the tag names, you can map them manually in the Map Tags to Styles window by choosing which style you want mapped to which tag. Either way you approach this process, it is generally much faster than manually formatting the copy within your layout. In this case, you will leave the unmapped styles as they are. Press OK.

4   Choose File > Save to save your work, then choose File > Close to close the file.

Using data merge

Data merge automates the creation of multiple versions of a project and populates areas of your layout with different content for each version. Data merge pulls variable content from a source file. The source file might contain a list of names, for instance, so you could easily populate your poster with the names of Feather Ridge ski trails first, then the names of Loon Mountain ski trails, followed by a version with the name of Snowmass trails.

In this exercise, you use data merge to create business cards for all Feather Ridge employees, quickly creating many versions of the same layout.

1   Using File > Open, open id003.indd from the id12lessons folder.

2   Choose File > Save As. In the Save As dialog box, navigate to the id12lessons folder and type **id003_done.indd** in the Name text field. Press Save.

This file is the general layout for the business cards. You need to add a graphic to the business card and then prepare the card for the data merge.

3   Press the Go to Bridge button (🖼) in the upper-right corner of your screen in InDesign to switch to the Adobe Bridge application.

4   In the Adobe Bridge application, navigate to the Images folder inside the id12lessons folder on your desktop.

5   Press the Switch to Compact Mode button (🖫) in the upper-left corner of Bridge. This reduces the size of the Bridge window so you can see it and InDesign simultaneously.

6   Drag the Snowflakes_Snippet.inds file from Bridge into your InDesign document and minimize the Bridge window.

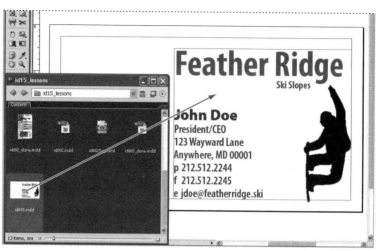

Switch to Compact mode in Adobe Bridge, then drag the snowflakes snippets item directly into the InDesign document.

XML Snippets

The file that you dragged into InDesign in step 6 of this exercise is called a snippet. A snippet is a single file that is a collection of objects that originated from InDesign. Snippets are extremely versatile because everything that you need is located within that one single file. Notice that the elements created by the snippet are a group of items. There are multiple frames containing images created by the snippet. This can't be done by simply placing a graphic.

An XML snippet is simply an XML file that describes the objects it contains, such as size, shape, location on the page, and link locations. Snippets aren't the only places that InDesign uses XML behind the scenes. In addition to the tagging process that you used in the beginning of this lesson, when you add an item to a library in InDesign CS3, InDesign creates an XML snippet in the process. Saving an InDesign CS3 file as an .inx (InDesign Interchange) file, saves the file in XML format so that previous versions of InDesign can interpret the file and open it. XML is what makes all these things possible.

7   Activate the Selection tool (✷) from the Tools panel and use it to position the snowflakes contained in the snippet file on the left side of the business card.

8   Choose Window > Automation > Data Merge to open the Data Merge panel.

9 From the Data Merge panel menu (-≡), choose Select Data Source. In the resulting Select Data Source dialog box, open buscardlist.csv from the id12lessons folder. The Data Merge panel now contains a list of fields that indicates all the available groups of specific information that can be merged into your document. Data merge can use either a .csv (comma separated value) or a .txt or .tab (tab delimited) text file; the difference in the formats is the type of delimiters used to separate the data.

Both .csv and .tab files can be exported from a spreadsheet using programs such as Microsoft Excel, or from databases such as Filemaker Pro.

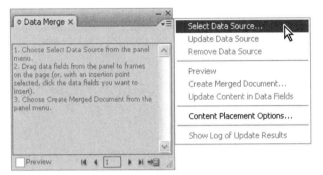

The Select Data Source option allows you to choose the source file that contains the data to merge into your layout.

To assist you in properly positioning the data fields, display the hidden characters in your document by pressing Ctrl+Alt+I (Windows) or Command+Option+I (Mac OS). If you can't see the hidden characters, make sure that you are not in Preview mode by clicking on the Normal mode button at the bottom of the Tools panel.

10 Add some data fields to your document to prepare it for the data merge. Using the Type tool, highlight the word *John*, and click once on Fname in the Data Merge panel.

11 Highlight the word *Doe*, and click once on Lname in the Data Merge panel.

Do not include spaces or returns when you highlight text to replace with a data field. Spaces and returns generally should be static, meaning they aren't pulled into your layout from the data source. Turning on the hidden characters in the document makes avoiding unwanted characters easier.

12 Select the title *President/CEO*, and click the Title field in the Data Merge panel. Select the line below the title, and click the Data Merge panel's Address field.

13 For the next line, highlight the word *Anywhere*, leaving out the comma, and click on the City field. Highlight *MD* (no spaces), and click on the State field. Finally highlight the five-digit zip code, 00001, and click on Zip in the Data Merge panel.

14 Repeat this process for the phone, fax, and e-mail copy, taking care not to include the tab at the beginning or the return at the end of each line. You're almost finished. Don't be too concerned if some of your copy runs into the graphic on the right side of the business card or even if some of the text becomes overset. This happens sometimes if the field names in the data file are particularly long. The double-angle bracket at the beginning (<<) and end (>>) of each field take up additional space.

This is what your card should look like after you have added all the data fields.

15 Press the Create Merged Document button (⇥) in the lower-right corner of the Data Merge panel to open the Create Merged Document dialog box. Leave the settings at their defaults, and press OK. You should receive a warning message that indicates that no overset text was generated. Press OK. InDesign displays your new merged document.

16 Open the Pages panel by choosing Window > Pages or by pressing the Pages button (⊞) in the dock and navigate through all the pages created in the merged document. Each one has the same basic components, but wherever you designated a merge field, new data appears on each respective business card.

17 Choose File > Save As. In the Save As dialog box, navigate to the id12lessons folder, type **id003_complete.indd** in the Name text field, then press Save.

By using data merge, you automated what would have been a tedious and time-consuming process had you created each card yourself. Using data merge furthermore eliminates typos and other mistakes (at least on your end) that could be costly if missed. Data merge in InDesign is not limited to text, you could have also defined an image field that would populate each card with a different image.

Self study

Practice tagging one of your existing documents and export the XML to repurpose in another document. Pre-tag a layout in a different orientation and then import your XML file to see the different possibilities that XML can create. If you or someone you know has extensive web knowledge, have them apply CSS (cascading style sheets) to your XML file to change the appearance of the content on the Web.

In this lesson, you used the Map Tags to Styles command to map tagged information to a Paragraph style to automate the formatting of content on your page. There is also a Map Styles to Tags option that does just the opposite. It takes a pre-styled layout that utilizes paragraph styles to format the copy and automates the tagging process by tagging elements based on the name of the paragraph style.

Create some InDesign snippets. For example, you could select one or more items in your InDesign layout and drag them to the Desktop of your computer. E-mail the newly created file to a co-worker who can drag it from the Desktop onto a blank document to see how InDesign recreates every element from the original document. One item to note: If you make a snippet out of InDesign elements that include an image, InDesign still looks at the path from where that original image is placed when you place that snippet into a new document, unless you embed the image.

InDesign Snippets

An InDesign Snippet is an XML file generated from within InDesign that allows you to repurpose commonly used elements throughout multiple documents in InDesign. If you are familiar with InDesign Libraries, Snippets work the same way but don't have to live inside of a Library. Snippets can be created in one of two ways:

1   Select an element(s) within an InDesign document and drag the item onto your Desktop. You may need to adjust your document window prior to doing this so you can see the Desktop behind your document. An InDesign Snippet file will be created.

2   Select an element(s) within an InDesign document and choose File > Export. In the resulting Export dialog box, choose InDesign Snippet from the Format menu and give the Snippet file a name. Press Save.

Once you've created some Snippets, you can reuse them by dragging them from an Explorer (Windows) or Finder (Mac OS) window and dropping them onto an open InDesign document. You can also place them like you would any other graphic file in InDesign. One of the great benefits of Snippets over an InDesign library is that you can browse them using the Adobe Bridge. This allows you to save the Snippet files to a central location on a server where several people can browse them at the same time.

Automate the placement of images as well as text during a data merge. You simply need to have the path to the image for each record within the source data file to make it work.

InDesign CS3 includes a new feature that automatically assembles a layout based on an XML input file. You can use Javascript or Applescript to automate the placement and positioning of files in an InDesign layout. This is an advanced topic; however, it opens virtually limitless options when working in an XML-based workflow.

Review

Questions

1 What does XML stand for?

2 How can you tell if an InDesign file contains tagged content?

3 Which XML component can be added to an XML element to provide additional information about the element, but does not show up in the content of an element?

4 Which type of file changes the structure of an XML file on import or export?

5 Where do you go in InDesign CS3 to adjust the XML structure of your document?

6 Which document formats can you use as a source for a data merge?

Answers

1 It stands for Extensible Markup Language.

2 Choose Show Tag Markers and Show Tagged Frames from the View > Structure menu.

3 An attribute.

4 An XSLT.

5 The Structure pane.

6 CSV (comma separated) and .txt or .tab (tab separated).

Index